PEACE AND CONFLICT SERIES
Ron Milam, General Editor

PEACE &
CONFLICT
S E R I E S

Also in the series:

Admirals Under Fire: The US Navy and the Vietnam War
by Edward J. Marolda

The Air War in Vietnam
by Michael E. Weaver

Crooked Bamboo: A Memoir from Inside the Diem Regime
by Nguyen Thai, edited by Justin Simundson

Girls Don't: A Woman's War in Vietnam
by Inette Miller

Rain in Our Hearts: Alpha Company in the Vietnam War
by James Allen Logue and Gary D. Ford

CHARGING A TYRANT

THE ARRAIGNMENT
OF SADDAM HUSSEIN

GREG SLAVONIC

TEXAS TECH UNIVERSITY PRESS

Copyright © 2023 by Texas Tech University Press

All rights reserved. No portion of this book may be reproduced in any form or by any means, including electronic storage and retrieval systems, except by explicit prior written permission of the publisher. Brief passages excerpted for review and critical purposes are excepted.

This book is typeset in EB Garamond. The paper used in this book meets the minimum requirements of ANSI/NISO Z39.48-1992 (R1997). ♾

Designed by Hannah Gaskamp
Cover design by Hannah Gaskamp

Library of Congress Cataloging-in-Publication Data

Names: Slavonic, Greg, author. Title: Charging a Tyrant: The Arraignment of Saddam Hussein / Greg Slavonic. Description: Lubbock: Texas Tech University Press, 2023. | Series: Peace and Conflict series | Includes bibliographical references and index. | Summary: "A firsthand chronicle of the arraignment of former Iraqi leader Saddam Hussein, offering never-before-released accounts of the legal proceedings"—Provided by publisher.
Identifiers: LCCN 2022032876 (print) | LCCN 2022032877 (ebook) |
ISBN 978-1-68283-164-9 (paperback) | ISBN 978-1-68283-165-6 (ebook)
Subjects: LCSH: Hussein, Saddam, 1937–2006. | Arraignment—Iraq. | Indictments—Iraq. |
Preliminary examinations (Criminal procedure)—Iraq.
Classification: LCC KMJ4632 .S53 2022 (print) | LCC KMJ4632 (ebook) |
DDC 345.567/072—dc23/eng/20220930
LC record available at https://lccn.loc.gov/2022032876
LC ebook record available at https://lccn.loc.gov/2022032877

Printed in the United States of America
23 24 25 26 27 28 29 30 31 / 9 8 7 6 5 4 3 2 1

Texas Tech University Press
Box 41037
Lubbock, Texas 79409-1037 USA
800.832.4042
ttup@ttu.edu
www.ttupress.org

This book is dedicated to my family: my wife Molly, my daughters Kara (Dresser) and Maggie (Orgel) and son Blake, my daughter-in-law Kasey Slavonic, and my seven grandchildren, Hogan and Harper Slavonic and Hank Dresser and the twins Ivy and Oliver Dresser and Marlow and Sebastian Orgel.

And to the men and women who wear the cloth of our great nation. They give so much and ask so little. God speed to all!

CONTENTS

ILLUSTRATIONS   IX

ACKNOWLEDGMENTS   XI

PART 1: CAPTURE

1: ARRAIGNMENT DAY   5

2: CAPTURE OF THE "ACE OF SPADES"   29

3: FOURTH AND FINAL COMBAT
   DEPLOYMENT   47

4: THE JOURNEY BEGINS   59

5: TRANSFER OF SOVEREIGNTY—
   HISTORIC EVENT   71

6: CASEY AND SANCHEZ—CHANGE OF
   COMMAND CEREMONY   83

7: AMANPOUR AND JENNINGS EPISODE   89

8: PREPARING FOR SADDAM AND
   OTHER HVDS' ARRIVAL   97

PART 2: THE ARRAIGNMENT

9: SADDAM HUSSEIN—A PRODUCT OF HIS
   ENVIRONMENT   109

10: ABID HAMID MAHMUD AL-TIKRITI   133

11: ALI HASSAN AL-MAJID AL-TIKRITI
("CHEMICAL ALI")   141

12: AZIZ SALEH AL-NUMAN   151

13: MUHAMMAD HAMZA AL-ZUBAYDI   155

14: BARZAN IBRAHIM HASAN AL-TIKRITI   161

15: SABIR ABDUL AZIZ AL-DOURI   175

16: SULTAN HASHIM AHMAD AL-TAI   181

17: KAMAL MUSTAFA SULTAN AL-TIKRITI   191

18: TAHA YASSIN RAMADAN   197

19: TARIQ AZIZ   203

20: WATBAN IBRAHIM HASAN AL-TIKRITI   215

21: NINAWA—A KILLING FIELD   221

POSTSCRIPT   235
NOTES   241
BIBLIOGRAPHY   257
INDEX   263

ILLUSTRATIONS

7   Key officials discuss Saddam's appearance after his day in court
7   Courtroom layout
10 The "perp walk": Saddam leaving bus and being escorted into courtroom
10 Saddam arriving to face Judge Ra'id
12 "Murderers' Row" as they leave the Rhino bus to enter the courtroom
13 "High Value Detainees" (HVDs) marching into courthouse
13 HVDs awaiting their turn in a separate holding room
15 Saddam looking directly at camera
16 Saddam being defiant
19 Saddam listening to judge
20 Saddam making a point
22 Saddam being loaded into the Rhino bus
22 Judge Ra'id reviewing paperwork
26 Author trying to get John Burns' attention during a break
26 Author visiting with the judge during a break
31 Poster advertising $25 million reward for capture of Saddam Hussein
65 Al Faw Palace, headquarters for Multi-National Force–Iraq, Camp Victory
66 Aerial view of Al Faw Palace and other facilities
73 Brig. Gen. Mark Kimmitt and Rear Adm. Greg Slavonic
74 Author with Rich Schmierer and Rob Tappan before Transfer of
    Sovereignty, rotunda of the Presidential Palace
75 Before Transfer of Sovereignty ceremony
78 Transfer of Sovereignty, June 28, 2004
85 Reception before the change of command ceremony
87 View of change of command ceremony from media pool's location
90 Outside view of the mosque used as the courtroom

90   Judge Ra'id arrives at the courthouse

93   Author with Christiane Amanpour and Peter Jennings

93   Court arraignment judge Ra'id

94   Author and Judge Ra'id before arraignment is to begin

98   All twelve High Value Detainees, June 15, 2004

134   Abid Hamid Mahmud al-Tikriti listens as judge reads charges

143   Ali Hassan al-Majid al-Tikriti ("Chemical Ali") arriving at waiting area

145   Chemical Ali listens to charges against him

146   Chemical Ali signing arraignment documents

152   Al-Numan preparing to enter courtroom

157   Muhammad Hamza al-Zubaydi arrives in the courtroom

165   Barzan Ibrahim Hasan al-Tikriti reacts to the judge's comments

166   Barzan pleading with the judge

176   Sabir Abdul Aziz al-Douri enters the courtroom

177   Sabir Abdul Aziz al-Douri listens to the judge

184   Sultan Hashim Ahmad al-Tai arriving in waiting room

185   Sultan Hashim Ahmad al-Tai ponders charges the judge reads to him

192   Kamal Mustafa Sultan al-Tikriti upon arrival in the waiting area

200   Taha Yassin Ramadan responds to a question from the judge

208   Tariq Aziz listens to Judge Ra'id

209   Tariq Aziz disputes the charges against him

218   Watban Ibrahim Hasan al-Tikriti listens to charges against him

ACKNOWLEDGMENTS

THIS BOOK WOULD NOT HAVE BEEN POSSIBLE WITHOUT THE generosity, support, and assistance of many people—some of whom are introduced within its pages, many who are not.

Travis Snyder, acquisition editor; Christie Perlmutter, editor; John Brock, marketing and sales manager; and the rest of the team at Texas Tech University Press all supplied the necessary guidance and support that made the entire project run smoothly.

Special thanks to friends and colleagues who provided their time, assistance, and insights at various stages of the writing and rewriting of the manuscript.

As for the reporting of this book, I am deeply indebted to many who took time to share their thoughts and experiences. I accept full responsibility for any error that may have crept into these pages despite the best efforts of so many people to inform me.

Several senior officers spent many hours reconstructing details of their experiences as they related to the project. Some of the people who helped me would prefer that I not recognize them in print.

In addition, I have many to thank for translating several hours of video so as to obtain the courtroom dialogue between the High Value Detainees (HVDs) and Judge Ra'id. Several individuals who helped with the translation project requested to remain anonymous, but two I can mention—Mr. and Mrs. Joe Mondalek—were fantastic in their assistance, along with Lyndon Whitmire and his law firm, who donated to my project by acquiring my last two translations.

Finally, this book would have neither started nor finished without my wife Molly. She pointed out my errors and spent hundreds of hours editing and re-editing the manuscript. For her patience and understanding, I will be eternally grateful. Her sister, Linda Poole, a retired schoolteacher, provided editing that was most helpful as well.

CHARGING A TYRANT

PART 1

CAPTURE

1

ARRAIGNMENT DAY

IN LEGAL JARGON, THE WORD "ARRAIGNMENT" TYPICALLY refers to a defendant's first appearance in court before a magistrate, in which the defendant is advised of the formal charge and called upon to enter a plea.[1]

This singular event—as pertains to former Iraqi president Saddam Hussein and eleven of his confederates—is recounted through my eyes and those of John Fisher Burns, pool reporter for the *New York Times*. The process would inform Saddam Hussein and the others of their rights and their status as defendants in a criminal case before the Iraqi Special Tribunal (IST). The occupation of Iraq had ended two days earlier; hence, the Iraqis established their legal custody of Saddam and the other High Value Detainees (HVDs) following the Iraqi return to sovereignty.

The primary objective of the July 1, 2004, arraignment was to demonstrate to the world via a seamless operation that the Iraqi Interim Government (IIG) was in control of the detainees and had a functioning court system.

The Deputy Commander of Detainee Operations, along with the IIG, agreed in advance that there was to be no "live" reporting from outside or inside the courtroom. This mandate was enacted for security purposes, primarily to ensure the safety of Saddam and the other defendants. The area could easily be identified and immediately targeted as the known location if there was live reporting. This site had in the past been hit by rockets and mortars.

I headed outside the courthouse—a mosque on Camp Victory not far from Multi-National Force–Iraq (MNF-I) headquarters—for a short walk around the building. Uniformed security personnel (US Military Police and Iraqi National Police) were all around the courthouse providing perimeter security. Col. David Phillips, commander of the 89th Military Police Brigade, was responsible for transporting Saddam and the other HVDs on this day, as well as for providing security. Col. Phillips reported to Maj. Gen. Geoff Miller, deputy commanding general, and Detainee Operations (Task Force 134), Multi-National Force–Iraq.

The HVDs would be transported from Camp Cropper, which was about two miles away, and Saddam would come from a specially made facility inside Camp Victory, the primary component of the Victory Base established in April 2003. It was named after the Victory Corps (V Corps) headquartered in Heidelberg, Germany. Saddam's "residence" was a bombed-out building down the road from Task Force 134. Surrounding the bottom floor of that building was concertina wire to make it secure.[2]

Colonel Phillips had several security worries during this period. Iraq had the Iraqi National Police to provide "visible" security and to escort Saddam and the HVDs from the transport bus into the courtroom. The Iraqis were unaware of whom they might be guarding or providing security for until that day. Phillips said, "Depending on whether they were Shi'a or Sunni, I had no idea how they would react when they saw him or were in Saddam's presence. This meant I needed backup US security in position."[3]

He went on to say, "I had two US sniper teams lined up and in position. I had snipers on rooftops of the surrounding buildings. They had line-of-site to the Rhino bus unloading spot and [were] ready to take aggressive action at the hint of any hostile action toward Saddam or the other HVDs when coming off the bus."[4] The Rhino bus (or Rhino Runner), as it was commonly referred to, was a type of armored bus used extensively in Iraq, especially on the infamous "Route Irish" between Baghdad International Airport (BIAP) and the Green Zone (the main thoroughfare in the center of the Iraqi capital). It was a customized vehicle used to transport VIPs, prisoners, civilian contractors, members of the media, and military personnel. The Rhino Runner was 360-degree fully protected (sides, front, back, roof, floor, and even glass).

I looked towards the half-circle drive where Saddam would arrive and saw a white ramp in place. The ramp would facilitate the unloading and loading of Saddam and the others since they would be wearing shackles. Col. Barry Johnson and his team collected all the media members' cell phones at a table outside and to the right of the entrance to the building prior to their entering the courthouse.

Key officials discuss Saddam's appearance after his day in court. Front row, left to right: Salem "Sam" Chalabi, Greg Kehoe, and Dr. Mowaffak al-Rubaie. John Burns, *New York Times* pool reporter (in white shirt), is behind them. (Photo from Combat Camera)

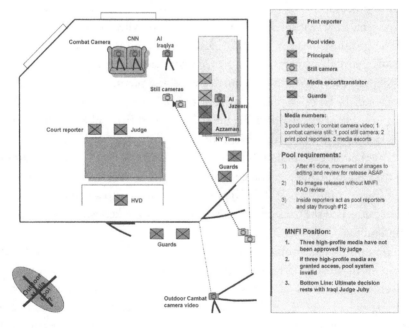

Courtroom layout. (Art credit to MNF–I)

Inside the courtroom, twenty individuals were waiting for Saddam's arrival. Judge Ra'id Juhi Hamadi al-Saedi and court clerks of the IST were in place. In front of the judge's desk (a tan four-legged table) was a wooden railing with one lone chair positioned directly opposite of where the judge would be seated. A similar table for the court reporters was placed to the right of the judge.

I strolled over and stood at the entrance of the long two-tiered jurors' box, which was at a 45-degree angle behind and to the left of Judge Ra'id's desk. Seated in the front row were officials of Iraq's interim government, including Salem "Sam" Chalabi, appointed the first general director of the Iraqi Special Tribunal; Dr. Mowaffak al-Rubaie, Iraq's new national security advisor; and Greg Kehoe, advisor to the IST. This was also where the print pool members were seated, including John Burns from the *New York Times* and a reporter from the Iraq-based *Azzaman*. My team had arranged for Burns, the assigned pool reporter, to have an Iraqi interpreter on one side translating the conversations between the judge and Saddam and the other HVDs during the court proceedings. The television crews were in place in the back of the room, including those from Iraq-based Al Iraqiya, Al Jazeera, and CNN. Karen Ballard, pool photographer for *Time* magazine, had her camera with telephoto lens and camera bag. And finally, the Combat Camera personnel were ready to proceed: two soldiers manned a television camera, and one photographer was present. All Combat Camera personnel were in civilian attire.

The ground rules for the two individuals responsible for still photography—Karen Ballard for *Time* and a Combat Camera representative—permitted them to move around the courtroom taking pictures, but they could not go beyond the wooden railing in front of the judge's desk. They could move on either side of and behind the judge but not in front of him. In addition, photographs of individuals—excluding Saddam and other HVDs—were not to show their faces. Concern for the safety of those pictured and their families was paramount. All images taken that day would be reviewed at the Combined Press Information Center (CPIC) prior to their release to any media. The television cameras at the back of the courtroom were to be kept stationary and with sound muted.

From my vantage point in the courtroom, I watched Saddam Hussein and eleven of his most notorious government officials/ministers and close advisors successively sit in this chair before us. In their positions of authority over the years, they had been the judges, juries, and executioners. Today would be the first time they would find themselves before an Iraqi judge, with the rule of law about to be enforced on them.

An unforeseen event occurred prior to Saddam's arrival, involving Christiane Amanpour. Due to a short transportation delay for Saddam, members of the media were requested to leave the courtroom and go out into the outer hallway. While John Burns was waiting there, someone noticed he was carrying a tape recorder. Recording devices were not allowed in the courtroom, so he was asked to surrender it to one of the military personnel who had collected all cell phones earlier. His recorder was kept in a safe place and returned to him once the proceedings had concluded.

Upon reentering the courtroom, Burns ran into his old friend Peter Jennings and had a brief exchange before returning to his seat. He saw that Amanpour had not left the courtroom as instructed and that she had taken Burns's assigned seat while he was in the hallway.

Burns said to her, "You can't do this because this is the pool reporter's seat. I have to have the seat next to this guy [the interpreter] and if I don't, I can't be the pool reporter." Amanpour failed to budge, simply saying she "did not recognize the authority of the military to make these assignments." She had gotten her seat and was going to hold on to it. I was attending to other media concerns and assumed that everyone knew the rules and were where they were supposed to be.[5]

Burns had had previous encounters with Amanpour. "This wasn't the first time I had seen Christiane capable of behaving very badly. She was a cohort of mine in Bosnia and she was a very young reporter on an upward arc." He continued, "I was totally chagrined she would behave like this because she knew what the consequences were for me."[6] Burns scurried to find a seat in the back row of the jurors' box to the right of his assigned place.

The planning was done; everything was in place. Apache helicopters flew over the makeshift courtroom at a low altitude. All eyes in the courtroom were trained on the large mahogany double doors. The expectations of those present this day were high. Thirty-five individuals had been waiting, some longer than others, for this moment to come.

Saddam then made his arrival. He departed the Rhino bus and was escorted by two Iraqi prison guards and four Iraqi security guards. They walked seventy-five feet to the entrance of the makeshift courthouse. The world would soon see a much different Saddam from that of some seven months earlier.

There were footsteps approaching, the first sounds the assembled group would hear. Those inside the courtroom were about to witness the first appearance by the former president of Iraq before the world since December 13, 2003. The clatter of the chains on the marble floor heralded Hussein's imminent approach.

The doors opened slowly, and in walked the former Iraqi President Saddam Hussein. He was handcuffed, but the shackles on his ankles were removed as he was escorted into the courtroom by two Iraqi security guards whose faces

The "perp walk": Saddam leaving the Rhino bus and being escorted into the court-room. (Photo from Combat Camera)

Saddam arriving to face Judge Ra'id. (Photo by Combat Camera)

were clearly visible to those present at the proceedings but were edited out in all photographs and video released later.

According to Burns, "The next twenty-six minutes were as compelling as any in a reporter's life. My notes, I realized later, were scribbled even less legibly than normal, reflecting the tension of the moment awaited, in a manner of speaking, since I reached Baghdad for the first time nearly fifteen years ago, when I imagined, hopelessly, like other Western journalists, that I might get an interview with Mr. Hussein."[7]

While this scene was unfolding inside, outside there was another event taking place which I would only find out about the next day.

Apparently, Saddam's arrival and exit from the Rhino bus and his escort to the entrance of the courthouse were being seen on live coverage on CNN and Fox News via cell phone. According to Col. Johnson, two CNN employees showed up outside the courthouse prior to Saddam's arrival. One was a producer, who happened to be Serbian, and the other a staffer. They told Johnson they had just come from another shoot and asked if they could upload some of their footage. Johnson was trying to work with them and facilitate their request. They knew the ground rules: no live reporting, no cell phones allowed in the courtroom. In fact, as previously noted, Johnson oversaw the collection of all cell phones prior to anyone entering the courtroom.[8]

Johnson left the two men and walked back to his office, which was about 200 meters from the mosque. As the colonel was leaving, Saddam arrived. When Johnson got to his office and began watching Fox News, he caught a live report of Saddam's arrival from outside the courthouse.[9] Apparently, a reporter was broadcasting, via a cell phone, Saddam's being escorted from the bus and led into the courthouse. Indeed, the reporter stated, "This is what we are seeing live."

Johnson later told me that his initial thought was that someone external to the event either "had eyes" on what was happening or had been placed outside the perimeter and was high enough that they could look down and report the events as they were unfolding.[10] He instructed one of his staff to call Fox News and notify them to "cease and desist" their coverage because they were violating the security procedures. Fox said they were getting their feed from CNN. At Johnson's request, they ended their feed immediately.[11]

Once Johnson knew it was CNN, he realized we had an internal problem. He asked the military police in charge of security to search the area around the mosque. In doing so, they opened the door to a porta-john located near the mosque and found the Serbian producer for CNN. He apparently had hidden inside when Col. Johnson left and was peeking out the door reporting Saddam's arrival with his cell phone.

He was immediately apprehended, and his cell phone was confiscated (it would be returned later). Johnson told the MPs to remove the producer and the other CNN person from the area. They were placed into a van and driven away.

"Murderers' Row" as they leave the Rhino bus to enter the courtroom. (Photo from media pool–Karen Ballard)

Johnson stated the "MPs reported back and said they [the CNN staffers] were laughing and thought it was all a joke, especially that they had violated the ground rules. They were able to report from the porta-john all the events outside before being caught."[12] Johnson would go on to say that he made an official call to CNN and gave them a warning. He told the network they would not have access to future operations if this behavior continued.

Eleven "High Value Detainees" (HVDs) marching into the courthouse. (R–L) Sabir Abdul Aziz al-Douri, Watban Ibrahim al-Hasan al-Tikriti, Taha Yassin Ramadan, Muhammed Hamza al-Zubaydi, Aziz Saleh al-Numan, Ali Hasan al-Majid, Saddam Hussein's top lieutenants, are escorted in shackles into the Iraqi courtroom. (Photo from Combat Camera)

HVDs awaiting their turn in a separate holding room. Left to right: Tariq Aziz, Kamal Mustafa, Abid Mahmud, Chemical Ali, Barzan Hasan. (Photo from Combat Camera)

Meanwhile, for almost six hours, with only three fifteen-minute breaks, John Burns would scribble his notes and then crosscheck with the interpreter the actual conversation between the judge and Saddam.[13] The *Times* reporter captured the scene as Hussein arrived inside the courtroom. According to Burns, it had been almost twenty-five years that week since Saddam "seized power in Baghdad. There stood Saddam Hussein al-Majid al-Tikriti, the man who awarded himself titles of honor and glory to fill a full page; the man who launched, or in some measure provoked, three disastrous wars; the man whose legacy runs to countless mass graves, and to hundreds of thousands of Iraqis killed, his very name synonymous, across much of the world, with a totalitarianism that turned the Iraqi state into a machine of torture and death."[14]

According to Greg Kehoe, all the detainees scheduled to appear in court had been going to wear orange jumpsuits. When Kehoe learned of the defendants' expected attire, he called Lt. Gen. Ricardo Sanchez and told him, "They need to be dressed appropriately." Jackets, slacks, shirts, and shoes were purchased for Saddam and the other HVDs to wear that day.[15]

Once Saddam was in the courtroom and seated, the other HVDs were taken from another Rhino bus, lined up, and marched into the courthouse. They were held in an adjacent conference room awaiting their turn before the judge.

Ballard, the media pool still photographer assigned to cover the arraignment, also emphasized the importance of this event. As Saddam entered the courtroom, she would be basically face to face with him and would shoot a photo that would capture the moment and would be published in newspapers around the world. As the former Iraqi president entered the courtroom, Ballard said, "I was concerned about accomplishing the goal which I knew was going to be a significant and historic day. I didn't want to screw it up. I wanted to make sure to get every shot. I was in a total 'photo zone.'"[16]

Burns recounted, "Saddam looked wasted, emaciated, bearded; footsteps uncertain, manner exhausted, eyes scanning left to right. His voice was husky at first, then oddly high-pitched, at moments nearly breaking." Saddam began "rubbing his eyes, finger to eyebrow, his hand placed on his cheek, the timbre of voice changed." This was a telling statement made by a reporter whose resume included many other significant events.[17]

Saddam was wearing a very dark charcoal pinstripe jacket, a white shirt open at the collar, brown trousers, and black shoes. His hair and beard were neatly trimmed. It was quite apparent, when contrasted with earlier photos of Saddam, that he was thinner than seven months ago when he was captured; his beard and hair were much grayer. He often stroked his beard and had heavy

Saddam looking directly at camera. (Photo by Combat Camera)

dark circles under his eyes. He looked around and appeared uneasy as he sat in front of the judge. His eyes moved back and forth, left to right, then focused on the jurors' area.

When the proceedings began, the former Iraqi ruler seemed preoccupied by the two-tiered bench to his right. Burns wrote about Saddam, "For the first few minutes or more, something to his right, toward the rear of the room, distracted him, so much so that the judge seemed to have only half his attention. Was it the presence of foreign reporters? Or was it the two senior officials of the

Saddam being defiant and pointing angrily. (Photo by media pool–Karen Ballard)

new Iraqi government who were sitting at the front of the cramped stall serving as a visitors' gallery?"[18]

Further according to Burns, "Officials of the new Iraqi government were seated with three American reporters and three American officials: two lawyers advising the Iraqi judge, and a United States Navy admiral acting as a spokesman who attended in tan chinos and a yellow, short-sleeved sports shirt."[19] (Note: My civilian attire that day was tan slacks (chinos) and a yellow short-sleeved golf shirt. These were the only civilian clothes I had brought with me when I deployed. I didn't think I would need more than a shirt and pair of slacks. So, from this point forward, when Burns would see me he would always refer to me jokingly as "the admiral in tan chinos and a yellow golf shirt.") In a later conversation, Burns shared with me that he felt Saddam knew almost everyone in the jurors' box but may have been curious about who I was. The yellow golf shirt seemed out of place, as most of the others were wearing coats and ties.[20]

For security reasons, an edited and six-hour-delayed broadcast of the court proceedings on Arab satellite television stations gave Iraqis their first look at the former dictator since his capture by the US military seven months earlier. They saw a Hussein whose mood ranged from nervousness and exasperation to contempt and defiance, and even flashes of anger. At times he seemed to lecture the young presiding judge. According to Burns, "Hussein often spoke with an unblinking stare, at times raising his chin and using hand gestures, like finger-pointing, that appeared forceful."[21] When Saddam was asked his name, he repeated it in full: "Saddam Hussein al-Majid, president of Iraq."

Once Saddam settled in and grew more comfortable with his environment, he became more like his old self, speaking with a commanding voice to declare that Kuwait was rightly a part of Iraq. Saddam began to challenge the judge, asking who he was and under what authority the latter was holding the hearing. The judge responded by saying that the tribunal that was established would be trying him and had been set up under the US-led occupation. Saddam continued, "So you are representing the coalition?" The judge replied, "No," and he went on to say, "I am an Iraqi representing the Iraqi judicial system."

The judge asked Saddam if he could afford a lawyer. Saddam responded, "The Americans say I have millions hidden in Switzerland. How can I not have money to pay for one?" He then went on to say, "I don't want to make you feel uneasy, but you know that this is all a theater by Bush, the criminal, to help him with his campaign." Burns shared his impressions of the proceedings. "In the courtroom, Hussein showed an insistent contempt for the American 'occupiers,' as he referred to them, and for what he implied was an attempt to dress up an American show trial as Iraqi justice."[22]

Hussein was very demanding at times and wanted to be referred to as "the (former) president." The judge instructed the clerk to add the title in parentheses into the transcript. Throughout the hearing, Saddam continued to assert: "I am Saddam Hussein, the president of Iraq." Thousands of Iraqis in Baghdad and throughout the Arab region would later watch Hussein speak at his hearing. It was reported that many Iraqi citizens said they were uneasy and angered at the former president's attitude toward the judge and the judicial process.

Judge Ra'id enumerated seven general charges against the former dictator. These included:

1. The premeditated killing of Kurds with chemical weapons in Halabja in Northern Iraq in March 1988.
2. The premeditated killing of a large number of Barzani—members of a prominent Iraqi Kurdish family—in 1983.
3. The premeditated killing of members of Iraqi political parties without lawful trials over the previous thirty years.
4. The premeditated killing of large numbers of Iraqi clerics in 1994.
5. The premeditated killing and displacement of Iraqi citizens and destruction of villages and homes in Northern Iraq in the Kurdish genocide (Anfal campaign, 1986–1988).
6. The premeditated killing of large numbers of Iraqis in 1991 (suppression of 1991 uprisings by Kurds and Shi'ites).
7. The 1990 invasion of Kuwait.

Saddam's deep, dark eyes looked toward the jurors' box as he listened while the judge read the charges against him.

Saddam's demeanor changed over the next twenty-six minutes. He went from being anxious to confrontational and belligerent. According to Burns, "His mood ranged from extreme uncertainty to exasperation, contempt, anger, and defiance."[23] Burns continued, "Over the next half-hour, he recovered something of his old presence and resolve, assuring that the stories that went around the world were mostly an unrepentant Mr. Hussein defying the court, condemning the American occupation and the Iraqis collaborating with it, and declaring himself the lawful president."[24]

As well, he pronounced Kuwait to be Iraq's legitimate territory and its leaders "animals," and he belittled the 1998 poison-gassing of Halabja, and his own alleged role, as something he had "heard on the radio, as though being accused of murdering 5,000 people in an afternoon was somehow an irrelevance or a bagatelle." The 67-year-old former ruler became agitated when the discussion came to the invasion of Kuwait, one of the broad charges against him. When the judge mentioned Kuwait, Saddam became very animated. He asserted, "The Kuwaitis said that it would make the Iraqi women's honor equal to ten dinars in the street." He

Saddam listening to the judge. (Photo by Combat Camera)

said, referring to himself in the third person, he "acted in his capacity as an honored Iraqi to defend Iraq and honor and revive its historical rights towards those dogs."[25]

At this point, Judge Ra'id admonished Saddam: "Don't be rash on anybody; you are in lawful proceedings." Saddam said that the responsibility for what he was saying was his. The judge interrupted Saddam and told him that any language that was outside the proper boundaries of politeness was not allowed in his courtroom.

Referring again to himself in the third person, Hussein said "that Saddam Hussein, who is the president of the Republic of Iraq, the General Commander of Armed Forces, and the armed forces went to Kuwait, right? In a formal way . . . then is it possible to level charges in a formal way and the defendant treated apart from the formal guarantees that are stated in the constitution and the law, including this law that you conduct the investigation according to it?"

According to the transcript, when the judge told Saddam that Iraqi law would govern the proceedings, the former President of Iraq remarked, "So now you are using the law that Saddam signed against Saddam." Saddam gestured with his hands while addressing the judge. Sometimes he took notes on a piece of yellow paper that he retrieved, along with a pen, from his pocket. None of the detainees were allowed legal counsel at the arraignment but would have counsel for the legal proceedings to follow.

As Saddam's arraignment was ending, Judge Ra'id instructed the court clerk

Saddam making a point. (Photo by Combat Camera)

to hand the defendant a sheet of paper to sign, as required under Iraqi procedural law, indicating that he had been informed of the charges and understood his rights. Saddam balked at putting his name on the document, saying he would not sign anything without a lawyer's attendance. Saddam said, "Please allow me not to sign until the lawyers are present. Anyhow, when you take a procedure to bring me here again, present me with all these papers in the presence of lawyers. Why would you behave in a manner that we might call hasty later?"

Saddam defied the court and refused to review or sign papers acknowledging the proceedings. The court signed the papers for him. The young investigating judge had battled Saddam throughout the arraignment on issues that involved the court's legitimacy and on the question of whether he should be designated on the papers as "President of the Republic of Iraq."

As I watched these judicial proceedings unfold, I flashed back to a movie I had seen several times (the first time as a ten-year-old boy). The title of the movie was *Judgment at Nuremberg.* It told the story of the International Military Tribunal (IMT) that took place in 1945–1946 in the Palace of Justice in Nuremberg, Germany, after World War II. The IMT tried surviving members of the military, political, and economic leadership of Nazi Germany with non-combatant war crimes against a civilian population. The crimes being charged at this arraignment in Iraq were eerily like those crimes against humanity at the Nuremberg trials. (Note: After the arraignment, the Iraqi High Tribunal (IHT) judges decided to try Saddam Hussein and other former Ba'athist leaders in a series of discrete cases, rather than in one mega-trial like Nuremberg or the Yugoslavia tribunal's massive case against Slobodan Milosevic. There are those who questioned the wisdom of this decision.)[26]

A very good friend of mine, Bobby Morgan, was drafted by the Army and sent to Nuremberg, Germany, in 1946 as part of the Army occupation of Germany. He recounted an experience he and a fellow soldier had on May 8, 1946, when they walked into the Palace of Justice to observe the day's events at the IMT.[27]

Morgan reflected, "We checked in at the entrance of the Palace of Justice and proceeded upstairs to gallery seating for visitors. We looked down upon this huge courtroom and we saw seated all thirty-three defendants in their section." The defendants who were close advisors to Hitler included Rudolf Hess, Alfred Rosenberg, Hermann Goering, Julius Streicher, Karl Doenitz, Franz von Papen, and Albert Speer, to name a few.[28] Morgan went on to say, "We put on the available headphones so we could understand what was being said. There were different headphones which translated different languages, and we selected the one for English. There was a lot of court talk. The judge was required to read all the charges each day to the defendants, and this took time."[29]

Morgan recounted, "I vividly remember one incident in the courtroom a day I was in attendance involving Goering. He was a huge man." Goering held many positions and titles within the Third Reich and was one of the close advisors to Adolf Hitler. He was found guilty of war crimes and crimes against humanity in territories occupied by German armed forces and in Austria, Czechoslovakia, and Italy and would later commit suicide instead of hanging.[30]

Morgan stated, "Behind the defendant section there stood several security guards shoulder to shoulder. On this day, Goering reacted to comments by the judge, stood up, and shook his fist at the judge and within a matter of seconds, one of the security guards came up from behind him, grabbed him, and pushed him back down into his seat." Morgan remembered the guard telling Goering, "Don't be shaking your fist at our judge." The guard then returned to his assigned position behind the defendants. "All of us in the gallery started cheering the guard and the action he took with Goering," Morgan said. "The judge then pounded his gavel several times on the desk saying, 'That will be enough of that.' We all smiled at each other and became quiet. We were proud of the action taken by the American guard."[31]

Relevantly, John Burns noted, "There were echoes of past war crimes trials at Nuremberg after World War II and at the Hague after the wars of the 1990s [Bosnian Serb] that ravaged the former Yugoslavia, when one after another of the men argued that he could not be held personally accountable for

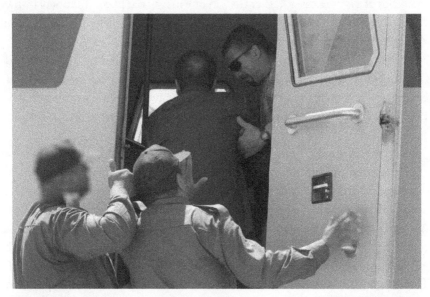

Saddam being loaded into the Rhino bus. (Photo by Combat Camera)

Judge Ra'id reviewing paperwork during one of the three breaks in the arraignment. (Photo by Combat Camera)

actions ordered by others, or carried out in the name of the 'leadership,' meaning Hussein and a handful of men in his innermost circle."[32]

Many members of Saddam's inner circle were to be in the courtroom that day. According to Burns, "All they had done, as several defendants argued, was to follow orders or assent to actions they had no power to halt, even as high-ranking military or intelligence officials or as members of the Revolutionary Command Council, the country's most powerful and feared political body."[33]

When the former president had finished his appearance before the judge, two guards assigned to escort not only Hussein but the other HVDs went to take him out of his chair to leave. He said to them, "Take it easy; I'm an old man."

As quickly as it had begun, it was over. Saddam was escorted out of the courtroom and back on the Rhino bus, where he would be transported to a helicopter that would return him to his secured holding area. He would not be seen again for several months until his first Iraqi tribunal. The preliminary charges read at the court proceedings formed the basis for a formal indictment. The investigative procedure would now begin.

Burns stated, "After Saddam departed the courtroom there was a short ten-minute break. The tension and drama seemed to suck the air out of the room." I left the courtroom and saw Amanpour. She told Burns that she and Jennings were returning to the Green Zone. They were not staying for the arraignments of the other detainees. Knowing this, Burns quickly got with the interpreter and went through his notes with him.[34] Burns rapidly wrote up his pool report and asked Amanpour if she would take it with her and hand it off to one of the military officers at LZ Washington and ask them to deliver it to the military press center (CPIC). She willingly took his notes from him, and he assumed she would follow the instructions that he provided. She did not. "Her malfeasance extended to the fact that when she went there, she did not [deliver the notes as requested]. She went on live on CNN for about two hours report-ing on what she had observed."[35]

At the conclusion of the almost six-hour arraignment, Burns finally returned to the Green Zone. He then went to the convention center, where he began to share his experience with the other journalists. Apparently, cameras were roll-ing, and his comments were being broadcast. He later learned that he was on the BBC and CNN. There was a clamor in the room from his colleagues when they said his pool notes never arrived at the CPIC.

"I was deeply, deeply upset by [Amanpour's] actions. It was not only a betrayal of me but the entire press corps by her actions that day," stated Burns. He continued, "I felt very strongly about that. She never apologized. I suppose if one reflected on that you'd have to say she had found her way to prominence in public life. She had been richly rewarded for it, and I suppose you might also say she had a career to make and that this was too good of an opportunity to miss. Her actions lacked honesty and character. In Bosnia some years earlier, I was helpful to her, since as a journalist I had far more experience than she did, and I helped her in any way that I could. But for her to act that way was most disappointing."[36]

I was unaware at the time of Amanpour's and Jennings's departure because I was distracted by a situation with Al Jazeera that had arisen regarding the television cameras. They were recording sound, which was a violation of the ground rules. When Amanpour and Jennings were granted access to the proceedings, they were instructed to remain for the entire arraignment. In reflecting back, I remember that Amanpour and Jennings nodded in agreement to the terms and proceeded into the courtroom. I should have placed a media escort with them during the entire event, but I did not. This is one reason why the military has a difficult time working with some journalists and media organizations. During my military career, I had the opportunity to work with some of the biggest names in television, newspaper, radio, and wire service, both American and international, and can only recall a few instances where a journalist was difficult or didn't play by the established ground rules—as Amanpour did on this occasion.

Saddam's trial and those of the others who appeared before the Iraqi Special Tribunal that day would not begin for months. The arraignments on Friday constituted the Iraqi equivalent of grand jury proceedings, at which evidence is weighed by a judge in the presence of the accused. If the judge finds that there is a case to answer, the charges are framed in detail, and the case goes to trial, with the judge commonly joined by a panel of other judges. A formal indictment with specific charges would follow later. The indictments would include war crimes, genocide, and crimes against humanity.[37]

It was reported in Amman, Jordan, that the lawyers who claimed to represent Hussein expressed outrage that they were not at his side for the hearing. "This is tyranny and absolute cruelty," said Ziad al-Khasawneh, who claimed that Hussein's wife, Sajidah, had hired him. He went on to demand, "How can this be called a trial if President Saddam Hussein, may God bless him, was denied his basic right to a lawyer?"[38]

A member of Hussein's defense team, Tim Hughes, said that the lawyers would argue that the trial could not be fair. He told CNN that they would argue that Hussein had immunity from prosecution because he was still Iraq's president, overthrown by an "illegitimate invasion." Legal representation at the arraignment appearance was denied Hussein, according to Hughes.[39]

"Saddam Hussein is going to say all sorts of things," the chief White House spokesman, Scott McClellan, said. "What's important is that justice is being served to Saddam Hussein and his band of oppressors by the Iraqi people in an Iraqi court." In my conversations with Jim Wilkinson, an assistant to National

Security Advisor Condoleezza Rice, he said the White House welcomed the beginning of judicial proceedings against the former dictator.[40]

President George W. Bush did not initially watch the television coverage of Hussein's court appearance, but at around midday, he stepped out of the Oval Office into an adjoining room to watch a short portion of the tape that was being replayed by one of the news networks. White House spokesman McClellan said that the president had no reaction to Hussein's comments.[41]

Except for NBC, all the US broadcast news divisions and cable news networks broke into normal programming to air the footage of Saddam. NBC's *Today* show did not air the footage, a decision it later reversed for the West Coast feed. "It [not originally showing the footage] was a mistake," a spokeswoman for *Today* would say.[42]

"On the images that rolled on Iraqi television every night until the Americans came, Mr. Hussein was always shown as indomitable, his presence diminishing all others. Until he picked up a cigar at a palace meeting, nobody else in his inner councils dared; when he spoke, top aides sat expectantly, head angled reverently, pencils poised. If he joked, all laughed; if his mood darkened, all would frown." Burns would write.[43] My personal observation of Saddam Hussein, the man in the courtroom, was that he looked like a shadow of the man I had previously seen on television and read about in magazines and newspapers. Of relevance, Greg Kehoe said he had a meeting with Saddam following the arraignment, revealing: "He thought he was going to be executed that day." This certainly makes sense, because this was the way he had handed out justice during his reign.[44]

Saddam's "enemies" frequently received similar treatment. Dr. Mowaffak al-Rubaie was one such recipient of Saddam's punishment. "Only later, from a burly Iraqi prison guard who clasped Hussein's right arm on his way in and out of the court, did Dr. al-Rubaie discover that Hussein was trying to get a fix on him, one of the two officials who sat watching Hussein from the lower tier of the stall." Hussein "asked the guard as he left, 'The man with the beard, was that Mowaffak al-Rubaie?' The guards told him 'Yes,' and he said, 'I thought so.'"

Dr. Rubaie, a neurologist on extended leave at the time from a medical post in London, said that he was seized from an operating room while still an intern in Baghdad in 1979, taken to a dungeon, tied up, and hung from the ceiling and rotated for hours.[45] After three stints in Saddam's jails, Dr. Rubaie fled to England and helped to find an Iraqi exile group and gain British citizenship. More than twenty years later, he still suffers from back pains and kidney ailments that he traces to being hung, beaten, and given electric shocks.[46] "By

Author trying to get John Burns's attention during one of the three breaks. (Photo from Slavonic collection)

Author visiting with the judge during a break. (Photo from Combat Camera)

bringing these men into a court, we've begun a huge psychological healing process," Dr. Rubaie said. "This is a new Iraq."[47]

"Here, at last, was the turning of the tables, the hunter turned hunted, the accuser accused," Burns stated.[48] This was just the beginning of the end. Saddam would find himself facing more judges, tribunals, and accusers over the course of the next thirty months leading up to his execution at the hands of an Iraqi justice system.

Once Judge Ra'id reconvened the proceedings, Burns was in his original seat with an interpreter at his side, the next phase of the arraignment. Eleven of Saddam's aides, including some of the most notorious figures of his regime and six of the ten Iraq's most wanted, would soon be arraigned.

The Arab world had never seen anything like this scene, which was broadcast repeatedly over the next twenty-four hours. In a region of the world accustomed to tyrants and despots, a seemingly invincible dictator was hauled before a court of his own citizens.[49] Burns said that Saddam "almost never appeared anywhere that made him accessible to ordinary Iraqis, sending out a team of doubles to maintain the pretense of being the people's tribune, while sparing him from assassins' threats, immured in his palaces; he was ever the grim but inaccessible colossus."[50]

The television broadcasts of the event showed only the back of the judge's head, and his name was not mentioned for security reasons. A few months later the world would learn that the man who read Saddam his rights and summarized the charges on the hot July day in Baghdad was thirty-five-year-old Ra'id Juhi Hamadi al-Sa'edi. The youthful judge was a graduate of Baghdad Law School. He came to the attention of the American authorities in 2003 while serving in Najaf when he courageously signed the indictment for notorious Shi'ite warlord Moqtada al-Sadr, charging him with murder. The public revelation of the Moqtada al-Sadr indictment placed the young judge and his family in great danger, and they were relocated for their protection to the Green Zone (or International Zone) in Baghdad. Because of his solid English and his unflappable demeanor, Ra'id Juhi became an obvious choice to head the Hussein investigation phase.[51]

At a luncheon at the Al Rasheed Hotel, Judge Ra'id was asked why he agreed to serve as the investigative judge for such a sensational and dangerous case. Judge Ra'id simply answered: "This is my job, my responsibility, my duty to my society." He added, "Many Iraqi people thought that there were no laws, no rules, no order, and we wanted to bring the rule of law and justice back to Iraq." When asked how he felt when he was face to face with one of the world's most ruthless dictators, Judge Ra'id merely shrugged his shoulders and said, "I just tried to think of him as an ordinary defendant."[52]

Spanning the next several months, Judge Ra'id would interview the defendants and compile a dossier against Saddam and the others containing more than a thousand pages of witness statements and incriminating documents— many bearing the former dictator's signature.[53]

2

CAPTURE OF THE "ACE OF SPADES"

ON JANUARY 19, 2003, 350 PERSONNEL ASSIGNED TO UNITED States Central Command (CENTCOM) located at MacDill Air Force Base in Tampa, Florida, were dispatched to set up CENTCOM's Forward Headquarters outside of Doha, Qatar, at As Sayliyah. The United States coalition forces initiated combat operations on March 19, 2003, with Operation Iraqi Freedom (OIF) under the leadership of Gen. Tommy Franks, US Army, Commander, and CENTCOM. The mission was to unseat Saddam Hussein and, in turn, to free the Iraqi people from the terror they had endured for many years under the former dictator.

Forty-five minutes after the attack, Bush addressed the US from the Oval Office. "On my orders, coalition forces have begun striking targets of military importance to undermine Saddam Hussein's ability to wage war," the president said. "Now that the conflict has begun, the only way to limit its duration is to apply decisive force."[1] Several hours later, Saddam appeared on television very much alive, in an army uniform and beret, fulminating against the American attack. Wearing glasses and reading from a notepad, Saddam spoke for seven minutes.[2]

Although Saddam was known to have body doubles, the suggestion that a surgically adjusted look-alike had delivered the address turned out to be lore. There was a simpler explanation for Saddam's wearing glasses. Abid Hamid Mahmud, Saddam's personal secretary, was apprehended after the collapse of the regime. He told US interrogators that Saddam showed up at his house. Saddam and Mahmud then went together to a safe house near the upscale Al-Mansur neighborhood in Baghdad. Hamid wrote the speech for Saddam by hand and ordered that it be videotaped. Usually, Saddam's speeches were printed in large text so he could easily read them, but no printer was available on this occasion, so Saddam put on his glasses to read the small handwriting.[3]

On April 11, 2003, US forces secured Baghdad, the capital of Iraq. Saddam had gone into hiding. It was thought that he was somewhere in Iraq; his capture was the top priority of the US military. At a press conference later that day, Army Brig. Gen. Vincent Brooks, deputy director of operations (and spokesman) at CENTCOM, made the first public announcement about the "deck of cards" in Iraq. These fifty-five cards were distributed to the troops as part of a major effort to focus on the hunt for Saddam and other high-level officials within the Iraq regime. Every card in the deck represented a "high-value target" (HVT) and together displayed the fifty-five most-wanted members of the Iraqi government.

Each card contained the wanted person's name, regime position, and (if available) photograph. Many of the photographs, however, were not current. The "Ace of Spades" was Saddam Hussein. The "Ace of Clubs" and "Ace of Hearts" were Saddam's sons Qusay and Uday. The "Ace of Diamonds" was Saddam's presidential secretary Abid Hamid Mahmud al-Tikriti. The backs of the cards featured a green military camouflage pattern. The playing cards would assist the troops in identifying the most-wanted members of Saddam's government, including high-ranking members of the Arab Socialist Ba'ath Party and Revolutionary Command Council.

Within a few weeks, the deck of cards proved to be a useful tool to the troops on the ground in assisting in the identification and capture of many of the HVTs. While many were captured and Saddam's sons Uday and Qusay were killed in a shoot-out, the Ace of Spades remained the most sought-after HVT. There was an ongoing campaign to capture Saddam and a $25 million bounty if apprehended. The capture of Saddam also included other considerations besides the reward—that is, safe conduct out of Iraq for the informant and his family.[4]

"From a religious point of view, it's illegal to hand over Saddam," said Mohammed Youssef, a 45-year-old Tikriti and father of eight who lost his leg during the 1980–1988 Iraq–Iran War. "Why? Because he is a Muslim, and the

Poster advertising $25 million reward for capture of Saddam Hussein. (Photo from Slavonic collection)

Americans are infidels." Talk in Tikrit of Saddam's prowess and dismissal of the American reward as a useless ploy was not entirely inspired by loyalty to the ousted leader. There was evidence in Tikrit of intimidation by hardcore Saddam supporters, which explains some of the quoted sentiment.

Among the contingency plans Saddam made before the war were arrangements for his own safekeeping if the need arose for him to go into hiding. Saddam had paid an estimated $1.3 billion to loyalists and tribal leaders in protection money he hoped would buy their allegiance in the event of his defeat.[5] Apart from having several safe houses in Baghdad, Saddam had hundreds more scattered around the country, with many of them being in the area around Tikrit, his tribal homeland, where he could rely on the unqualified support of his fellow tribesmen.[6]

Following the collapse of Saddam's regime, dozens of family members and senior Ba'athists fled to Syria and Jordan. An Iraqi businessman who worked closely with Saddam's regime claimed that he helped transfer "tens of millions of dollars" from a bank account run by Saddam's family in Jordan to the Iraqi embassy in Damascus shortly before hostilities commenced.[7] Conversely, Ambassador L. Paul Bremer, the top US civilian administrator, said that the coalition would not rest until Saddam's fate was determined and reassured Iraqis that he would never again rule their country. "He may be alive, but he is not coming back. I think the noose is going to tighten around his neck. His days are finished," Bremer said.

A young man by the name of S. Sgt. Eric Maddox would soon become part of history along with several other members of his team. Sgt. Maddox was raised in Sapulpa, Oklahoma, a community just west of Tulsa. He graduated from the University of Oklahoma and joined the US Army in 1999. He began his military career as a paratrooper in the Army's 82nd Airborne Division. Prior to September 11, 2001, he was assigned to the US Embassy in Beijing.[8]

In early 2003, Maddox volunteered to be a military interrogator and entered an extensive training program. Upon completion of his training, he was deployed to Iraq in July 2003, where he joined other intelligence analysts and interrogators. Their assignment was to obtain actionable intelligence, including leads that could be used to find the "deck of cards" persons within the insurgency. During the next six months, Maddox would be involved in key events that led to Saddam's eventual capture.[9]

Upon landing at Baghdad International Airport (BIAP), Maddox came under the authority of Joint Special Operations Command (JSOC), a component command of the US Special Operations Command (USSOCOM). He was immediately assigned to Task Force 121 (TF 121) that was headed by Rear Adm. Bill McRaven and was dispatched to Saddam's hometown of Tikrit, 95 miles north of Baghdad.[10]

Maddox then reported to a seven-man Delta Force element under the leadership of a Special Operations Force (SOF) senior commander to whom I will refer as "Lt. Col. Alan Troy," which is a pseudonym. (Members of his SOF team prefer their names not be mentioned due to security reasons and for the safety of their families.) Troy was an experienced SOF operator and a trusted leader who could tackle tough assignments successfully. Maddox was assigned as an interrogator for his team. The other team interrogators included Troy's senior non-commissioned officer (NCO) Jim Johnson (pseudonym) and the lead interrogator/interpreter Aziz al-Adel (pseudonym), a Jordanian American.

A Delta element is composed mostly of Army SOF operators supported by interrogators and CIA analysts.[11] They are trained in the art of hostage rescue and high-risk sensitive operations. This team was tasked with finding and capturing high-value targets (especially those included in the famous deck of cards) and gathering information through interrogation. Over the next six months, Maddox, Johnson, and al-Adel interrogated more than 300 prisoners who were captured on raids by the Delta element or other Special Forces teams.

Maddox quickly recognized that Army-instructed interrogation techniques wouldn't be effective in Tikrit. The Army had taught interrogators to "overwhelm subjects with damning information" that would convince the captured prisoners to surrender information. Hunting for hidden links in the terrorist network, however, required untested tactics. Maddox had limited time—a mere six months—to accomplish this mission. Moreover, he had to overcome the history that Saddam's regime left behind. Many Iraqis had learned under Saddam's reign that when his forces needed information, they forced confessions from their suspects. If Saddam's interrogators did not obtain the desired information, then the Iraqis would be executed.

In September 2003, Lt. Col. Troy needed a new strategy for finding actionable intelligence. The three interrogators did most of the questioning in Baghdad and Fallujah. After months of chasing down hundreds of leads, valuable information was uncovered.[12] In early November, the work of al-Adel led Troy's team to raid a small fish farm near Tikrit. They were hoping to find Mohammed Ibrahim al-Muslit, an insurgent commander and one of Saddam's right-hand men. Troy's team knew that Ibrahim and his brother owned the farm. As fate would have it, Ibrahim was not at the farm on the occasion of the "hit," but Troy's team did capture three targets, including the fish farmer. The information obtained on this hit would lead to the eventual capture of Mohammed Ibrahim al-Muslit and his son in the Sunni area of Baghdad.

In early December, Troy's Special Forces unit set out to capture Ibrahim's close associate from information obtained from the fish farmer. On this night they made three hits and successfully captured six males. The latter were brought to a special operations command compound located at BIAP. This was a temporary holding facility where initial interrogation was done.

During the two-hour interrogation session of the six males, something surprising happened. One of the individuals told the interrogators they had already captured Ibrahim. How could this have happened? Due to a stroke of luck, the unit had Ibrahim in custody and didn't even know it.[13] Once it was determined and validated that they had Ibrahim, Troy received a call from Johnson and al-Adel informing him: "We have Mohammed Ibrahim!" Troy said, "That's good news." They then told him, "And he is willing to show us where Saddam is located." Troy followed up, "That's even better."[14]

So, Troy's team went and got al-Muslit and began to interrogate him. Ibrahim was 5'10" and husky, with short jet-black hair and dark brown eyes. Ibrahim, like so many Iraqis, feared for the safety of his family if he were to share information about Saddam or his whereabouts.[15]

It took Johnson, al-Adel, and Maddox two hours to break one of the key insurgents in Iraq. Ibrahim had to be made to talk quickly since the tour in Iraq of one of the interrogators, Maddox, was drawing to a close. He had to leave Iraq within a few hours; his deployment had come to an end.

During the interrogation process, the prisoner began to negotiate with his captors. Ibrahim said he would tell them where Saddam was located and would decline the reward money. The only stipulation was he that wanted his son—who was also captured on the raid—to be released.[16] Troy said, "I can agree to your request, but *only* after we can confirm we have captured Saddam Hussein."[17]

Ibrahim eventually said in a low, hoarse whisper to the interrogators, "He [Saddam] is at a farm in Ad-Dawr. It is south of Tikrit, just east of the river [Tigris]."

"Whose farm?" one of the interrogators asked.

Ibrahim responded, "It belongs to a man named Qies Niemic Jasim."

According to Troy, this is where Maddox came in handy. He was able to fill in some gaps and provide family history, which was helpful because a lot of the records and files were destroyed during the pre-invasion phase of the war. Troy stated, "We did the best we could with the HUMIT (human intelligence) we had, which allowed us to go after many targets."

Troy then took a map, laid it on the table, and asked Ibrahim to show them the location where they could find Saddam. "You can find him west of Trikit in this area." Troy thought for a minute; the location Ibrahim pointed to was not west of Tikrit. Iraqis are notoriously bad at reading maps, as evidenced by the fact that Saddam's actual location was southeast of Tikrit and not west. Regardless, Ibrahim acceded, "I will take you."

As Maddox was reflecting on the previous two hours, one of the aircrew-men stuck his head in the door and said, "It's time to go. The admiral is waiting at the flight line."[18] Rear Adm. Bill McRaven was the commander of the entire Special Forces task force in Iraq. McRaven would later earn his fourth star and command the USSOCOM in Tampa, Florida.

Maddox was due to give a briefing later that day in Doha, Qatar. He rushed to the runway and boarded the C-17. He shouted a greeting to Rear Adm. McRaven, and the admiral nodded as he headed to the cargo hold, but with the noise from revving engines, it was difficult to hear anything.[19]

Once the doors closed, Rear Adm. McRaven made his way to the back of the plane with his staff of analysts and assistants.

"Good to see you, Sergeant Maddox," he said. "Are you ready to give that brief?"

"Yes, sir," Maddox replied. "But I think you should know the situation has changed. We captured Mohammed Ibrahim last night and he's given us a location for Saddam." McRaven stared at him blankly.[20] The admiral had been dealing with a flood of information daily. If what Maddox was telling him was true, he probably assumed that he would have already heard it from higher up in the chain of command. Prior to landing, Maddox walked Rear Adm. McRaven through the interrogation process and the information Troy's team had acquired. The admiral was finally processing the information.[21]

Upon landing, Rear Adm. McRaven called headquarters for details of the upcoming operation and where it was to be conducted. McRaven turned to his staff and said, "We're going back, just as soon as they gas this thing up. There is no way in hell I'm going to be out of Iraq when we bring in the big guy."[22]

Back at the SOF facility, Troy decided to fly Ibrahim up with the Delta element to Tikrit and make him show them exactly where Saddam was located. Once in the area, Troy began "close target recognition" to identify Saddam's location.[23] Operation Red Dawn was launched in the town of Ad-Dawr on Saturday evening (local time), December 13, 2003.

The admiral returned to Iraq and Maddox stayed behind in Doha to give his brief. He got some well-deserved rest that night but was anxious to know details about the raid. Maddox awoke early and was taken to CENTCOM Forward headquarters where he would brief Brig. Gen. John Custer, the J2 (Intelligence) CENTCOM.[24]

Lt. Col. Troy had conducted many of these hits over the past three months and was not very optimistic that Saddam would be at this location. In fact, this operation acknowledged two possibilities where the HVTs could be located.[25] Troy called Col. Jim Hickey with the 4th Infantry Division (4th ID) to ride alongside him during both hits. The 4th ID, based out of Fort Carson, Colorado, has had a long and distinguished military history dating back to World War I and through World War II at Normandy and Vietnam in the late '60s.

Troy looked at the map and told Hickey he ONLY needed 4th ID perimeter security approximately 2,000 meters' distance from the two-target area so as to keep people from getting any closer and to prevent other targets escaping the area. The area was "terrain dependent."[26]

According to Troy, Hickey insisted on providing additional 4th ID personnel to support Troy's team on the hits, but Troy was able to persuade him not to add more 4th ID personnel, and NONE inside the perimeter. The only support Troy and his Delta element needed was for 4th ID to provide *limited inner cordon assistance and other perimeter security support as needed.*[27]

Troy had two targets to hit based on his intelligence. Hence, his two teams hit each target. As the on-scene commander, Troy positioned himself in the middle of both operations to have optimal situational awareness. As both operations began, MH-6 Little Birds, UH-60 Black Hawks, and an MC-130 circled overhead.

Ibrahim was with one of the teams and, once coming upon Qies Niemic Jasim—the man who lived at the farm—Ibrahim began yelling at him to show them where Saddam was hiding. Ibrahim knew the exact spot but was reluctant to be the one to pinpoint it; he wanted Qies to do the deed. It became apparent to Ibrahim that it was going to be up to him to show the location. He moved to an area just meters away from where the team was concentrated and began inconspicuously kicking the ground. Two of the team members noticed that he was slowly uncovering a piece of rope. He had taken them to the exact spot.

The team dug up the rope to reveal a trap door. One of the members of Lt. Col. Troy's team pulled the rope and the Styrofoam lid came off, bringing with it a lid that covered a spider hole approximately six feet wide by eight feet deep.[28] A dirty, bearded man could be seen at the bottom of the spider hole. A team member ordered him to hold up his hands. The man hiding inside was Saddam Hussein. With both hands raised, Saddam poked his head out of the hole. The fugitive would never have been found here if not for Ibrahim, Saddam's bodyguard, and the work of several key interrogators.

The second assault element was notified that the search for HVT Saddam Hussein was successful and complete, and they were to return to the safe house. Col. Hickey left Troy and DID NOT accompany the Delta elements back to the safe house. Troy showed the author many photos of his team at the safe house with Saddam, but there were NO 4th ID members at the safe house—the latter only provided perimeter security.[29]

Col. Hickey radioed back to headquarters and said, "They got him!" This was not an accurate report, since it was unconfirmed: Lt. Col. Troy's team still had additional testing to verify whom they had captured. It should be pointed out again that Saddam had many doubles during his reign who provided both security and safety for him. Was this individual whom Troy's Delta element captured the Iraqi president or was it one of these doubles?

Once at the safe house, Col. Troy and his teams went through the protocols to ensure they had the necessary evidence to support Saddam's capture. Saddam looked bewildered and tired. They examined him for identifying marks. They examined his tattoos—three blue dots near his wrist, a symbol of his tribe—and noted on his waist a scar from a previous gunshot wound. But the most important evidence was his DNA, which was a match with that of his two sons. It all checked out. They had their confirmation.

On December 13, at around midnight, the Ace of Spades was captured. Armed with a 9mm Glock pistol and two AK-47 assault rifles, Saddam was in possession of $450,000 in cash (US hundred-dollar bills) in a green metal box and a box of Cuban cigars. He did not resist capture. He said to his captors, "I'm Saddam Hussein. I'm the president of Iraq. I'm willing to negotiate."[30] According to Troy, "I gave Col. Hickey the $450,000 to 4th ID *so his group could have something from the capture.* I asked him to turn it over to the proper authorities."[31]

To celebrate their success, Lt. Col. Troy's team gathered in the safe house to look at Saddam and to prepare to transport him to the south. Now, the question remained: what to do with their special guest? Although difficult to believe, there was not a plan in place for how to proceed when Saddam was captured. The assumption was that he would *not* be captured but that he would face the same death as his two sons: he would go down in a gunfight.

Troy called Baghdad to talk with his boss, Rear Adm. McRaven, who had returned from Doha. Troy confirmed with McRaven that they had Saddam and were awaiting further instructions. McRaven instructed him to bring Saddam to BIAP for security reasons.

Two hours had passed. Troy told his teams to load up the two waiting UH-60 Black Hawk helicopters with the HVDs; they were headed back to Baghdad. (Note: Once HVTs were captured, they became high-value detainees.) Ibrahim, whose head was covered with a black hood, was escorted to one helicopter and Saddam, whose head was similarly covered, was loaded in the other. Each helicopter had four operators on board for security.[32]

Both helicopters landed at BIAP, and the on-ground security personnel went to the first helicopter and unloaded and escorted the HVT onboard they assumed was Saddam, but who was actually Ibrahim. Upon seeing this, Troy shook his head and took Saddam by the arm and followed the security detail to the temporary screening facility (TSF). Saddam was given a medical examination by military doctors and placed in solitary confinement. They still needed to take a confirming DNA sample and cross-check it with that of his two sons.

The Camp Cropper compound was located to the right of the main entrance of BIAP and was clearly visible. The footprint of Cropper was roughly the shape of a square. There were four barracks-style buildings on the compound. One of these was an administration building. Three rows of parallel buildings with a courtyard between were used to hold other prisoners. These were older existing one-story buildings, which were former officers' quarters. A motel-style door on the outside opened into divided single-room cells for holding prisoners. Another building, separated from the others, was used as holding cells for HVDs. Individual rooms—not open cells—were made available for this group. There were thirty to forty feet between those buildings, with a common area for detainee use.[33]

Further back in the compound was a separate building about the size of a large car garage. It was a stand-alone, nondescript facility that was out of sight from the other buildings in the area; other detainees would never see it. This would be Saddam's new residence.[34]

Saddam arrived at BIAP with his hands zip-tied in front and a sandbag over his head so that he remained unaware of his location. He was walked into a small room, stood up against the wall, and stripped of his hood.

"Who are you?" asked the interpreter.

Slightly disoriented, the HVD looked around. "I'm Saddam Hussein, the president of Iraq," he said. "Why are you doing this to me?"

"We are going to give you a physical," said the interpreter. "Is there anything wrong with you?"

"I think I have an injury to the side of my head and a cut in my mouth," replied Saddam.[35]

"What other problems do you have?"

"I have high blood pressure and I need my medicines."

"We'll get your medicines for you," the interpreted assured him.[36]

According to Lt. Gen. Ricardo Sanchez, Commander Joint Task Force 7 (CJTF-7), "We gave Saddam a short physical exam. I was present in the room along with a security guard, a physician's assistant, an interpreter, and a cameraman [to document the prisoner's physical condition]."[37]

The exam lasted approximately fifteen minutes. According to Sanchez, "Other than a couple of bruises, the prisoner was in pretty good physical condition." He continued, "Over the next four or five hours, there was some confusion regarding Saddam's status: Was he a prisoner of war and subject to the Geneva Conventions?" Shortly thereafter, Sanchez received a call from Gen. John Abizaid informing him to treat Saddam in accordance with the Geneva Conventions.[38]

Troy said there was another cross-check to ensure that this was indeed Saddam. Once at BIAP, some HVDs who had been close to Saddam were brought to the facility to identify him: Tariq Aziz, Abid Mahmud, Chemical Ali, and one of his stepbrothers. Each prisoner was taken to an adjacent room, given a headset, and asked to view a television monitor to look at a man in the room. The man they were to identify was slouched on an Army cot in a windowless room. Each man identified the individual as Saddam Hussein, except for Aziz. Once he heard his voice, however, he too verified the man in the adjacent room as his former boss, Saddam Hussein.[39]

Maddox was in Doha awaiting word of the success or failure of capturing Saddam. Maddox asked his driver, Sgt. Peters, numerous times if he had heard anything about Operation Red Dawn. Finally, Maddox asked an Army major, "Did anything happen last night?"[40]

The major replied, "What do you mean?"

"Did they get anyone on the raid last night?"

The major craned his head out to see if anyone was within hearing distance. "Yeah," he said in a low whisper. "We got him."[41]

Maddox didn't know what to do, whether to laugh or cry. He didn't make a sound; he just stood there. He had spent many long months trying to get to this moment. He was thinking of all the dead ends and frustrating failures over those months. He had worked closely with many of his team members, and they had become good friends.[42]

Maddox was a big fan of college football, especially the University of Oklahoma (his alma mater), but at this moment he was thinking about Barry Sanders, the great running back for OU's archrival Oklahoma State. He considered him the greatest football player he had ever seen. Maddox thought, "'It wasn't his record of accomplishments that came to mind but the way he would handle himself after he scored a touchdown. He never danced or dropped to his knees or showboated in any way. He'd simply hand the ball to the referee and jog to the sidelines.' Whenever he heard Sanders interviewed, he was humble about his achievements, no matter how impressive they were."[43]

As Maddox stood in the hallway at 8 a.m. (local time) on December 14, 2003, he told himself one thing, "Remember Barry Sanders." Then he was grabbed by his good friend Lee, who said, "You did it, Eric! Holy shit! You did it."[44]

The Army major filled them in on the details of the raid, recounting how two different targets were hit based on intel gathered. Maddox's briefing with Brig. Gen. Custer was canceled, but there were several analysts at CENTCOM Forward who wanted to talk with Maddox. He was peppered with many questions: "What approach worked best for you in interrogating?" "What can Saddam tell us?" "Will Saddam talk to us?" Later that day, Maddox expected to be called back to Iraq, but instead, he boarded a commercial flight to London. Shortly after touching down at Heathrow, the news finally broke.[45]

Back in Washington, DC, Secretary of Defense Donald Rumsfeld spoke with Gen. John Abizaid, Commander CENTCOM, and called President Bush and said he believed they had captured Saddam. Before announcing this news to the world, US officials needed to be 100 percent sure. Secretary of State Condoleezza Rice called Secretary Rumsfeld and confirmed the earlier report: it was Saddam.[46]

Of course, everyone remembers seeing several seconds of video and the famous still photograph showing a heavily bearded Saddam blinking under the bright lights while being examined by military doctors. These few seconds of video and this still photo released by the military were the only images of Saddam since the invasion. The next time the world would see Saddam would be July 1, 2004, for his famous, high-profile court arraignment.

On December 14, 2003, at 3 p.m. (local time), Ambassador Bremer held a formal press conference announcing the capture of Saddam Hussein. "Ladies and gentlemen, we got him!" he declared. Those three words were suggested to him by his Arabic-speaking British press aide, Charles Heatley, just before he went on stage. Heatley told him, "They would be easy to translate." The effect was immediate and dramatic.[47]

After a few further remarks, Bremer introduced Gen. Sanchez, who provided additional details about the location of the capture, along with a short video clip of the capture site.[48] The press conference lasted about thirty minutes, and as the group left the stage there was ringing applause. Following the press event, Bremer led the group of four senior Iraqi politicians to meet Saddam at a secret location near the airport. They were Adnan Pachachi, Adel Mahdi, Ahmad Chalabi, and Mowaffak al-Rubaie.[49]

Adnan Pachachi was the former Iraqi Foreign Minister and now the acting president for the Governing Council (GC). He had opposed the coalition invasion and occupation of Iraq. To avoid the impending war, Pachachi was involved in creating an exile deal for Saddam through the United Arab Emirates (UAE). Saddam allegedly accepted the eleventh-hour offer to flee into exile weeks ahead of the US-led 2003 invasion, but Arab League officials scuttled the proposal. The exile initiative was spearheaded by the late president of the UAE, Sheikh Zayed bin Sultan Al Nahyan, at an emergency Arab summit held in Egypt in February 2003. This account corresponded with testimony from Sheikh Zayed's son in a documentary interview aired by Al-Arabiya TV.[50]

Adel Mahdi was an Iraqi Shi'a politician and economist. He was formerly the finance minister in the interim government and a member of the powerful Shi'a Party of the Supreme Islamic Iraqi Council.

Ahmad Chalabi was the former president of the GC of Iraq and a graduate of MIT and University of Chicago.

Mowaffak al-Rubaie was appointed as one of the twenty-five-member Iraqi Governing Council by the Coalition Provisional Authority (CPA) in July 2003. He was the head of the Dawa Party's international section and was prolific in organizing opposition conferences, publications highlighting Saddam's atrocities, and fundraising events in order to assist Saddam's countless victims. Al-Rubaie was a pivotal figure in the movement from its very beginning, which brought him into direct conflict with Saddam's regime. He was tortured on three separate occasions. The day after leaving Iraq to complete his medical studies in the United Kingdom, he was sentenced to death in absentia. In April 2004, he was appointed National Security Advisor (NSA) by the CPA. He held this post for its full five-year term until April 2009, when he was appointed an MP in Iraq's Council of Representatives

(Iraq's parliament). He held that position until the parliament's dissolution in March 2010.[51]

Ambassador Paul Bremer and Lt. Gen. Ricardo Sanchez, the top civilian and military Americans in the country, and the four Iraqi dignitaries reached the helipad where the helicopter was waiting to take them to BIAP, a twenty-minute flight. The group then arrived at the detention facility. Sanchez asked the four Iraqis if they wanted to see Saddam on the TV monitor or in person. They responded that they wanted to confront him in person. They were led down a dim corridor about thirty feet long, painted in drab military yellow, and stopped at the end before a blank metal door on the left. The door opened to reveal a brightly lit, oddly shaped room, about eight feet wide and probably twice that long.

Saddam then received his first official visitors while in American custody. The four Iraqis filed into the narrow room. The Americans stayed at the doorway. To the right of the door, slouched on an Army cot, wearing white Arab pajamas and a blue winter parka over his shoulders, sat Saddam Hussein. Beside one foot stood a rectangular carton of orange juice with a pink straw sticking out.[52] Saddam watched the group from beneath hooded eyelids. An Arabic-speaking American soldier stood protectively at Saddam's right shoulder, no doubt under orders to intervene if any of the Iraqis lunged for the prisoner.[53]

"He just woke up, sir," the guard said to Sanchez. "I gave him some juice."

The mood was solemn. The Iraqis began to ask Saddam pointed questions about why he had committed such horrific crimes against his own people. "What other leaders in the world used chemical weapons against his civilians?" "Why did the two hundred thousand Kurds have to die, and five thousand villages be bulldozed during the Anfal campaigns?" Mowaffak al-Rubaie, who was serving as the national security advisor, would be in the courtroom to witness Saddam's court arraignment on July 1 and the execution by hanging some thirty-six months later. (As an aside, al-Rubaie has the rope used to execute Saddam in his Baghdad home.)[54]

Chalabi grabbed one of the folding chairs and placed it at the very edge of the area that separated the visitors from Saddam so that he could peer down on him. Pachachi sat in front and Dr. Mahdi moved a chair behind the table, as though still in awe of the dictator. Mowaffak al-Rubaie declined to sit. He paced, glowering at the prisoner. "Saddam Hussein!" he shouted. "Saddam Hussein, you are cursed by God! You are cursed by God!"[55]

Saddam raised his face, glowering in the bright light. "Who are you to curse me, you traitor who has come with the Americans?" Saddam then turned to Pachachi, the foreign minister Saddam had sent into exile with a price on his head decades earlier. "My friend, Dr. Adnan," Saddam said, his tone softening, "why have you come with these traitors? You are not one of them. You are one of us."[56]

When Pachachi ignored the snare, Saddam made a show of scanning the other faces. "Who will introduce me to these great leaders of the New Iraq?" he asked contemptuously.[57]

Speaking from behind the table, Adel Mahdi pierced Saddam's sarcasm. "How do you explain the Anfal operation and Halabja?" He was referring to the brutal campaign of repression and the use of chemical weapons against the Kurds. "Why did you give the orders?" Mahdi demanded.[58]

"They were traitors and Iranians," Saddam muttered.

Now all four Iraqis were shouting questions well laced with insults at Saddam. For a moment he looked stunned. For decades no one had spoken to him in this way and lived to talk about it. He only listened.

"Why didn't you have the courage to fight or at least die trying?" al-Rubaie shouted.

Saddam refused to answer him at first and instead turned to Sanchez and asked, "If you were in my place would you have tried to resist?" Saddam then turned back to al-Rubaie and answered scornfully, "And what do you know of combat, anyway?"

Al-Rubaie was not intimidated. "At least your sons fought before they were killed."[59]

He continued with his line of questions regarding several prominent Ba'athists whom Saddam had ordered killed in the early 1980s. "Why did you do it?"

"That's just street talk," the former president replied coldly. "And what business is that to you? They were Ba'athists."

Then Pachachi leaned forward. "And why did you invade Kuwait? That began Iraq's slide into disaster."

Saddam almost smirked. "When I get something in my head, I act," he responded. "That's just the way I am."[60]

The questions went back and forth and continued for several minutes. Eventually, Chalabi rose and strode angrily from the room. The others followed. As al-Rubaie passed Saddam's cot, he glared down. "Saddam Hussein, you are cursed by God," he repeated. "How will you meet your creator?"

Saddam responded calmly, "I will meet him with a clear conscience and as a believer."

Any hope that the former dictator could be turned around and used to help persuade the insurgents to lay down their arms had been dashed. Chalabi repeated and again, "He's learned nothing . . . nothing!"[61]

Al-Rubaie recounted that Saddam's mood shifted as the group prepared to leave. "He expected to be tortured, to be hanged, or he expected Sanchez to pull out his pistol and empty three or four bullets into his head. That was Saddam's idea of justice . . . that's what he expected because that is how he ran Iraq."[62]

Members of the FBI were present to debrief Saddam after his capture. He told agents that he was more worried about looking weak to Iran than being removed by the coalition. He never thought the United States would follow through on their promise to disarm him by force.[63]

As Sgt. Maddox sat in the Heathrow airport pub awaiting his flight back to the US, he was watching the press conference intently, and many thoughts ran through his mind. He listened to the excitement and buzz around him. He was keyed up, too, but at the same time dead tired. The people in the bar had no idea who was sitting with them on that historic day. Later, Maddox was recognized for his crucial contribution to the capture of Saddam. Porter Goss, Director of the Central Intelligence Agency, presented Maddox with the National Intelligence Medal of Achievement for his role in the capture of Saddam Hussein.[64]

In addition, the US Army presented Maddox, Johnson, and al-Adel with the Legion of Merit Medal, which is rarely awarded to non-commissioned officers.

Saddam Hussein was finally captured: the man who started a nine-year war against Iran, used chemical weapons against the Kurds of his country, developed biological weapons capable of killing most of the people of the Middle East, threatened and then invaded Kuwait and started the Gulf War, and came close to making an atomic bomb. And, within his country, he executed people at random, imprisoned and tortured thousands of others, and placed all power in the hands of his family and relations and allowed them to steal, rape, and murder scores of innocents.[65]

The reaction across the world was immediate. President Bush said that Saddam "would face the justice he denied to millions. For the Ba'athist Party holdouts responsible for the violence, there will be no return to the corrupt power and privilege they once held." Secretary of Defense Donald Rumsfeld stated, "Here was a man who was photographed hundreds of times shooting off rifles and showing how tough he was, and in fact, he wasn't very tough, he was cowering in a hole in the ground, and had a pistol and didn't use it, and certainly did not put up any fight at all."[66]

Prime Minister Tony Blair of Great Britain was President Bush's strongest Iraq War ally. He called the capture good news for all Iraqis, saying, "It removes the shadow that has been hanging over them for too long."[67]

POSTSCRIPT TO SADDAM'S CAPTURE

Lt. Col. Troy had a series of conversations with Ibrahim after Saddam's capture. During one of these conversations, Ibrahim asked Troy about receiving the $25 million bounty placed on Saddam's seizure. He felt he was entitled to it since he provided information that led a team to Saddam. Troy reminded Ibrahim that he did not come forward and volunteer the information. He only shared what he knew about Saddam's location after he was already in custody of the US government. Plus, he had negotiated for the release of his son only after the capture of Saddam.[68]

Ibrahim was eventually sent to jail and his son was released and went to Jordan.

Troy felt there was still something not right with Ibrahim's story. He wondered why Ibrahim had been so willing to give up his boss. Troy ordered his team back to the farmhouse on December 17 and soon noticed there were several empty holes in the ground. The team continued digging in the area. Troy had a hunch that proved accurate. They dug up four holes and uncovered $12 million. Based on the existence of other holes they found, Troy estimated there was another $24 million missing. Interesting to note is that the $450,000 (in $100 bills) they found with Saddam that Troy gave to Col. Hickey and the $12 million (also $100 bills) they found while digging were all sequential numbers.[69]

Col. Troy received an invitation to meet with President George Bush. In preparation for the meeting, he had Saddam's pistol that was with him when he was captured encased in a beautiful shadow box with a brass plate inscribed with the words "Captured Pistol of Saddam Hussein – December 13, 2003." Troy was unable to list his team's names due to security reasons, so he had each team member involved in the capture sign their names on the back side of the pistol. Troy and three Delta members went to the White House and presented President Bush with the pistol.[70]

As recounted in President Bush's book, *Decision Points*, "The president asked Col. Troy and his team to tell him the story of the hunt and who was involved in the actual capture."[71] Troy outlined the story of how the Delta element operation came together and how HIS team made the two hits and captured Saddam.[72] President Bush would go on to say, "This pistol always reminded me that a brutal dictator, responsible for so much death and suffering, had surrendered to our troops." There was only one person with the power to avoid war, and he (Saddam) chose not to use it. For all his deception of the world, the person Saddam ultimately deceived the most was himself.[73] The president told Troy and his team that "he would display the gift in the private study off the Oval Office and one day in my presidential library."[74]

When Maddox returned to Washington, DC, he was asked to do several debriefs, including with Vice Adm. Lowell Jacoby, Director, Defense Intelligence Agency; Gen. Pete Pace, Vice Chairman, Joint Chiefs of Staff; Donald Rumsfeld, Secretary of Defense; and Lt. Gen. John Alexander, head of Army Intelligence. As Maddox began his brief with Gen. Alexander, he was quickly interrupted when the general pulled out a newspaper clipping from the *New York Times*. "What is this article referring to?" Maddox couldn't believe it. Another organization had rushed in so quickly to take the credit: the 4th ID. Maddox never imagined the 4th ID would begin taking credit for the capture, but they did.[75]

According to Maddox, "The media was not allowed anywhere near our operations. Whenever we got a big catch in Tikrit, we would turn the HVTs over to the 4th ID. They would brief the press. But no one in the 4th ID had anything to do with directly capturing Saddam." Their role was to secure the perimeter of the search area.[76]

Saddam was NOT turned over to 4th ID, according to Lt. Col. Troy and Sgt. Maddox. Hence, the commander for 4th ID has taken credit for "leading" the assault force capturing Saddam. He has said "the media will often frame things to sensationalize" events. Of course, I have worked with the media in three combat zones, and I know how important it is to set the record straight every time there is an interview or speech on a particular event or misperceptions will continue.[77] As with any high-profile event, groups arrive on the scene after the fact, claiming greater participation than was the case, standing by the site and taking pictures, holding captured money, etc.

I'm reminded of the story of a good friend, Clendon Thomas, who was an All-American halfback at the University of Oklahoma. Thomas played on OU's 1955 and 1956 championship teams and played eleven years in the National Football League with the Los Angeles Rams and Pittsburgh Steelers where he was All-Pro.

His story is about the famous 1957 football game between OU and Notre Dame. Notre Dame came into Norman, Oklahoma, and beat the Sooners 7–0, snapping the Sooners' forty-seven-game winning streak. At that time, it was the longest winning streak in college football history. More than fifty years have passed since that fateful day in Norman, but OU fans still come up to Thomas and tell him they were at that game and saw the streak come to an end. Thomas says, "The stadium only held 62,000, but there must have been 300,000 there that day because so many people say they were there."

3

FOURTH AND FINAL COMBAT DEPLOYMENT

I HAD JUST WRAPPED UP MY THIRD SENIOR LEADERSHIP CON-ference in Washington, DC, February 4–8, 2003. These conferences were designed to bring together my community senior leadership for a series of briefings and lectures from naval leaders—active and retired—who would share their leadership experiences and "best practices" in leading men and women whether in peace or combat. Some of the previous guest presenters included Cmdr. Kirk Lippold, skipper of the USS *Cole*; Navy Master Diver Carl Brashear; Cmdr. (Ret.) Lloyd "Pete" Bucher, skipper of the USS *Pueblo*; Medal of Honor recipients Lt. (Ret.) Tom Norris and Capt. (Ret.) Tom Hudner; and the first American shot down over North Vietnam and one of the longest-serving prisoners of war (POW), Lt. Everett "Erv" Alvarez Jr.; numerous flag officers also attended the event. Feedback from the community from these events was always very positive, and there were many takeaways from the lectures.

A week and a half later, I flew from Oklahoma City to New Orleans for a series of Navy meetings. They started with lunch in the French Quarter. During the meal, I received a call from a Washington, DC, number but was unsure of who was calling. After lunch and a follow-up meeting that lasted about an hour, I headed to the hotel and checked in. I began returning telephone calls and checking paperwork, which was never-ending.

Among the many phone messages was one from Capt. Frank Thorp (who would later be promoted to Rear Admiral and be the Navy's Chief of Information) in Washington, DC. Thorp was the special assistant to the Chairman Joint Chiefs of Staff for Public Affairs (Gen. Richard Myers). I had an office call and lunch with Thorp in the Pentagon a few days prior to the leadership conference, plus he was one of my guest speakers at the conference. Then Lt. Thorp and I had met in November 1990 prior to and returning from Operation Desert Shield/Desert Storm, when he served as the aide to Rear Admiral Brent Baker, Navy's Chief of Information. During my office call, we discussed several topics, one of which was "if he ever needed someone to go down range [Iraq] to just call."

I finally connected with Thorp later that afternoon. When he answered the telephone, I said, "Frank, this is Greg Slavonic."

He said, "Admiral, how are you?"

I said, "Fine. I'm in New Orleans for a series of flag officer meetings."

After a few minutes, he said, "I've got a question to ask you: I need you to go to Iraq and relieve Brig. Gen. Mark Kimmitt."

I responded, "Are you serious?"

He said, "Yes."

"When would I deploy?" was my response.

"I don't know for sure, but will probably know in few months," was his answer.

"Sounds good; count me in."

In a conversation in early May, Capt. Thorp indicated I would need to first come to Washington, DC, for processing that would take about a week. While the processing was underway, I would be in the Pentagon attending a series of meetings and briefings, which Thorp had put together.

I tried to read as much as I could about the current state of affairs in Iraq and remember one story noting that the head of Iraq's war crimes tribunal said the US had pledged to hand over Saddam Hussein and about 100 other suspects to Iraqi authorities before July 1—if they were already in Iraqi custody. Salem Chalabi, head of the IST, said, "The coalition will hand them over if we are able to hold them in custody." He continued, "Mr. Hussein would definitely be handed over before July 1, when Iraq assumes sovereignty from the US-led occupiers."

The story went on to say that US officials, who were holding Saddam in an undisclosed location, disputed the report. Secretary of State Colin Powell said he knew nothing about the reports regarding a transfer of custody by July 1. State Department spokesman Richard Boucher also said that he did not know of any decision on when the coalition would hand over the ousted Iraqi leader.

The US estimated that Saddam Hussein's regime killed at least 300,000 Iraqis. Some human rights groups asserted the number was closer to one million. After reading the reports and many others about Saddam and his killing machine, I wondered if I would ever actually be face to face with this former dictator. In a couple of months, I would.

My orders arrived May 20 for 365 days (unless released sooner). Thorp had told me this was a six- or seven-month deployment. When I asked Thorp: "Why me for this job?", he told me it was due to the work in 1990–1991, and he thought I was the best person for the Baghdad assignment. My orders read "Position title: Director of Public Affairs/Strategic Communicator, Baghdad, Iraq–United States Central Command, CJTF-7/MNF-I." Since it was uncertain when I would return home, my wife, Molly, and I decided she would accompany me to Washington, DC, for the week of meetings.

This would be my final overseas combat deployment, with my retirement looming only thirteen months away. The first had been to the Vietnam War aboard the USS *Constellation* (CVA 64; nickname "Connie") in 1972, where we supported Operation Linebacker in the mining of Haiphong Harbor and the bombing of Hanoi and other North Vietnam targets. The second deployment was in 1973 for nine-and-a-half months where *Constellation* was on station to ensure that the peace treaty signed on January 23 was enforced. Connie's presence was also to secure the safe return of POWs stateside to their families from Hanoi. The third deployment was to support Operation Desert Shield/Desert Storm in late 1990 to mid-1991, mentioned earlier. Now, in 2004, I was returning to a region of the world that the US and its coalition partners had had the opportunity to finish in 1991, but that politics had not allowed for closure.

This was our last week together. Molly and I departed later that afternoon. I picked up the rental car and headed to the Marriott Residence Inn in Crystal City, which was within walking distance or one metro stop from the Pentagon. Monday was a holiday (Memorial Day) and we took this opportunity to visit and tour the newly opened World War II Memorial and spend time in Old Town Alexandria. We had dinner at our favorite restaurant in Old Town, which was located on the Potomac River and gives a great view of DC at night.

Tuesday morning, June 1, I reported to Capt. Thorp's office to see what he had planned for me. On his staff was another old friend who was a member of the Joint PA staff I had met in San Diego six years earlier, Cdr. Dawn Cutler (she would later be promoted to rear admiral and named the Navy's Chief of Information (CHINFO). We had a chance to visit and catch up on old times. We went over the schedule, and it was impressive. Thorp had arranged briefings/office calls with many of the top military leaders. I had only met a few of them and was looking forward to the meetings. I then headed over to the Washington Navy Yard and reported to the Navy Military Processing Station (NMPS), which would get me ready with the required paperwork to deploy. I also needed to walk over to the medical clinic for my physical and shots—all part of the overseas processing one goes through.

Over the next four days I had several briefings/office calls with:

- Gen. Richard Myers, Chairman of the Joint Chiefs of Staff (CJCS).
- Gen. Peter Pace, Vice Chairman of the Joint Chiefs of Staff.
- Gen. George Casey, Jr., Vice Chief of Staff, US Army.
- Brig. Gen. Vincent K. Brooks, who served as the Deputy Director of Operations and Spokesman for Operation Iraqi Freedom, CENTCOM Forward in Doha, Qatar. Later he was promoted to general and served as Command General US Army Pacific. Thorp and Brooks worked closely together when they were both deployed to Doha prior to the commencement of combat operations in Iraq in March 2003.
- Lt. Gen. Norton A. Schwartz, Director of Operation (J-3), Joint Staff. He would later be promoted to general and Chief of Staff for the Air Force.
- Vice Adm. Timothy J. Keating, Director Joint Staff. He would later be promoted to admiral and served as Commander, US Northern Command.
- Hon. Larry DiRita, Acting Principal Deputy Assistant Secretary of Defense for Public Affairs.
- Hon. Bryan Whitman, Principal Deputy Assistant Secretary of Defense for Media Operations.
- Brig. Gen. Mary Ann Krussa-Dossin, Director of Public Affairs, US Marine Corps.
- Brig. Gen. Ron Rand, Director of Public Affairs Secretary of the Air Force.
- Rear Adm. Terry "T" McCreary, Navy's Chief of Information.

- Capt. Greg Smith, in charge of public affairs for Joint Forces Command and who later would be promoted to rear admiral and named CHINFO.
- Col. Guy Shields, Deputy Chief of Public Affairs, US Army.

Of all these encounters, three were the most memorable to me, and I still have vivid recollections of them. The first was my meeting with Gen. Myers, CJCS, who was Thorp's boss. This was my first meeting Tuesday afternoon, and Thorp accompanied me as he would on most senior officer meetings. I knew the Chairman was a Kansas State graduate and I understood Thorp had a good working relationship with him. We entered the outer office and Thorp told the secretary we were there for our 2 p.m. meeting. The Chairman greeted us, introductions were made, and we were invited to sit at a small table. The Chairman and Thorp talked about some issues and then the Chairman looked at me and said, "We have a problem I need you to address and fix when you arrive in Iraq."

I said, "Yes, sir. How can I be of assistance?"

He said they had a "combat camera issue. We need to get those images out of Iraq in a timelier manner and get them out to the media." He said that he and Frank had talked about this issue and felt it needed to be fixed.

I said, "Sir, once I get on the ground and evaluate the situation, I will get back with Capt. Thorp with a plan of action." After about thirty-five minutes, the meeting concluded. The Chairman wished me well and we departed the office.

Later that week was the next meeting that was of particular interest for me. It was with Gen. Casey, who would later serve and retire as the 44th US Army Chief of Staff, the highest-ranking officer in the US Army. It was anticipated that Casey would officially be named in a few days the Commanding General of Multi-National Force–Iraq (MNF-I), the newly established four-star command in which I would be assigned once in Iraq. He would soon relieve Lt. Gen. Ricardo Sanchez.

Gen. Casey graduated from Georgetown University with a BS in international relations in 1970 and received his Army commission following graduation. He went on to earn an MA degree in international relations from the University of Denver. His father, George W. Casey Sr., was a West Point graduate who rose to the rank of major general and served in two conflicts (the Korean and Vietnam Wars). Casey Sr. commanded the 1st Cavalry Division in Vietnam and was killed on July 7, 1970, when his command helicopter crashed in South Vietnam en route to a hospital to visit wounded US soldiers. He was the first general officer killed in the Vietnam War.

Rear Adm. McCreary accompanied me to the meeting, which was scheduled for June 3 at 3 p.m. Gen. Casey would be the person I'd be working for in Iraq, and I was looking forward to meeting my new boss. I didn't know anything about him other than that he was US Army, and I knew the Army had a different view of strategic communications and public affairs than did the Navy. On the walk down to his office, McCreary raved about the general and mentioned how they had worked together on the Joint Staff. "Greg, you will enjoy working with him," McCreary said.

We arrived at his outer office and told his secretary we were there to see Gen. Casey. She asked us to be seated, saying that it would be just a moment. She entered Casey's office, returned after a couple of minutes, and said, "The general will see you." As we walked in, the general greeted McCreary like they were long-lost friends. I introduced myself and we shook hands. Casey invited us to sit on the sofa and he sat on a chair. McCreary was between Casey and me. For the next fifteen minutes, McCreary and Casey talked about Joint Staff, where people were, etc. Casey never said anything to me. He didn't even look at me. I've been in enough of these types of meetings to know and sense when something was not quite right. McCreary then talked about Iraq and how he saw the communications landscape. Casey and he engaged in another five-minute discussion. I was not included. As our meeting was drawing to an end Casey looked at me and said, "I will see you in Iraq." That was it. It was a thirty-minute meeting and that was the extent of our interaction. We stood, he shook McCreary's hand and then mine, and then we departed his office. McCreary told me not to worry about anything and reiterated it by saying, "You will enjoy working for him." I did my best not to pre-judge this initial meeting, but I did not have a good feeling about my upcoming working situation with Casey.

The last meeting of interest was with Gen. Peter Pace, Vice Chairman, Joint Chiefs of Staff and who would later become Chairman, Joint Chiefs of Staff. The meeting was scheduled on Friday, June 4, at 2 p.m. Due to Gen. Pace's busy schedule, this meeting was rescheduled twice, but it was the most interesting of the entire group. As Thorp and I entered his office, he greeted us with a handshake, and I introduced myself. He invited us to sit at a table to the right of the entrance to his office. I had never met Pace before but found that he was a very down-to-earth person and most informative. He provided an excellent overview of what to expect and after about thirty-five minutes, he rose from the table and went to his desk, opened the middle drawer, and returned with a business card and his challenge coin. A challenge coin is a small coin or medallion, bearing the organization's insignia or emblem. Historically, the coin is presented by unit commanders in recognition of special achievement by a member of that unit. These coins are also exchanged in recognition of a visit of a unit commander to an organization. He presented me with his coin and wished me luck. He said if there was ever anything I needed while I was deployed to call him, and he would do his best to support me. (There were two instances when I should have called him and did not. I have second-guessed myself regarding not making those telephone calls many, many times.)

He took his business card, turned it over, and wrote two phone numbers on it. As he was writing he said, "Give this card to your wife, and if she ever has any questions or problems while you're deployed, have her call me. These are my cell and home numbers."

I thought for a second and, as he started to hand the card to me, I said, "General, my wife is outside in the hallway waiting for me, and I think this would mean more to her coming from you than from me." My wife Molly had met me for lunch and then accompanied me to the Pentagon.

He said, "Great." As he opened his office door, he turned to the left and opened a cabinet and looked at me and said, "Do you think she would like this [pointing to a stuffed bear] or this [silver circular jewelry case]?" The case was about three-and-a-half inches in diameter and one inch tall, with a "Chairman JCS" crest on the top.

I looked at him and said, "The silver case."

As we exited his outer office, there must have been three or four 3-star and 2-star officers stacked up waiting for their meeting with him. He was calm and focused. We turned to the right, walked about fifteen feet, and entered the Joint Chiefs of Staff Corridor. Molly was walking in the long corridor, looking at and reading about one of the paintings on the wall of the former Chairman of the Joint Chiefs of Staff. It is a corridor of immense military history. As we turned the corner I called her name, and she came walking toward us. I said, "Molly, I would like you to meet Gen. Peter Pace. He's a Marine."

He said, "Molly, please accept this gift from me."

She said, "Thank you," and then continued, "My brother-in-law served with the Marines in Vietnam and received three Purple Hearts."

Gen. Pace said, "Really, you should be proud of his service."

She said, "I am."

Gen. Pace then went on to present her with his business card and told her that his work, home, and cell numbers were on the card and if there was anything she ever needed or if she ever had any questions, she could call him any time. She said, "Thank you." He turned to me and again wished me well and returned to his office. I would have another office call with Gen. Pace seven months later when I returned from Iraq.

Thorp and I returned to his office, where Barbara Starr was waiting. Starr was the CNN Pentagon reporter. Thorp introduced me to her, and we had a brief and social discussion. She wished me well, and I told her that if there was anything I could do for her just to call me. She said, "I will."

Molly waited in the outer office while I went in with Thorp to say good-bye and he wished me luck. We would have several conversations and exchange many e-mails over the coming months.

My last stop and meeting that Friday was with Master Chief Gwen Wallmark at the Washington Navy Yard. We arrived at her office at around 3 p.m. and she had almost everything ready to go. She and her staff were flexible and accommodating. She said, "Admiral, good luck. Call if there is anything I can help you with or anything you may need once you're in Iraq." I said I would.

Molly was flying out Sunday morning and I was flying out the next day for my next processing station: Fort Benning, Georgia, a US Army post outside of Columbus, which many service personnel needed to pass through prior to deployment to Iraq or Afghanistan.

Sunday, June 6, after I took Molly to the airport and she departed Washington, DC, the world learned that the fortieth president of the United States, Ronald Reagan, had died. When I heard this news, I had a strong feeling that his passing was going to impact my deployment schedule but needed to wait and see.

Fort Benning would be the next-to-last stop before deploying to Iraq. I knew what to expect, and most everything had already been accomplished in DC. My plan upon completing my processing/training at Fort Benning was to depart on Thursday and drive to US Central Command, MacDill Air Force Base, in Tampa, Florida, for my final day of briefings on Friday, June 11. This would be with Capt. Hal Pittman. Pittman was Director of Public Affairs for CENTCOM and would later be promoted to rear admiral. His boss was Gen. John Abizaid, Commander, US CENTCOM. I had hoped to depart early Saturday, June 12, for Iraq. Well, sometimes the best-laid plans don't always come together, and one needs to remain flexible and adaptive to the situation presented.

I departed Washington, DC, on Monday, June 7. The flight departed a little after 10 a.m. and flew to Atlanta's Hartsfield International Airport. Once I landed, I picked up my rental car. I loaded my gear into the car, which consisted of two large roller bags, and headed to Columbus, Georgia, the home of Fort Benning.

It was announced mid-day on Monday that President Reagan's funeral would be held June 11 at the Reagan Library. This meant Friday would more than likely be a national holiday and would probably result in the postpone-ment of my meetings at CENTCOM.

I arrived at Fort Benning in the afternoon. Fort Benning is known for its Infantry and Armor Schools, and thousands of soldiers have been trained at this facility. I checked into my quarters, which were located near officer hous-ing, and went on a long run that took me along South Lumpkin Road. I remem-bered this road well from scenes of the movie *We Were Soldiers* that were filmed there. In one scene, Lt. Col. Hal Moore, played by Mel Gibson, woke up, kissed his wife good-bye, and walked out of his quarters and down the street in the early morning darkness preparing to deploy to Vietnam in 1965. This scene was vivid in my mind.

I called Molly that evening and said, "What do you think about flying to Tampa on Thursday?" I continued, "I am pretty sure I will be finished mid-morning Thursday and will be driving to Tampa. I can pick you up at the airport if you can arrive around 5 p.m." I also said, "I called CENTCOM [MacDill Air Force Base] and Friday will be a holiday for the military due to the funeral, and my meeting will be pushed to Monday."

The next day, Tuesday, June 8, I was picked at my quarters and escorted by Capt. Brenda Crummell, a squared-away young Army soldier, and taken to the CONUS Replacement Center (CRC) site to begin my processing. She would be my escort and driver while I was at Fort Benning.

I was the only flag officer (admiral) going through the in-processing for about thirty individuals including five sailors and one Navy commander. After I arrived at the auditorium, we received a briefing of what to expect during this week. We were then taken to another room to begin the administrative and medical processing. I had already been through this in Washington, DC, so it went rather fast. Once I was finished, I spoke with the person in charge and said I had intended to depart Fort Benning on Thursday and drive to CENTCOM, if that was possible. He said he would check on it and get back with me but didn't think there would be a problem with this plan.

I returned to my quarters, changed clothes, and went on a long run. June at Fort Benning can be warm and humid, as was the case on this day. I called Molly and told her to schedule a flight to Tampa. I would arrive in time to pick her up around 5:30 p.m.

On Wednesday, June 9, Capt. Crummell picked me up at 7:45 a.m. for the second day of processing. On this day, everyone would receive clothing: mission-oriented protective posture (MOPP) gear, helmet, protective vest with Kevlar insert plates, and personal weapons. I declined to be issued a Beretta 9mm. I had purchased the carry case (per my orders), but I did not want all the hassle that accompanied carrying a weapon on a commercial aircraft, so I chose to be issued this weapon upon my arrival in Iraq. This proved to be a wise decision.

On Wednesday after lunch, Capt. Crummell took me to the firing range for small arms qualification. In my case, it was for the 9mm Beretta. I told the person in charge that I had already qualified about a year ago and had my paperwork. I thought I had this box checked. The range master said, "Sir, you still need to qualify again here."

I said, "Okay." I knew I needed a minimum score of 160 to pass, which I was sure I could easily do. I passed and was on my way.

I packed that evening and prepared to shove off at around 11 a.m. the next day. Thursday morning, I was picked up by Capt. Crummell for the last time and taken to the auditorium for a training video. After watching the video, I was escorted to the admin section, was told my training was complete, and received a large manila envelope with my paperwork and endorsed orders. Endorsed orders are critical to being paid, and you must have this paperwork. The young Capt. Crummell took me back to my quarters and I thanked her for all her assistance. I loaded the car and went to billeting to check out. I was on my way out of Fort Benning by around 11 a.m. and on my way to Tampa. It was about a six-and-a-half-hour drive. If there were no traffic issues or mechanical problems the timing was good for me to be at Tampa International Airport just in time for Molly's scheduled flight arrival.

Her flight was on time, and I greeted her at the Southwest Airlines baggage claim area. We headed for the Bachelor Officer Quarters (BOQ) at MacDill AFB and arrived around 6:30 p.m. I had called earlier and reserved a BOQ room for four days with a checkout on Tuesday, June 15. I had stayed at MacDill before; they had great officers' quarters and the base was fantastic. It was located right on Tampa Bay.

The next day, Friday, June 11, the government was shut down, so Molly and I toured the area beaches. I had been to MacDill several times but never ventured too far off base, so it was fun to go and visit several beach cities. Saturday and Sunday we did much the same. We had quality time together and really enjoyed each other and the area. On Sunday evening we had dinner with Rear Adm. Bill Payne, a Navy SEAL with whom I had become friends. Molly and I met Bill at a local restaurant not far from the base. It was good to see a fellow shipmate, and our evening included good conversation and his insights about Iraq.

Lt. Cmdr. Lindsay Kough arrived later that night at MacDill. I had invited Kough to accompany me to Iraq for the early portion of my deployment. His orders were cut, and he was ready to go. He would be my personal security detail (PSD). Mark Kimmitt had a PSD team, but I did not expect him to offer them to me. As it turned out I was correct.

Monday morning, I arrived at the CENTCOM Public Affairs shop and met Deputy Public Affairs Officer Lt. Col. John Robinson. He was covering for Capt. Hal Pittman, who was traveling with Gen. John Abizaid throughout the CENTCOM AOR (area of responsibility). Capt. Pittman had arranged a meeting for me at 9 a.m. with Maj. Gen. Steve Whitcomb, Chief of Staff, and USCENTCOM. The Deputy Commander-in-Chief (DCINC) was unavailable. Whitcomb briefed me on the operational environment in Iraq and the transition from CJTF-7 to MNF-I and MNC-I (Multi-National Corps–Iraq). MNF-I would be the four-star command I would be working for, and the MNC-I would be headed up by a Lt. Gen. Tom Metz, a three-star. Corps would be responsible for the day-to-day combat operations. The meeting lasted about two hours and was very informative.

Afterward, I returned to the CENTCOM PA office to visit with the staff and acquire their insights and thoughts about how things were going in Iraq and any suggestions they might have on how best to improve the situation. In addition, the staff was most helpful in acquiring airline tickets to Doha, Qatar, for Lt. Cmdr. Kough and me. Travel to Doha was required for a final set of briefings before going into Iraq.

Since this was my last day with Molly and I was finished with all the meetings, I decided to secure for the day at around 2 p.m. I also needed to go to the Base Exchange to get a haircut and a few other toiletries items that I needed to take with me. Molly and I had an enjoyable dinner at a local restaurant, which would be—again—our last night together.

I had a restless night. I was anxious about my upcoming deployment. I got up early Tuesday morning, June 15, and had a late breakfast with Molly and Kough. We returned to BOQ, checked out, and headed to the airport to return the rental car, check luggage, and go through the international check-in. Molly's flight departed before mine. Kough's flight left later than mine. I took Molly to her gate, kissed her good-bye, and said I would call her from Doha.

4

THE JOURNEY BEGINS

THE AMERICAN AIRLINES FLIGHTS FROM TAMPA TO CHICAGO and then to Heathrow (London) were eventful and challenging due to flight delays leaving Chicago.

I was not aware of the afternoon thunderstorms that regularly rolled into Tampa that time of year; my flight to Chicago was delayed an hour. If I had known this I would have arranged for an earlier departure. The American Airlines flight was scheduled to depart Tampa at 3:57 p.m. and arrive in Chicago at 5:44 p.m. Since it was delayed, I was concerned about making my connecting flight. The American agent said I had a 50/50 chance of making my connection. This was not good news, especially since it was an international flight.

American Airlines flight #1651 finally departed at 5 p.m. and the MD-80 was headed to Chicago's O'Hare International Airport. It did not land until 6:15 p.m. I could still make my connecting flight to London, which was departing at 6:30 p.m. When we landed, I quickly deplaned and ran to my connecting gate. Whew, I made it. I gave the attendant my ticket, boarded the plane, and took my seat. I took a deep breath, sat back, and closed my eyes.

Then, about five minutes later I heard someone say, "Mr. Slavonic." I opened my eyes to see a flight attendant who asked, "Would you please come with me?" I thought to myself, "What is this about?" We arrived at the ticket counter, where an American Airlines attendant said, "We're sorry, but your luggage did not make it and we can't allow you to fly without your luggage."

I said, "I ran all the way to this gate, made it, and you're telling me my luggage did not make it?"

She said, "Yes, and we're extremely sorry." I told her I had a connecting flight from Heathrow to Doha, Qatar, and asked if I would be able to make that flight. She replied, "It's highly unlikely, but we will do our best to get you on the next flight to London." Little did I know this was only the beginning of this travel saga to Doha.

I finally got a seat on the second flight to London, which departed at 9:15 p.m. that night. I could not do anything about my connecting flight until I arrived in London. So again, I gave the gate attendant my ticket and boarded the plane. And again, I closed my eyes, trying to relax and not show my frustration with American Airlines. In a few minutes, I heard the flight attendant ask, "Mr. Slavonic, would you please come with me?"

I said, "What is this about? Am I getting bumped from this flight too?"

She said, "No, but we need to talk to you." This was just great; what could this be?

When I got to the desk, an American Airlines agent said, "We are extremely sorry to tell you this, but we need you to come with us. One of your bags got caught on the conveyor belt, which loads baggage into the luggage storage area, and everything in the bag is on the tarmac. We need you to come down and gather everything up and see what might be missing."

As the agent escorted me down to the tarmac, I was thinking, "I have flown thousands and thousands of miles during my military career, and I have never had something like this happen before." When I arrived underneath the 777 aircraft, there was my duffle bag—ripped to shreds, and much of the contents, including my clothing, torn or covered in black grease. I asked the agent where my other bag was because I had an extra duffle bag inside it. They found that bag and I opened it, retrieved the extra bag, and began stuffing everything on the tarmac into the extra bag. I would worry about replacing these items once in Baghdad. At least I had a couple of uniforms, boots, socks, a Kevlar vest and a helmet, and a few other items that would allow me to attend my meetings—IF I ever got to Doha.

After about thirty minutes, I got everything together and said, "Okay, that's it." The American Airlines agent apologized again as we walked back to the terminal and up the ramp and she took me back to my seat. I had grease on my slacks and my hands. Of course, I had been sweating due to the humid night in Chicago.

I went into the bathroom to wash my hands and face and returned to my seat and prepared for takeoff. The doors closed at 9:55 p.m. and the plane began to taxi down the runway. Within a few seconds we lifted off and headed to London for the nine-hour flight. I closed my eyes and went to sleep for a few hours.

We landed at Heathrow at 11:30 a.m. (local time), and I immediately headed to the American Airlines ticket counter to see what options were available. After about an hour of back-and-forth with other airlines, checking schedules, etc., they finally got me a seat on Qatar Airlines. I was a little leery of flying on this airline, but this was "the best worst option available." The flight did not leave for nine hours. Wow . . . nine-hour layover. What to do? Then I thought, how about the American Airlines' Admirals Club? I located the club and went to the desk, where I explained my situation and the difficulties I had experienced with American Airlines—and I included that I was headed to Iraq. I requested access to the club, which, after about a fifteen-minute conversation, was granted. It was worth my time and effort to pursue this course because sitting in the Admirals Club was far more comfortable and restful than the main terminal as I waited for my upcoming flight. It also gave me time to call Molly and recount the nightmare of air travel from Tampa to Chicago to London.

Then I reflected back on my mission during the First Gulf War in Dhahran, Saudi Arabia, a similar work assignment to the one ahead. This time I would be in charge of around seventy-plus personnel, but there were NO Navy sailors. I did not know any of the individuals who would be working for me, nor did I know any of the general officers with whom I would be working.

Before leaving Tampa I acquired 90-days' orders with the appropriate accounting data for three Navy Reserve public affairs officers plus my senior chief. All of these individuals, whom I knew and had worked with in the past, were to join me and help organize the public affairs staff.

I would learn shortly after arriving in Baghdad that Rear Adm. McCreary, CHINFO, along with Vice Adm. John Cotton, Commander, Navy Reserve Force, canceled the orders for all four individuals. Once receiving this information, I called McCreary and asked why he canceled the orders. He said that I "did not need these individuals; I had all the public affairs officers to do my job." He had no idea of the environment nor what skill sets I needed to be successful. Unfortunately, Cotton deferred to McCreary on the orders, and neither one of them had the professional courtesy to call me in advance and discuss my needs in theater prior to cancelling these orders.

In addition, the real unknown would be how Gen. Casey and I would connect and work together. Again, I did not have a good feeling about this relationship, and my feeling proved to be accurate.

It was finally time to board Qatar Airlines and my flight to Doha. It was uneventful but pleasant; good food, good service—all around a great flight. After another nine hours, we landed at 6:20 a.m. (local time) in Doha on Thursday, June 17. It had seemed like a weeklong adventure but had only been three days. I was greeted at Doha International Airport by Major David Farlow, a member of Pittman's PA staff. We headed to the baggage area. Guess what? My luggage did not arrive! Apparently, it was not on the plane with me. How could you have a nine-hour layover in London and your bags not make it onto the airplane? It was just more frustration.

The next flight from London would arrive in four hours, and the Qatar Airlines agent assured me my bags would be on this flight. We headed to Camp As Sayliyah CENTCOM Forward headquarters, where I checked into a BOQ room. Maj. Farlow had the key and took me to Suite 13 in Bldg. 104. It was good to get a room, an hour of quiet time, and a shower. Maj. Farlow returned to pick me up a few hours later, so we could travel back to the airport to retrieve my luggage. My bags had made it. We loaded them in the SUV and returned to As Sayliyah.

Kough would arrive a few hours later and would be picked up by the staff. We connected for dinner. After dinner we headed to the club for happy hour and our "three beers minimum" with one new friend, Lt. Col. "Stretch" Rodney, and a fellow shipmate and friend, Navy Cdr. Dave Culler. Beer of choice was Foster's.

I then spent some time preparing for my meetings for the next morning. There was a luncheon planned for the following day, and I needed to be ready to fly to Baghdad International Airport (BIAP). The next day would be a busy one and I went to bed early.

The PA staff had arranged a luncheon at the request of the ABC News team at the Ritz Carlton in downtown Doha. When we arrived at the front door, a Rolls Royce had just pulled up and the young man at the valet was getting ready to park it. In attendance at the luncheon were Clark Bentson and Carolyn Durand with ABC News, along with Lt. Col. Rodney, Lt. Cdr. Culler, and Maj. Farlow. What a beautiful hotel. We dined on the thirtieth floor and the view was incredible! We talked about the media currently in Baghdad, some of their challenges regarding access, etc. It was good to have this luncheon; I felt I was back in the game.

When we returned from lunch, I got into my uniform for a series of office calls with CENTCOM senior staff: Maj. Gen. John Sattler, J-3 (who would later be promoted to Lt. Gen. and command I Marine Expeditionary Force); Brig. Gen. George Troutman, III, J-5; and Col. Plush, STRATCOMS.

The PA staff got Kough and me on a flight to Baghdad, departing Friday, June 18, at 7:30 p.m. The flight was aboard a C-130. Farlow took us to the terminal about ninety minutes early, which was not a problem. Within about thirty minutes of arriving at the terminal, a flight landed and into the terminal walked a brigadier general and his staff. They saw us and stopped. The general said, "Hello, my name is Gary Harrell." Three members of his staff introduced themselves.

I said, "General, my name is Greg Slavonic, and this is Lt. Cmdr. Lindsay Kough." Brig. Gen. Harrell was a special operator (Green Beret), and when he saw Kough's Navy SEAL Trident on his uniform, Harrell wanted to chat. Gen. Harrell was Commander, Special Operations Command, and USCENTCOM. He was a remarkable individual. He helped rescue US hostage Kurt Muse from a Panamanian jail in 1989 and hunt down Colombian drug lord Pablo Escobar. He searched for mobile Iraqi Scud missile launchers in the First Gulf War in 1991 (which I greatly appreciate because I was on the receiving end of many of those missiles inbound into Dhahran, Saudi Arabia). He was also the commander during the 1993 battle for Mogadishu. The event was chronicled in the book and movie *Black Hawk Down*.

We boarded the airplane around 7:30 p.m. and took off heading west. Once we crossed into Iraq airspace, the plane went black, and the pilots wore night vision goggles. I was invited into the cockpit to chat with the pilots and look at the lights below. I knew this was "game on" and I was not sure when I would return stateside. After about thirty minutes in the cockpit, the pilots said, "Admiral, you need to go back to your seat. We're going to be landing in about twenty minutes."

As we approached BIAP and began our descent, it was protocol to make a quick corkscrew maneuver and to land from approximately 10,000 feet. This was required to ensure the aircraft was not a bigger target and could avoid any type of missile or small gunfire that might be fired.

We arrived around 10 p.m. and were greeted by an Air Force colonel and taken to his office. We knew that Baghdad had been informed of our arrival and that someone from my new team would arrive shortly. Well, they were there but could not find us. They went back to the Green Zone thinking we had not arrived at BIAP. At midnight the colonel asked if we wanted to stay at BIAP and that he would call the Green Zone in the morning. It was late, and we agreed to the proposal. He took us to a transit quarters, which was a plywood two-bedroom building. It looked like something you would see on a Boy Scout outing, but it did have a cot and running water. I had stayed in much worse. Once we stowed our bags, he asked us if we wanted to join him for "midrats" (midnight rations) at the dining facility. We had not eaten since around 4 p.m., so Kough and I looked at each other and said, "Sure, lead the way."

We had a small meal and more conversation and returned to our temporary lodging around 2 a.m. Just as the colonel was leaving, he asked if we wanted to join him at 6 a.m. for command's daily two-mile run. I had totally lost track of time and quickly replied, "You bet; can you pick us up?"

He said, "Sure, I'll be here at 5:45 a.m."

"Great, we'll see you then," I responded.

The colonel left. I looked at Kough and could tell that he was not up for the run in the morning. He said, "Admiral, I'm a swimmer, not a runner."

I said, "I know, but this will do you good." That was a mistake. 5:30 a.m. came too early and before we knew it, we were picked up and headed to the track. I thought I was in pretty good shape, but those two miles killed me. It was probably a combination of lack of sleep, travel, etc. We both finally got through this torture and went to breakfast. After eating, we went back to our quarters, showered, and waited to be picked up.

At around 8 a.m., Maj. John Wagner and 2nd Lt. Brian Melanephy arrived at the terminal to welcome and pick us up. We loaded our gear into the minivan and drove to our temporary quarters, loaded our baggage, and headed to Camp Victory, which is only a couple of miles from BIAP.

My first full day in Iraq was busy. Wagner and I have remained friends over the years since and stay in regular contact. Wagner and Melanephy took Kough and me to the Joint Visitors Lodging facility where we stowed our gear. Then they took us to Camp Victory headquarters at Al Faw Palace to begin check-in, handing off the orders and processing credentials. I acquired all the badges I would need to have access to facilities and places I would travel.

Since I spent a great deal of time at Al Faw Palace I learned as much as I could about the complex. The palace itself was a former resort of Saddam Hussein and was very ornate. It was made primarily of marble, glass, wood, and brass. Many of the banisters were constructed of gypsum, and the Arabic script within was made to look like gold but was actually gilded brass. There were more than sixty rooms and twenty-nine bathrooms. Many rooms were converted into offices for MNF-I and MNC-I. The palace complex, with 450,000 square feet of space, was located approximately three miles from Baghdad International Airport (formerly called Saddam Hussein International Airport). It was also referred to as the Water Palace. There was a picturesque manmade lake surrounding the palace along with numerous small palaces and villas used by Saddam's friends. They enjoyed fishing and duck hunting at the lavish resort.

Al Faw Palace (Water Palace), headquarters for Multi-National Force–Iraq, located at Camp Victory. (Photo from Slavonic collection)

I was assigned one of these villas when I first arrived in Iraq. I occupied it for about two weeks before moving into my permanent quarters in a trailer behind Saddam's Presidential Palace in the Green Zone. The villa was near the helicopter land area and perimeter road that surrounded the palace.

The palace complex and villas experienced some light damage during the March 2003 US coalition attack on Baghdad and the subsequent bombings. There was speculation that military planners limited bombings of those facilities for them to be used later as military headquarters. The high walls surrounding the complex and several security towers provided surveillance and made it ideally suited for a command headquarters.

Al Faw Palace construction was commissioned by Saddam to commemorate the sacrifices made by the Iraqi Army during the Iran–Iraq War in regaining the Al-Faw Peninsula, located in southern Iraq. In February 1986, the Iranian Army successfully launched a 30,000-man amphibious-style attack across the Shatt al-Arab River that captured the area as part of a plan to cut off Iraqi oil export. Hussein vowed to retake the Al-Faw Peninsula at all costs. It would take the Iraqi Army two years to recapture the lost ground. Mustard gas and other chemical weapons were used on 8,000 to 10,000 Iranian troops during this period. Thousands of Iraqi soldiers died in the Al-Faw Peninsula campaign.

Aerial view of Al Faw Palace and other connecting facilities. (Photo from briefing on June 24, 2004)

Al Faw was one of Saddam's ninety-nine palaces throughout Iraq. During the occupation they each served as headquarters for various regional US and coalition commands due to their location and size. Since I spent time at Camp Victory and in the Green Zone (Presidential Palace), I required an office at both locations.

My Camp Victory office on the third floor of the palace was a modest but functional space for my needs. It consisted of a desk, three chairs, and a computer along with a large map of the country of Iraq on the wall. The palace itself was truly an incredible facility and I was fortunate to have an office both at Victory and in the Green Zone.

Later that day I met Maj. Gen. Joe Weber, Chief of Staff, Multi-National Force–Iraq (MNF–I) (later he would be promoted to Lt. Gen. and Commander, US Marine Corps Forces Command, US Marine Corps Bases Atlantic & Commanding General Fleet Marine Forces Atlantic). Weber and I talked regularly during my deployment, and he provided me much-needed guidance and insight. He was a 1972 Texas A&M graduate. We had Big 12 college football in common and enjoyed discussing recruiting and the upcoming season.

I had been informed by Wagner that the next day we would travel to the Green Zone, and he would need to arrange transportation for me since I did not have my own vehicle (Humvee). Every flag or general office had a vehicle but, like everything else, as I would soon learn, would not be that easy to acquire. That being the case, I asked Weber for a ride the next day over to the Saddam's Presidential Palace in the Green Zone. The Coalition Provisional Authority and Brig. Gen. Mark Kimmitt, whom I would relieve, was in the Green Zone Palace. I had meetings scheduled with Kimmitt and Dan Senor (spokesman for the Coalition Provisional Authority). They both delivered the daily televised media briefing.

Weber said, "Sure, be in front of Victory at 0900 and I'll give you a ride over." I said, "Great, I'll see you in the morning."

After I had finished up my processing and met some other staff members, it was lunch time. We walked from the palace to the large dining facility, about quarter of a mile away. The dining tent was about one-third the size of a football field and would serve three meals a day to the troops. We got in line and filled our trays through the serving line. The food looked really good. We took our trays and sat down at a table with a group of soldiers and began eating.

Within a few minutes we heard a whistling sound. The talking stopped . . . and then an explosion. A mortar round had landed about 150 meters from the dining facility. Within a few seconds talking resumed, and then in a few minutes the same sound. The entire tent got quiet and soldiers started to rise and bend down . . . and then an explosion. Another mortar!

I looked at Kough, who said, "Sir, don't worry. As long as you can hear them that's a good sign."

I said, "Thanks, that's comforting." Another few minutes passed, conversations started again, then the same sound, soldiers started heading under the tables, and there was another explosion. This one was louder and closer. I looked at Kough, Wagner, and Melanephy and asked if we needed to go to a bunker; they said that we needed to stay put. Table conversation started up again, but I had lost my appetite. It was a very memorable first lunch at Camp Victory in Iraq. This was only the beginning of many more unforgettable events during my last deployment.

We walked back to the palace for the balance of the afternoon to look at my office and check on the computers that had been ordered for me.

Kough and I went to dinner with Wagner and Melanephy. After dinner they took us back to the Joint Visitors lodging facility. During dinner Wagner said, "Sir, do you know about Route Irish?"

I said, "No."

Wagner smiled and said, "It will be an experience."

Route Irish was barely seven miles long. It was a stretch of road between

Camp Victory and the Green Zone. It was a four-lane road on which impro-vised explosive devices (IED) were commonplace. One had to travel this road daily to get to either the US or British embassies in the Green Zone. It was reported to be the most dangerous stretch of road in Iraq. Snipers would lie in ambush and suicide bombers lurked ready to attack a convoy. It was also known as "Ambush Alley" or "RPG (rocket-propelled grenade) Alley." I had daily meetings at Camp Victory that required daily "convoy" travel back and forth from Victory to the Green Zone along Route Irish. Our convoy consisted of my "up-armored" Humvee and a white Dodge Caravan as we traveled daily on this dangerous section of highway. While in Baghdad, I would make well over 120 round trips up and down this highway (day and night), and only by the grace of God did we not experience more than a few incidents. But every time I hear AC/DC's song "Highway to Hell" I reflect on these daily road trips.

The next morning, Wagner and Melanephy picked us up again and we went to breakfast. We were at the front of the palace a few minutes before 9 a.m. Weber had three hummers all equipped with 50-caliber guns mounted on top with trigger pullers. He had brought his personal security detail from his pre-vious command. Kough was in the lead vehicle, and I loaded up with Weber in his. After I got in, I put my helmet on and secured my seat belt. Weber did the same. He also removed his Beretta 9mm from his holster, cocked it, and placed it on his lap. He looked at me and said, "Greg, see that bag in front of you?"

I said, "Yes."

He said, "It is full of frag [fragmentation] grenades. If we run into a problem, pull down the window, open the bag, pull the pin, and start throwing those out the window." Frag grenades are standard grenades designed to disperse small projectiles or fragments on detonation. They can deliver significant damage.

I said, "Got it." This would be my first trip on Route Irish. These first two days in Iraq were only a snapshot of what I would experience during my tour in Iraq.

A few weeks later, I shifted my permanent living quarters from Camp Victory to an area behind the Presidential Palace into one of the many trailers located there. This made life much easier with my quarters closer to my work. The trail-ers were home for contractors, State Department employees, and the military, including many of the coalition forces. I was assigned a trailer approximately thirty feet by sixty feet. It was divided into two living quarters joined by a shower, sink, and toilet. The occupant on the other side of the trailer was an Army 0-6.

The majority of my job concentrated on working with a sixty-five-person team. The team manned the Combined Press Information Center (CPIC), located in the Baghdad Convention Center. The CPIC would provide support for the journalists in Baghdad. The journalists would meet daily for updates on combat operations or inquire about embedding opportunities. In addition, newly arriving journalists were required to be credentialed at the CPIC once they entered Baghdad. CPIC became an important work center for all the news the US and the world received. The news was supported from this facility. This was the center of the universe for me.

The entire time I was in Baghdad, I worked seven days a week. Each day began at 5 a.m. The day, usually, began with a run and would end sometime between 10 p.m. and 1 a.m. If there were rocket attacks—and those were common either during the day or in the evening—then the interrupted workflow would change my daily schedule.

My trailer was a stone's throw away from the Tigris River in the Green Zone. Once an incoming rocket was detected, sirens would sound, and everyone was supposed to move quickly from the trailers into the palace. The size and structure of the palace provided necessary shelter. It could hold many soldiers and contractors. It provided far better protection than the prefab trailers behind the palace in which many lived.

For example, the skin of my trailer was very thin. In August 2004, the Summer Olympic Games were underway in Greece. The Iraqi soccer team was experiencing much success. When they were victorious, thousands of Iraqi citizens would go outside and begin firing their AK-47s, pistols, etc., into the air to celebrate the victory. When these rounds landed on my trailer I was reminded of a hailstorm in Oklahoma; the pinging sound would last a few minutes then subside. This "celebratory fire" occurred each night the Iraqi soccer team won.

Once a rocket attack was over and the "all clear" sounded, you could return to your living quarters. Some nights a subsequent attack would follow shortly after the all-clear sounded. Then, it was back to the palace again. While you could sleep in the palace if you wanted, it would be on the floor.

In July, after about two weeks of living in the Green Zone, I was tired at the end of every day. Once I did get to my trailer, I lay down in my bed, often in my uniform, and fell asleep. There were times when the sirens sounded that I would reach over, pick up the protective vest beside my bed, pull it over me, and go back to sleep. I rationalized the act of staying in my trailer by thinking, "If it is my time to go, then the good Lord will take me." A good four- or five-hour rest was rare, and I needed to take advantage of sleep every night.

5

TRANSFER OF SOVEREIGNTY– HISTORIC EVENT

IT WAS MONDAY, JUNE 28, 2004. I'D BEEN IN IRAQ A WEEK, but it seemed longer. It was only two days until the Transfer of Sovereignty (TOS) and two days until Saddam's arraignment. There was still a lot of preparation to do, in addition to the daily briefings and press releases, which were starting to multiply every day.

The TOS was a pivotal event for the US and Iraq. This was to be the official transfer of control of Iraq from the United States to an Interim Iraqi Government. This event had to take place prior to the arraignments for Saddam and the other HVDs on July 1, 2004.

The TOS would officially put the Iraqi government in charge and enable the judicial process to move forward for those who committed crimes against Iraqi civilians. This change would show the world that Iraq was in control and responsibility for its future. The Iraqi government would demonstrate that it had the ability to begin the legal process, which would allow justice to be served.

An agreement signed in mid-November 2003 by the top US civilian adminis-trator, Ambassador Paul Bremer, and the Iraqi Governing Council envisioned a three-step process leading to the establishment of a provisional Iraqi government by July 1, 2004.[1] First, the Governing Council and the Coalition Provisional Authority (CPA) had to agree on a "fundamental law" that would govern the transition period. The law was to be in place by the end of February 2003 and would set out the scope and structure of the interim government. Second, pro-visional caucuses had to choose a transitional assembly by the end of May. This transitional assembly would elect a sovereign government by the end of June. And third, the CPA would be abolished, although US and coalition troops were expected to remain in the country for an undetermined period of time.[2]

In addition, President Bush made a speech before the US Army War College in Carlisle, Pennsylvania, on May 24, that outlined five steps toward a free and democratic Iraq:

- Hand over authority to a sovereign Iraqi government.
- Help establish the stability and security in Iraq that democ-racy requires.
- Continue rebuilding Iraq's infrastructure.
- Encourage more international support.
- Move toward free, national elections that would bring forward new leaders empowered by the Iraqi people.

Lt. Melanephy picked me up at my Camp Victory quarters at 8 a.m. We headed out the gate and down Route Irish to the Green Zone for a series of meetings. Lt. Melanephy let me off at the palace entrance and I walked through the large, beautiful foyer with a ceiling of some twenty feet high. I veered to my right into the Green Room, which was part of the Coalition Provisional Authority spaces. The large room was occupied 90 percent by State Department employees. My desk was at the far end of the room. This would be my "office" for the next three months. I was the only flag or general officer of the approximately thirty-five assigned to MNF-I who did not have their own office. I had to fend for myself in finding a workspace, and if it were not for the State Department's willingness to share, I would not have had a workstation. Brig. Gen. Kimmitt did not secure an office or even a desk for me prior to my arrival.

On my way to the Green Room, I ran into Rob Tappan, Head of CPA Strategic Communications, and his newly arrived relief Richard (Rich) Schmierer. (The latter would later be named ambassador to Oman.) They said, "Admiral, did you hear?"

Brig. Gen. Mark Kimmitt and Rear Adm. Greg Slavonic. (Photo from Slavonic collection)

I said, "Hear what?"

Tappan said, "It was decided early this morning that the transfer of sovereignty would take place at 10 this morning."

I said, "Really?"

He replied, "Rich and I are going to drive over in about thirty minutes. Do you want to join us?"

I said, "Yes, thank you. Where should I meet you?"

Tappan said, "Right here."

This was still closely held information, and the media were informed at 9 a.m. that Prime Minister Allawi and Ambassador Paul Bremer would have comments for the press at the government building at 10 a.m. Moving up TOS was still not public information, although rumors were circulated quickly. The week before, militants had conducted a campaign of car bombings, kidnappings, and other violence against Iraqis. According to the Bush administration, these events had taken place to disrupt the TOS.[3]

I headed to my desk with Melanephy and told him to move my morning meetings to that afternoon. I then met Tappan and Schmierer and we loaded into their car and headed over for the mile-long ride to the former

Author (left) in discussion with Rich Schmierer (middle) and Rob Tappan (right) about Transfer of Sovereignty, rotunda of the Presidential Palace. (Photo from Slavonic collection)

Iraqi Governing Council building. It was a five-minute drive; upon arriving, we parked the car and walked about a hundred yards to the entrance of the building. We all entered the building. Tappan walked in and quickly positioned himself outside Allawi's office. Schmierer and I asked an Iraqi security officer where the event was to take place. He directed us to a large room with floor-length drapes on all windows and a marble floor.

As we entered the room, we found seated the six senior US and Iraqi officials: Ambassador Paul Bremer, Iraqi Chief Justice Midhat al-Mahmoudi, Iraqi Prime Minister (PM) Iyad Allawi, Iraqi President Ghazi al-Yawer, Deputy Prime Minister (DPM) Barham Saleh, and David Richmond, Bremer's Deputy and Special Representative from the United Kingdom. They appeared to be in assigned seating.

Seated on a light gold sofa to my right were State Department official Bremer and President al-Yawer. Bremer was wearing a charcoal suit, a white shirt with a blue tie, a white pocket square in his left coat pocket, and his military boots. He was a career diplomat and was Presidential Envoy to Iraq from May 2003 to June 2004. During his twenty-three years at the State Department, he served on the personal staffs of six secretaries of state and on four continents. In the 1980s, he was Ambassador to the Netherlands and Ambassador at Large for Counterterrorism.[4]

The scene minutes before the Transfer of Sovereignty ceremony. (Photo from media pool–Karen Ballard)

Seated to Bremer's left was David Richmond. He had only arrived in Iraq at the end of March from the UK. He had taken over for Sir Jeremy Greenstock as Britain's special representative to Baghdad. He too was wearing a charcoal suit with a light blue shirt and a maroon tie.

To Richmond's left was President al-Yawer, born in Mosul in 1958. He was a prominent Sunni and a member of the Shammar tribe, which includes Shi'ites. The Shammar tribe was one of the largest tribes in the Gulf Region. He was also related to the Saudi royal family. He studied in Saudi Arabia and at Georgetown University in the US. He was a Saudi businessman and served as IGC President. Al-Yawer was seen as more in tune with the current state of affairs in Iraq and with Iraqi values and culture. He had become widely popular as a champion of the Sunni minority. He preferred wearing traditional Arab dress, which on this day was a long gold-colored robe, a long-sleeve white shirt underneath, and a white headdress.

To Bremer's right was PM Allawi. He had thinning gray hair and was seated in a light gold chair. He was wearing a pinstripe charcoal suit, white shirt, and gray tie. Allawi was born in Baghdad in 1945. He was a US-backed Shi'ite Muslim with military and CIA connections who had been exiled to the United Kingdom and was a consultant to United Nations organizations. His power base, the Jordanian-based opposition group Iraqi National Accord—made up largely of former members of Saddam's Ba'ath Party and former military men—stressed secularism and included Sunnis and Shi'ites. Allawi had a PhD in medicine from the University of London. He was a neurosurgeon who survived an ax attack in London that British authorities attributed to Saddam Hussein's agents.[5] He served as IGC president.

To Allawi's right was Chief Justice al-Mahmoudi, who was seated in a matching light gold chair. He was small in stature with gray hair, wearing a light gray suit, a white shirt, and a maroon tie. Following the 2003 invasion of Iraq, al-Mahmoudi was made a supervisor, or minister, for the Ministry of Justice by the Coalition Provisional Authority on June 12, 2003. He was later appointed Vice President of the Court of Cassation before being appointed as Chairman of the Federal Court of Cassation.

To al-Mahmoudi's right was DPM Saleh. He was a tall balding man with a mustache, wearing glasses and a light gray suit with a dark tie. He was born in Iraqi Kurdistan in 1950 and had close ties to the Americans. In 1976, he joined and became a leader of one of the main Iraqi Kurdish groups, the Patriotic Union of Kurdistan (PUK). He was arrested twice by the Iraqi Secret Police and left Iraq in 1979. He became a PUK spokesman in London and then became PUK Ambassador to the US from 1991 to 2001. He had a PhD in statistics from the University of Liverpool. He recently had served as Regional Administrator for Suleimaniya, Iraq.

Behind Saleh was a large mahogany desk that divided the VIPs from the group of journalists already gathered in the room when we arrived. There were several pieces of correspondence on the desk. There was much anticipation about what was going to take place in about five minutes. The CPA staff had collected everybody's cell phones when the media had arrived at the building so that they could not report the event in real time, nor immediately after.[6]

Tappan, Schmierer, and I were standing in the back of the room but still had an excellent view of the entire scene, including the dignitaries seated on the sofa and chairs. They were carrying on small talk amongst themselves in very low tones.

I looked to my left where there were approximately twenty journalists positioned to cover the event. I recognized only a few of them: Bret Baier, Fox News; Peter Jennings, ABC News; Greg Palkot, Fox News; and Christiane Amanpour, CNN. I looked down and saw in one of the few chairs in the front row Brig. Gen. Kimmitt. He happened to turn, and we made eye contact. The expression on his face was one of total surprise. I had seen and talked with Kimmitt over the past two days, and he never mentioned that the TOS was possibly being moved up, nor did he even try to contact me that morning to invite me to attend with him when it became official.

There were only two uniformed military officers in the room for this official event, Brig. Gen. Kimmitt and me. Since I was new to the journalists there—and Kimmitt had told them he was the "only military officer in the room" to observe the historic event—this is how the media reported the attendance.

From the first day we met, it was apparent that he was not going to be the least bit helpful in my transition. The reason for this was that another one-star Air Force general was coming to be the spokesperson for MNF-I. Acting as spokesperson was one of Kimmitt's two assigned jobs. Kimmitt had determined that he would hand over everything he had acquired during his tour in Iraq—including his Humvee, his aide, a three-person security detail, and an office that consisted of two rooms, desks, a refrigerator, filing cabinets, etc.—to the Air Force general upon his arrival. Apparently, they had known each other in the past and had recently been in communication. Kimmitt never tried to reach out to me to provide any assistance with my transition in Baghdad. The Air Force one-star would not arrive until around July 1 but had everything he would need already in place when he did arrive. Bottom line, the turnover between Kimmitt and me was less than desirable.

To Capt. Thorp's credit, he put together a great lineup of office calls and briefings for me prior to my deployment. I had somewhat expected Kimmitt would do the same when I arrived in Iraq, but this was not the case. Kimmitt never arranged office calls with Bremer, Sanchez, or other senior officers for me. Hence, I never personally met Bremer, and my first meeting with Sanchez came about when I did not attend my first General Officer/Flag Officer (GO/FO) morning briefing. He knew through his staff that I had arrived, and he sent word via his aide: "Admiral, you missed the morning meeting. Lt. Gen. Sanchez was wondering where you were." I did not offer any excuse but told the aide that I would be there the following morning.

I noticed one of the photographers moving freely around the room, shooting pictures and capturing the events of the morning. Her name was Karen Ballard, from *Time* magazine. Our paths would cross again at the arraignment. Ballard would later say she had heard whispers through the CPA about the possible arraignment of Saddam Hussein within the next few days. She had been in Iraq for six weeks and it was time for her to go home, but what an opportunity awaited her—if she could get that assignment. She thus had a dilemma: should she take the next scheduled flight out of Baghdad and return stateside or gamble on being selected as the photographer to cover the arraignment? The TOS was significant, but adding in Saddam's arraignment would be incredible. She made her decision, deciding to give up her seat on the aircraft and trying to sell Kimmitt on why she should be the still photographer for the arraignment.

Transfer of Sovereignty, June 28, 2004. L–R: Iraqi Deputy Prime Minister Barham Saleh, Iraqi Chief Justice Midhat al-Mahmoudi, Iraqi Prime Minister Iyad Allawi, Ambassador Paul Bremer, Deputy and Special Representative David Richmond, and Iraqi President Ghazi al-Yawer. (Photo by from media pool–Karen Ballard)

She headed to Kimmitt's office and requested the assignment. The next day she learned she had been selected.

There were approximately two dozen journalists, both US and Iraqi, in attendance at the TOS. One photographer was leaning on the desk with a tele-photo lens, and another was standing at the far end of the desk.

After things had quieted down and everyone was in the room that was invited, Bremer then stood, as did the others. He opened a blue Moroccan leather folder and read a letter that he had signed that morning, formally trans-ferring sovereignty to the Iraqi people and their government. Bremer then said, "We welcome Iraq's step to take its rightful place of equality and honor among the nations of the world."[7]

Displaying some emotion, Bremer handed the folder to Iraqi Chief Justice al-Mahmoudi, who appeared to preside over the ceremony. With the passing of the documents, Justice al-Mahmoudi administered the oath to the prime minister on a red Qur'an. The land that was once ruled by a dictator named Saddam Hussein now received official sovereignty from the US administrators in a secret ceremony. Some 467 days earlier, the US, along with coalition forces, had invaded Iraq. Now, with the ceremony concluded, the dignitaries sat down in their places. Later in the day, Prime Minister Allawi would deliver his inaugural address to the Nation of Iraq.

An Iraqi with dark hair, gray mustache, and beard, in a light tan suit and brown tie and holding a small notepad, called the invited media present in the room to ask questions.

Al Iraqiya, an Iraqi satellite TV channel located in Baghdad, was the first media invited to ask a question, but they had a small technical problem that had to be resolved.

The next journalist who had an opportunity to ask a question was US Fox News reporter Greg Palkot. His question was directed to Ambassador Bremer.

Greg Palkot: "Mr. Ambassador, fourteen months in, was it all worth it for you and the Iraqi people? What are your hopes for Iraq? And what, perhaps, might be your regrets, to have happened in the past?"

Ambassador Paul Bremer: "You know there is no question that the liberation of Iraq was a great and noble thing. My last day's visit in Iraq, yesterday, was to the town al-Hilla. It is the site of the biggest mass graves. Anybody who has any doubts about whether Iraq is a better place today than it was fourteen months ago should go down and see the mass graves at Hilla or visit Halabja where Saddam gassed thousands of people or see any of the torture chambers or rape rooms around this country. Anybody who has seen those things as I have, and know what I know, knows Iraq is a much better place, albeit a different place. No doubt there will be challenges ahead, but I'm delighted to have been able to play a role here in the stabilization part of Operation Iraqi Freedom."

Al Iraqiya (translated): "Mr. Ambassador, your mission in Iraq has ended and Mr. [John] Negroponte has assumed responsibilities. Will the authority of Mr. Negroponte as ambassador of the United States be different from the mission of other US ambassadors in other countries?"

AMB Bremer: "No, Ambassador Negroponte will soon arrive, but we are moving through regular diplomatic relations with a sovereign, independent government just as we have in some 120 countries around the world. He will work closely with the government, the president, and the prime minister, in the implementation of our very large new construction program. And he will, of course, be working closely with Multi-National Forces and Iraqi security forces."

Peter Jennings: "Mr. Prime Minister, I'm Peter Jennings with ABC. This historic occasion appears to have taken place two days before the world expected it to happen. Was this in part your determination to control the opposition to the government, somewhat on balance? And if that is the case, can you tell us a little more about your early efforts now, to restrain the insurgency?"

Prime Minister Allawi: "No, this is, in fact, something that we have been working towards achieving as early as possible. We have been laying down these strategies for the security of this country. And to protect our people we have been transferring sovereignty of these areas to various ministries. Two days ago, we finalized the Transfer of Sovereignty to the remaining eleven ministries. So, this is something I have asked the coalition to expedite. We are sure that the Iraqi authority, now the government of Iraq, will be handling the situation for the security of the country. And this is a great day for us, and Iraq for the first time will deal with its own problems."

Peter Jennings: "What is one of the first thing you want to do as the sovereign prime minister?"

PM Allawi: "The first thing is really to ensure the safety of our people and to ensure the safety of the country, and we will be addressing the nation today, expressing our vision to the nation. And our views and strategies. So, this will be the first thing I will do today."

Christiane Amanpour: "Mr. Prime Minister, you've been talking about security and saying you're going to address the nation today. Can you please tell us precisely what you will do differently that the world's most powerful nation has not been able to do in fifteen months?"

PM Allawi: "The most powerful military in the world has helped us in liberating our country and we are very grateful. And we appreciate what the United States, Britain, and other members of the coalition have done. The blood that has been spilled here in Iraq was spilled for a very good reason, for the defense of values, of freedom, and democracy, and fighting terrorism. And we intend to continue doing so. So, frankly, the security of our country now lies in our hands basically, we have the support of Multi-National Forces, and we look forward to their continued support. We have measures that will be declared today and tomorrow to enhance and ensure our security and it is something that we will carry forward."

Christiane Amanpour: "Can you tell us [inaudible] . . ."

As Amanpour attempted to ask another question, the press conference moderator interrupted and said, "Last question, Al Jazeera. Go ahead."

PM Allawi: "I'll tell you later."

Al Jazeera reporter (translated): "Mr. Prime Minister, you have spoken with the *Washington Post* recently, and you have said the elections could be impacted by the violence."

PM Allawi: "This statement was taken out of context. We have made an adjusted statement. The Iraqi government is determined to go ahead with the election on January 2 next year [2005] and we are consistent with that."

As video cameras continued recording, the historic event was documented. At 10:26 a.m. local time, legal sovereignty was passed to Iraq. The ceremony was over. Bremer shook hands with al-Mahmoudi, Allawi, al-Yawer, and Saleh and everyone headed out. Bremer was in the middle flanked by Allawi on his right and Yawer on his left with Saleh trailing. And all were escorted by a security detail down the long hallway.

They exited the building, walking down four flights of steps. At the end of the walkway, Bremer turned and again said good-bye to Allawi, al-Yawer, Saleh, and other Iraqi officials who attended the ceremony. Shaking hands with Allawi, Bremer said, "You have your country now. It's in your hands. Take good care of it."[8]

As soon as this event concluded, Brig. Gen. Kimmitt and Dan Senor conducted a press conference in an adjourning room to answer additional questions. The media still did not have possession of their cell phones. Just before the press conference started, Christiane Amanpour strenuously objected to giving up her phone. Kimmitt said, "These are the rules." She stayed put and the press conference started. The press conference lasted about thirty minutes and then the journalists departed. Tappan, Schmierer, and I returned to the palace.

Back in the palace there was a buzz of activity. Several CPA employees in the Green Room said, "Bremer is leaving the country along with several staff members." Within about thirty minutes of his return to the palace, Bremer walked out of his office and into the rotunda area with Lt. Gen. Sanchez. They were escorted by two plainclothes security personnel, one leading the way and one following. They passed through the airport-style metal detector; Bremer was smiling along with Lt. Gen. Sanchez. In the large rotunda, applause broke out.

The Green Room was located across from Bremer's office. A semicircle of former CPA employees, military and other contractors, had begun to form around the rotunda along the outer edge of the room. Bremer signaled for Sanchez to join him as they walked around randomly shaking the hands of those who had waited to say good-bye to their former boss. The ambassador stopped and spent additional time with those he knew. Many of these individuals had worked for months to reach this day.

A line had formed as Bremer exited the palace. He and several other staff members were escorted to Landing Zone (LZ) Washington, and he was given a protective green camouflage vest to wear as he boarded one of two waiting US Army CH-47 Chinook tandem rotor heavy-lift helicopters with several staff members. DPM Saleh accompanied him. Once onboard the helicopter, he put on his ear protection and sat in the long red cargo seat, which ran the length of the helicopter, for the twenty-minute flight to BIAP. He sat calmly with his wire-rimmed sunglasses resting on his head, wearing a long-sleeve white shirt and presidential cuff links, with his suit coat on his lap. His hands were on his knees, and he gazed levelly at the area outside. To his right was Saleh in his suit looking outside too. The noise inside was so loud that it was impossible to have a conversation. The rear door of the helicopter was down, and the view of the palace and Baghdad passed in the distance.

Once on the ground, Bremer exited the helicopter, took off his vest, and put on his suit jacket. Carrying his black briefcase, he was accompanied by his security detail, one on either side, with Saleh to the terminal and a cooled VIP room. Once inside, he greeted the last of many congressional delegations (CODELs), led by California Republican Congressman Duncan Hunter, chairman of the House Armed Services Committee and a staunch supporter of the liberation of Iraq.[9]

A group numbering about twenty gathered in the large room for a reception. Others in attendance included Sanchez and other CPA officials. Bremer was laughing and joking with the group. After a short stay in the room, he said his good-byes and was escorted out to the terminal. He made his way to the Air Force C-130 Hercules aircraft waiting for him along with the press. Two different markings on the side of the aircraft had been covered over with tape. Saleh, who was escorting him, was to his right. A security detail of five with automatic weapons surrounded him as they approached the aircraft.

Bremer shook Saleh's hand and ascended into the aircraft following his security detail. Once on the top step, grabbing the side rail, he turned and waved one last time to Saleh, turned back and entered the aircraft, and the crew closed the door.

The press was escorted back to the terminal. Bremer waited on the plane for about fifteen minutes until the press had departed. Then he crawled up and over the plane's fully loaded cargo bay and ran down the tailgate ramp. He dashed fifty yards across the baking tarmac to a waiting Chinook, where his small personal staff was waiting.[10]

The Chinook lifted off once he was inside and flew for about five minutes to another area of the airport where he and his staff deplaned and immediately boarded a small US government jet. He departed Iraq for his return to the US. His mission in Iraq was complete.

The new US ambassador, John Negroponte, arrived Monday. Our paths would cross several times. We would find ourselves attending and sitting next to each other at Catholic Mass services.

Gen. George Casey arrived the following day.

6

CASEY AND SANCHEZ— CHANGE OF COMMAND CEREMONY

JULY 1, 2004, BEGAN WITH MY ATTENDANCE AT THE 6:30 A.M. daily Battle Update Assessment (BUA) general/flag officer briefing. The meeting was conducted by Lt. Gen. Ricardo Sanchez at Camp Victory in the Al Faw Palace. The Al Faw Palace served as headquarters to Sanchez's Commander Joint Task Force-7 (CJTF-7). This meeting was shorter than usual due to the ceremony that would follow in a few hours. This would be Sanchez's last morning briefing.

There was a great deal of work to be done by variously assigned staff in preparation for the upcoming change of command event. The ceremony was to be held in the large first-floor rotunda of the Al Faw Palace. The ornate space featured several large columns reaching all the way to the three-story ceiling. There was marble on the floor and walls and gold-inlay writing throughout the palace.

On this day, Gen. George Casey Jr. would succeed Lt. Gen. Sanchez and take command of 165,000 allied troops, 140,000 of which were US forces. This was a historic event. There had not been a US occupation of a country or a military command transition on this scale since World War II. In addition, this elaborate Army ceremony was steeped in military tradition. The highlight event of note was when Generals John Abizaid (Commander US Central Command) and Casey walked over to the mass formation of coalition members, escorted the senior Iraqi general to the front of the formation, and then saluted him together as a sign of respect not only to him but to the newly sovereign nation of Iraq.[1]

On May 15, 2004, CJTF-7 was split into two components. The Al Faw Palace would serve as the headquarters for both Multi-National Force–Iraq (MNF-I) and Multi-National Corps–Iraq (MNC-I). MNF-I would be the new four-star headquarters, responsible for the strategic international, political, and military interface directing the Iraqi theater of operations. MNF-I would also coordinate with CENTCOM and other national and international agencies. MNC-I was now a subordinate unit of MNF-I focusing on operational and tactical warfighting operations. MNC-I would be commanded by Lt. Gen. Tom Metz, who was second in command under Sanchez at CJTF-7. Metz was a 1971 West Point graduate. He had a distinguished career that would span forty years. In November 2001, Metz assumed command of the 24th Infantry Division (Mechanized). During his command of the 24th ID, Metz was chosen to serve for four months beginning in October 2002 as the Chief of Staff, CENTCOM, during Operation Enduring Freedom.[2]

Before the ceremony began, I met another Navy flag officer attending the event, Rear Adm. Chuck Kubic. He was the commander of the 1st Naval Construction Division and the 1st Marine Expeditionary Force Engineer Group during Operation Iraqi Freedom. He and I sat together, and I got his perspective on the ongoing Seabee operations in Iraq.

In addition, two busloads or more of approximately seventy-five members of the media were escorted to the event from the Green Zone to Camp Victory. A Green Zone military unit called the Steel Dragons dispatched high-powered weapons protection via Humvees in front of and behind the buses.

Gen. Sanchez graduated from Texas A&I University at Kingsville in 1973. In 1991, then-Lt. Col. Sanchez served as a battalion commander during Operation Desert Storm. He successfully led his unit of the 197th Infantry Brigade (Mechanized) to Basra, Iraq. On July 10, 2001, now a lieutenant general, Sanchez became commander of V Corps' 1st Armored Division. He held that position for nearly two years before assuming command of the entire corps on June 14, 2003. On that date, he also became commander CJTF-7.

Sanchez held the top military position in Iraq during what was arguably one of the most critical periods of the war: the year after the fall of Saddam's

At a reception the night before the change of command ceremony to welcome a congressional delegation from Washington, DC. Friend of the author Senator Don Nickles (R-OK), a member of the delegation. (Photo from Slavonic collection)

regime. During this period, the insurgency took root and began its counterattack. Notable highlights during his tenure as commander in Iraq included the killing of Uday and Qusay Hussein and the capture of Saddam Hussein.

The change of command event started at 10 a.m. and concluded shortly after 11 a.m. There were approximately 250 in attendance. This included a large group of media bussed over from the Green Zone. I witnessed on this day my first Army change-of-command ceremony.

There were several dignitaries in town including the new incoming Ambassador to Iraq John Negroponte and US Senators Joe Lieberman (D-CT) and Don Nickles (R-OK), as well as more than thirty-five generals, admirals, colonels, and Navy captains. I had seen and visited with Senator Nickles the day before at a reception for his delegation.

Critical to the success in Iraq was ongoing communication and a strong relationship between the military and government officials in charge of our civilian efforts. Ambassador Paul Bremer was head of the Coalition Provisional Authority in Iraq. According to journalist Thomas Ricks, in his book *Fiasco*, "There was general agreement on both the civilian and military sides that their leaders in Iraq, Bremer, and Sanchez, were profoundly unhappy with each other."[3]

"'It was very clear they [Bremer and Sanchez] hated each other,' recalled a senior administrative official. . . . '[T]hey lived in the same palace and didn't talk to each other.'"[4] This lack of unity in leadership has been cited as one of the major failures in this critical period of the Iraq War. I never personally witnessed issues between Sanchez and Bremer but was told of the failed relationship between the two. During my four-day series of briefings in the Pentagon prior to my deployment, it was emphasized to me, on more than one occasion by several senior officers, that it was critical for me to engage with my State Department counterpart and establish a solid working relationship. Fortunately for me and my staff, we enjoyed an excellent working relationship with everyone from the State Department.

Many felt Gen. Sanchez would receive his 4-star and take command of MNF-I. This speculation ended when Abu Ghraib made the news in the spring of 2004, prior to my deployment. The Abu Ghraib prison was located near BIAP. It was the site where Saddam killed many of his enemies. In the fall of 2003, the prison became a holding pen for a variety of inmates and criminals who were mixed in with suspected insurgents. Many of the soldiers assigned to this facility were not properly trained or supervised in the application of interrogation procedures. Reports on the scandal blamed the conditions on inadequate manpower and the lack of a plan to handle the number of detainees at the prison. The repercussions of the prison scandal were felt throughout Iraq, the Arab world, and the US military. The scandal became propaganda for international terrorists.[5]

Maj. Gen. Antonio Taguba was directed to investigate the abuses at the prison. The "Taguba Report" concluded that although Sanchez was not directly involved in the abuses, there was evidence that some degree of culpability resided with him. Media along with senior government officials had been highly critical of the US military's failure to hold senior officers accountable. Blame for abuses at Abu Ghraib and other detention centers was placed on only a few individuals of the lowest rank.

With the ceremony winding down, 1st Sgt Steve Valley, media escort for the event, was hoping to prolong his morning mission with a stop at a remote makeshift courthouse up the road from Camp Victory, where Saddam Hussein was to make his first court appearance since being captured. According to Valley, "The CPIC and many other public affairs leaders wanted to bring the busload of media to the courthouse to document Saddam's 'perp' walk in arm and leg chains so the world could finally see that he was no longer the powerful tyrant

View of the change of command ceremony from the media pool's location. (Photo from Maj. John Wagner)

he was in the past." He went on to say, "My plan was to surprise the media with a quick stop and shoot B-roll video and photographs and then head back with our convoy escorts to the Green Zone." Valley said, "I never got the telephone call to allow the driver to head that direction, so we loaded up on the bus and returned to the CPIC."

7

AMANPOUR AND JENNINGS EPISODE

FOLLOWING THE CHANGE OF COMMAND CEREMONY, SADDAM'S arraignment was less than two hours away. My aide, Lt. Brian Melanephy, found me and reported, "Admiral, I think you might have a problem. There are two journalists in your conference room who want to visit with you."

I said, "Who are they?"

Melanephy responded, "Sir, it's Christiane Amanpour and Peter Jennings."

Amanpour was CNN's chief international correspondent in Baghdad. I had met her in Dhahran, during the First Gulf War, in December 1990, but our paths had not crossed since I arrived in Iraq. I had attended the transfer of sovereignty ceremony earlier in the week and remembered well the interaction between Kimmitt and Senor regarding Christiane's cell phone.

Amanpour and Jennings were at Camp Victory to cover the change of command ceremony, which was open to the entire press corps. I felt that this was only a cover and that their primary reason to be at the palace was to be close to the location where Saddam's court arraignment was to take place.

Given the sensitive nature of this event, coupled with the tight security, it was decided early on to establish a media pool to cover the arraignment

Outside view of the mosque housing the courtroom a few hours before Saddam's arraignment. (Photo from Slavonic collection)

Judge Ra'id arrives at the courthouse. (Photo from Combat Camera)

proceedings. This meant that only a few media representatives would witness the event in person. The final decision of who could be in the courtroom ultimately rested with the Iraqi judge, after military input.

Amanpour knew of this arrangement because CNN was a television pool member. Since she was not selected to cover this event as the pool reporter, she was going to try and gain access inside the courtroom. MNF-I's position was that if other media members were granted access to the courtroom, the pool system was invalid. It would create problems.

As we headed to the conference room, I had a good idea of what they wanted to talk about. I knew this was not going to be a pleasant conversation. I intentionally took the three flights of stairs, instead of the elevator, from the foyer up to the conference room to gather my thoughts and determine how best to approach the situation.

When I arrived at the conference room, Amanpour and Jennings stood, and we exchanged greetings. The CNN reporter did not remember me from Dhahran. That was not surprising given the number of military public affairs officers from all the armed services that she encountered since 1990, and now in Iraq. After about five minutes of small talk, Amanpour took the lead and opened the discussion on why they wanted to meet with me. She thought I was her last resort in gaining them access to the courtroom.

Jennings let her do all the talking in their attempt to persuade me to allow them access to Saddam's arraignment. I reiterated what had been decided regarding access and told them that the media pool had been selected several days before and that those selected would cover this event for the entire press corps. She knew all of this but said she had DOD approval for access and for me to call the Pentagon. Of course, this was unrealistic given the time difference, and the clock was ticking for me. The proceedings were due to begin at 1 p.m. and one of the requirements for US personnel in the courtroom was that there were to be NO military in uniform. I still needed to change into civilian clothes and get to the courtroom to ensure all media were in place and had everything they needed prior to the arrival of the star prisoner.

I made a decision and told Amanpour and Jennings, "Let's go to the courthouse and talk to the judge regarding allowing you access." I thought this was the best strategy because, in earlier conversations with the presiding judge, we were on the same page regarding the pool system and the media's role during the arraignment. While he had control of the proceedings, I would oversee the media pool inside his courtroom. He understood the media pool concept and approved it. He had already reviewed the list of media allowed in the courtroom and understood that they had all been vetted and were approved to be present that day. The total number of individuals was around twenty, but fewer than twelve would be in the courtroom for the entire proceedings.

I thought that once I had the opportunity to confer with the judge and explain that these two reporters were not on the vetted list, nor selected for the media pool, he would deny them access to his courtroom. I believed the case would be closed and Amanpour and Jennings would be escorted out. I told them I needed to change clothes and would meet them at the courtroom. I did not tell them the courtroom location, nor did I instruct them to follow me. I left them to change my clothes, and then Lt. Melanephy drove me to the court-house in our Humvee. And there they were, standing outside: Amanpour and Jennings. So much for the "secure location."

When I arrived, I looked at my watch and saw that it was 12:40 p.m., twenty minutes before the first Rhino bus was due to deliver Saddam. As we entered the courtroom together, I spotted Judge Ra'id Juhi Hamadi al-Saedi speaking with his clerk. I asked if I might have a few minutes of his time and he agreed. I introduced him to Amanpour and Jennings, explaining why I had brought them to his courtroom and hoping to remind him why they should not be allowed access to the proceedings. I told the judge that they were not selected pool members and that allowing them access would cause problems with other members of the press. I felt this would be a short conversation and his decision would come quickly.

Judge Ra'id, a graduate of Baghdad Law School, was thirty-five years old and built like a football player. He was originally one of the investigative judges of the Central Criminal Court of Iraq (CCCI), Iraq's newly established criminal court for ordinary crimes. Judge Ra'id had come to the attention of American authorities in 2003 while serving in Najaf when he courageously signed an indictment for the notorious Shi'ite warlord Muqtada al-Sadr, charging him with murder. The public revelation of the al-Sadr indictment placed the young judge and his family in great danger, and they were relocated for their protec-tion to the Green Zone in Baghdad, where they resided until the end of the Dujail trial. With his solid command of English and his unflappable demeanor, Judge Ra'id became an obvious choice to head the investigative phase.[1]

During my conversation with the judge, I noticed to my right Salem "Sam" Chalabi, the first general director of the Iraqi Special Tribunal, having a conver-sation with another Iraqi. The tribunal was established in 2003, shortly after Saddam's capture, and would be the judicial organization to try him and other members of his regime for crimes against humanity. Chalabi's appointment was made by Ambassador Bremer before Iraq was under Iraqi leadership. Chalabi graduated from Yale University in 1985 and in 1993 received a law degree from

Author in conversation with Christiane Amanpour, international news reporter for CNN, and Peter Jennings, ABC news anchor, prior to entering courtroom to meet with Judge Ra'id. Al Faw Palace is in the distance over Jennings's
left shoulder. (Photo from Slavonic collection)

Court arraignment judge Ra'id. (Photo from
Combat Camera)

Author and the judge before arraignment was to begin. (Photo from Slavonic collection)

Northwestern University School of Law. He worked in New York as a corporate securities attorney. His appointment was widely criticized for perceived nepotism. His uncle, Ahmad Chalabi, was deeply involved in the US-led war against Iraq and Hussein, and Chalabi lacked any significant trial experience.

Chalabi remained standing close by and was obviously listening to my conversation with the judge. I did not feel his presence to be a problem, nor did I anticipate his injecting himself into the conversation. But it was, and he did. It soon became apparent that Chalabi was starstruck with Amanpour and Jennings. He never took his eyes off them while I was talking with the judge. When I concluded my conversation, Chalabi came over, pulled the judge aside, spoke softly in his ear, and after a few minutes the judge came back and said, "Okay, they are allowed in my courtroom."

Allowing Amanpour and Jennings admittance into the courtroom would soon prove to be a strategic error on my part. The fallout of the judge's decision to allow them access would not be well received by other members of the Baghdad press corps. Their displeasure with me came up at other high-profile pool events, which were arranged by my staff. Needless to say, hindsight being 20/20, I should never have allowed either journalist to meet with Judge Ra'id.

Back at the Combined Press Information Center (CPIC), the fallout would occur within a few hours. Since this was a "media pool" arrangement, other members of the media were waiting at CPIC to receive media reports and video upon return of the media pool. According to 1st Sgt Valley, "When Amanpour and Jennings arrived first and started feedback to their networks, the rest of the media thought the military gave preferential treatment to these two journalists because of who they were. In actuality, we did not, and the media began complaining about the situation because other media had heard we gave these two individuals special treatment in return for positive stories." He went on to say, "Better yet, speculation swirled that they paid money to the American military to get in the courtroom when we really had nothing to do with it at all. Once the media learned the real story, they ended up taking their frustration out on each other." He said later, "Someone from another jealous media outlet went to the roof of the CPIC Convention Center and inflicted damage to CNN's satellite dish for a little bit of revenge. CNN blamed members of the CPIC for the damage."[2]

8

PREPARING FOR SADDAM AND OTHER HVDS' ARRIVAL

THE HVD HEARINGS WERE QUICKLY APPROACHING, BEGIN-ning with the arraignment of Saddam Hussein. They were going to be held under iron-tight security. This was in line with President Bush's decision that insisted on maintaining the HVDs under American security. The detainees had remained under US guard even after their transfer to the legal custody of Iraq, a few days earlier.

According to Col. (Ret.) Barry Johnson, public affairs officer for Maj. Gen. Geoffrey Miller, Deputy Commander of Detainee Operations, Multi-National Force–Iraq, "It was determined for security reasons that Camp Victory would be the best location for the arraignment." There was ample security within Victory. The building selected to provide a courtroom for the arraignment was a small nearby mosque. It was not perfect but certainly met the desired requirements.[1]

The building was redesigned both to be a courthouse and to feature a

12 HVD'S TRANSFERRED TO IRAQI LEGAL CUSTODY 201015JUN04

Photo of all twelve HVDs taken June 15, 2004. Note: Zubaydi and Barzan are misidentified. (Photo from MNF-I briefing)

courtroom. It was octagon shaped, with a central courtroom thirty feet by thirty feet that would have been better to be larger. The conference room intended to hold the HVDs was about fifteen feet wide and twenty feet in length. In addition, there was a smaller room to hold Saddam once he was in the building, two other support rooms, and a large entry hall. One room was designated for communications and the other for security. The building would also be used for future hearings. The headquarters for Detainee Operations, Task Force 134 (TF 134) was about a hundred yards from the courthouse.

Johnson and Miller had previously worked together at Joint Task Force-Guantanamo Bay (JTF-GTMO). Miller was the commanding general (CG) from August 2002 to September 2003, and Johnson was his public affairs officer (PAO). They worked well together, and Miller had the utmost trust and confidence in Johnson's ability to interact with the media.

Miller was given orders to come to Iraq and clean up the Abu Ghraib prison mess. He had earned the reputation of having an ability to resolve issues and he worked well with people. Upon hearing the news of Miller's new assignment, Johnson reached out to him to see if he could support Miller at his new command. Miller assented, and they were working together again.

The arraignments were going to be time sensitive. Secretary of Defense Donald Rumsfeld approved the HVD list. MNF-I transferred legal control of selected HVDs to the Iraqi judicial system to support the prosecution of these criminals using the rule of law. MNF-I would maintain physical custody of the detainees, including ensuring their safety and security, until such time as they were relieved of the mission. At the specific request of the Minister of Justice (MOJ) and Iraqi Interim Government (IIG), this was an agreed-upon action.

The authority for US forces to have custodial support included control of Saddam and other HVDs. This authority was outlined in the Memorandum of Understanding (MOU) between US Contingent of Multi-National Force–Iraq and the Ministry of Justice of Iraq.

The MOU outlined legal custody to prosecute the defendants. Johnson stated, "We were often asked by journalists about this agreement, and I often stated this document provided legal authority by which the US continued to hold HVDs during trials." The document also provided responsibility for the transportation of these individuals to and from the courtroom. Saddam and other HVDs were held at Camp Cropper, located near BIAP.

The week before the arraignment Johnson said, "I invited Bakhtiar Amin, a Kurd and the new Minister of International Human Rights, to Camp Cropper to see Saddam and the other HVDs." He continued, "Our rationale for allowing him to come and visit Saddam was to allow him to see that he and the other HVDs were being treated humanely." Johnson went on, "Amin was the point of contact for families to address concerns, and we had developed a good relationship with him."[2]

Johnson said, "We knew full well he would not keep his visit and the location to himself, and shortly after there was a story published about Saddam and where he was being held at Camp Cropper. Amin enjoyed talking to the media, and of course we did not 'confirm or deny' the story." Johnson continued, "We never did state publicly, for obvious reasons, the location of where Saddam and other HVDs were being held. All the news leading up to the July 1 arraignment had him being held everywhere within Baghdad." He concluded, "We were good with that conjecture. This suited our needs on where he was being held."[3]

Coordination for the custody and control of Saddam and the other HVDs was the responsibility of the 89th Military Police (MP) under the command of Col. Barry Phillips (later to be promoted to Brig. Gen). A native of Cleveland, Ohio, and a graduate of Bowling Green State University, Phillips served in myriad assignments within the Military Police Corps.

He assumed command of the 89th MP in December 2003. His command provided military police combat support across the theater from Basra to Mosul.

They ran the Iraq National Police Academy, which produced more than 6,000 new police officers. In addition, his brigade provided protective custody for the 3,800 members of the Mujahedin e-Khalq (MEK) and the ammunition facility at Camp Ashraf. His brigade also performed the restoration sixty days earlier on the mosque, turning it into a makeshift courtroom and courthouse.

On the day of the arraignment, Col. Phillips' brigade would be responsible for transporting Saddam and the other eleven HVDs via Rhino bus from their holding facilities to the makeshift courtroom at Camp Victory. Escorting the buses were four Humvees and an ambulance.

After Saddam's capture, he was kept at Camp Cropper. Then, in February 2003, he was moved to the "lost lake" location located on the Camp Victory complex, on the eastern edge of one of the lakes that had a drawbridge. It was about one kilometer from TF 134 and not far from the courthouse. This facility was built to US specifications and was a maximum-security facility.[4]

Phillips put an MP platoon in place whose mission was to maintain custody of and security for #1 (Saddam). "When I first acquired him [Saddam], I put a Puerto Rico National Guard unit in charge and told them only to speak Spanish. Later, they were relieved by an English-speaking platoon."[5] The other eleven HVDs were housed at Camp Cropper, located on the other side of Camp Victory a few kilometers away.

The planning process for Saddam's court appearance began around the first of June. Johnson thought that he had the lead on selecting the media pool for Saddam's arraignment and not Brig. Gen. Mark Kimmitt. Kimmitt was a West Point graduate and the Deputy Director for Operations/Chief Military Spokesman. Johnson said he handpicked a journalist and photographer with whom he had worked on the Abu Ghraib issue. According to Johnson, "I selected the media members. Once I had my primary media list, I sent it to Miller, and he approved it. I thought it was a done deal."[6]

The print journalist Johnson selected was Steven Komarow. He was a long-standing foreign journalist with a good reputation, a former AP reporter with whom Johnson had worked. Johnson respected Komarow's journalistic talents. Johnson said, "I completely trusted him. He would get it right." All the journalists understood the ground rules and were reputable members of the Baghdad Press Corps.[7] Hence, Johnson stated, "I was under the impression the list had been approved. I then notified Steven Komarow of his selection. I briefed him on what he was going to cover: the arraignment of Saddam Hussein."

Selecting members for a media pool is usually an easy process. I've put many of these together during my career, but this pool selection took a different twist. According to Johnson, he would later learn that there was a procedure already in place regarding the formation of a media pool within the Coalition Press Information Center (CPIC). A list was established weekly that provided each media member an equal opportunity to be selected for this type of event. Johnson said, "We didn't use the system that was in place and the one the journalists agreed to." Johnson continued that Kimmitt "had already made the selection, declaring this was what the White House wanted." He commented, "I was totally unaware the media pool had been selected by Kimmitt."[8]

A few days later, Kimmitt told Johnson that he was talking to Condoleezza Rice's office, and they said, "They wanted John Burns and Karen Ballard [photographer] as the print journalist and photographer respectively." Both individuals were Kimmitt favorites. Johnson said, "It is my feeling the White House didn't really care who the media were inside the courtroom, but Kimmitt injected their names into the conversation so as to confirm their pool selection."

There was already a "strong negative relationship between Miller and Kimmitt," according to Johnson. Both had been artillery officers, and each knew of the other during their careers. Johnson stated, "Kimmitt had the reputation of treating people like crap and Miller wanted to protect me from him." Miller told him, "If he [Kimmitt] ever had any issues with me, he needed to come and address them with Miller directly."

As an aside, the first time I met Miller was at a late June General Officer/ Flag Officer (GO/FO) monthly commanders conference held at Camp Victory. I saw Kimmitt, and when he saw me, Kimmitt made my formal introduction to Miller. I felt Miller and I never really got off to a good start, due to my being "painted with the Kimmitt brush."

Johnson and I enjoyed a good working relationship during my time at MNF-I. Four days prior to my departure from MNF-I, I requested an office call with Miller, whom I respected. We had a very positive final conversation, and he even presented me with his personal two-star coin.

The media pool members selected for the courtroom event consisted of the following:

- A US print journalist, John Fisher Burns of the *New York Times*, Baghdad Bureau Chief, a Pulitzer Prize winner and well respected. He arrived in Baghdad during the lead-up to the war in 2003 and had written extensively on the war and the subsequent liberation. He was sent to China in 1971 to be among one of a few Western journalists in China during the Cultural Revolution. Burns joined the *New York Times* in 1975 and was assigned to and headed several of the paper's foreign bureaus. Burns received a Pulitzer in 1997 "for his courageous and insightful coverage of the harrowing regime imposed on Afghanistan by the Taliban."

- An Iraqi print journalist, a reporter from *Azzaman* ("Time"), an Arabic daily and self-declared "independent" newspaper printed in Great Britain and distributed throughout the Arab community. It was widely read throughout Baghdad and regarded as a valuable source of information. *Azzaman* took a more centered approach in its reporting and editorials, rather than being pro-coalition. The paper published anti-coalition pieces that labeled the US presence in Iraq as an occupying force. Basically, it was a liberal, non-religious-based, western paper providing local and international news, sports, fashion, and arts. This kind of newspaper was not available in Baghdad during the Saddam regime.

- Three television cameramen (no TV reporters)—one US, one Iraqi, and one from another Arab station. Since the dialogue between the judge and the defendants would only be in Arabic, it was decided there would only be video and NO audio. The US pool member was CNN. The Iraqi was Al Iraqiya, a satellite TV channel that used to be part of the Iraqi Media Network and was founded and funded by the coalition. Al Iraqiya was a local Baghdad media source that broadcast in English and Arabic. Al Iraqiya worked in cooperation with the CPA in broadcasting information and instructions to the Iraqi population regarding various reconstruction efforts and public announcements. Their programming consisted of news, CPA announcements, CPA reconstruction meetings, movies, cartoons, and sports. Its office was in the Baghdad Convention Center (in the Green Zone). The Arab station was Al Jazeera, based in Doha, Qatar. It covered regional and international news and had an extensive Arabic audience in the Middle East, as well as an active website that ran updates of international regional news. The station reported on foreign policy, education, sciences, the arts, culture, history, and sports.

- One still photographer, Karen Ballard from *Time* magazine, who had been embedded with Gen. Tommy Franks as he moved into Iraq in 2003. She was a respected photographer at the White House, on Capitol Hill, and in the Middle East. She later worked on a number of feature films, including *Quantum of Solace*, *The Expendables*, and *Jack Reacher*, as the main unit photographer.

- Two Combat Camera members: one video/cameraman and one photographer.

Of course, all media members selected for this event were required to sign and follow the "pool rules."

Another interesting twist occurred the evening before the arraignment. Col. Phillips received a call from Col. Mark Warren, the lawyer for CJTF-7. He was calling Phillips to tell him to expect a call from Commanding General (CG) Sanchez within the next few minutes.

Shortly thereafter, the telephone rang, Phillips answered it. "Col. Phillips, what are you going to dress the HVDs in for their court arraignment?" Sanchez asked.

Phillips responded, "Well, right now we have them in their orange jumpsuits."

Sanchez said, "No, no; this is not going to work. Get them in suits, ties, and [dress] shoes."

Phillips then asked, "Sir, suits and ties?"

"You heard me. Get them in suits and ties. You have to make them presentable."[9]

Phillips immediately called Colonel Warren and said, "Hell, where am I going to get suits, ties, and shoes at this hour?"

Warren said, "Do whatever you have to do."

Phillips thought for a few minutes. How was he going to achieve what the CG wanted thirty-six hours before the arraignment?

Phillips immediately sent out a team to go and get the measurements for Saddam and the eleven other HVDs. Within a short while, they returned with all the numbers. I called into my office one of my interpreters, a US citizen who grew up in Baghdad who had come to the US as a young boy. He knew his way around Baghdad, which would be critical to the success of this project.

I told him I needed him to go downtown and into the bazaars to buy twelve suits, shirts, pairs of shoes, and ties, and provided all the measurements. He would be dropped off at a predetermined location and picked up at the same location. But before taking him downtown I went to Capt. Cullen Sheppard, my brigade lawyer (JAG), and said, "I need to make a withdrawal from my Commanders Emergency Response Program (CERP) funds. I need $10,000 in cash."

(Note: During the Iraq War, battalion commanders were allocated packets of $100 bills and authorized to use them for anything from repairing a schoolhouse to paying off ex-rebels or blood money. Much has been written about the use of these funds.[10] Marisa Sullivan, deputy director of the Institute for the Study of War, asserted that CERP helped put people to work who would otherwise be susceptible to joining the insurgency and that the economic development the funds helped spark was critical in bringing security to the local environment. "Without CERP there would be not the kind of counterinsurgency success we saw in Iraq during and after the surge," she said.)

The young officer told Phillips, "Sir, you can't do this!" Despite the objection, Phillips took the money ($10,000 in brand-new $100 bills), gave it to his interpreter, and had a vehicle waiting for him that took him downtown and dropped him off.

Within a few hours, the interpreter returned. Phillips pulled together a team and divided up the clothes, first deciding what Saddam would wear, then giving the HVDs the balance of the clothing.

The young lawyer asked, "How much did we get back? Where are the receipts?" Phillips told him, "We're not asking for change. We got a hell of a deal! He came back alive." Phillips had accomplished his mission. Saddam and the HVDs would not be wearing orange jumpsuits but jackets, shirts, and shoes.[11]

I had several nightly conversations with Jim Wilkinson, an assistant to National Security Advisor Condoleezza Rice, leading up to July 1. He and I had become friends over the previous three years. Jim knew Baghdad and the region quite well. He was Gen. Tommy Franks' Director of Strategic Communications before and during Operations Iraqi Freedom.[12]

According to Gen. Franks, in his book *American Soldier*, "I'd asked Donald Rumsfeld and his public relations assistant, Torie [Victoria] Clarke, for a skilled PR man, as the buildup for a possible major operation in Iraq progressed." He went on to say, "I don't deal well with the media. That's more Norm Schwarzkopf's style. I need someone press-savvy to help me navigate the rapids." Two weeks later Wilkinson was named to the position. During that two-week period, Wilkinson called me several times, and we discussed his role and many of the challenges that lay ahead of him.[13]

Wilkinson was a lieutenant in the Navy Reserve public affairs community and would also oversee the Joint Information Bureau (JIB) located in

CENTCOM Forward headquarters in Doha, Qatar. The JIB was the lead element in disseminating all the news to the world regarding daily combat operations from Operation Iraqi Freedom.

One day, Jim called and asked if I might help get a young man assigned to him who had worked on President Clinton's communications staff. Lt. Mark Kitchens had a particular skill set that was needed in the JIB to assist with the daily briefings. Lt. Kitchens was also in the Navy Reserve, and I knew him well. He too would soon be deployed to CENTCOM but at the reluctance of the Navy's Chief of Information. As the senior Navy PAO, the chief had determined the JIB was to be manned ONLY by active-duty public affairs officers and NOT with any Navy Reserve PAOs.[14]

Wilkinson was solid and knew how to work with the media. Franks recounted how Wilkinson once told him, "You're going to learn to love the media, General." Franks never did, but he did come to trust Jim Wilkinson.[15] I was envious of Wilkinson because Gen. Casey and I never had that kind of a relationship.

It was my opinion that Kimmitt had conversations with Wilkinson regarding the media pool prior to my arrival. My conversations with Wilkinson mostly dealt with the outside media pool positions. One media location was outside the courthouse to capture the unloading of the HVDs, and the other was inside the courthouse.

Wilkinson and I also discussed the "perp walk" (preparatory walk or "walking the perp"). According to Col. Johnson, the perp walk is a common custom of American law enforcement. It is the practice of taking an arrested suspect through a public place at some point after the arrest, creating an opportunity for the media to take photographs and video. The defendant is typically handcuffed or otherwise restrained and sometimes dressed in prison garb. Within the United States, the perp walk is most closely associated with New York City. Originally only those accused of violent street crimes were subjected to it. After Rudy Giuliani had accused white-collar criminals to be perp-walked in the 1980s, the practice was extended to almost every defendant. Law enforcement agencies often coordinate with the media in scheduling and arranging the walk. It has been criticized as a form of public humiliation that violates a defendant's right to privacy and is prejudicial to the presumption of innocence. On the other hand, it has been defended as promoting transparency in the criminal justice system.[16]

I lobbied hard for the outside media position. I thought it was important to capture the scene of Saddam's departure, along with that of the other HVDs, from the Rhino bus. I wanted to demonstrate that Saddam was in Iraqi control, cuffed but being treated with dignity as a prisoner.

Of course, there was a concern voiced by Iraqi guards who did not want their faces shown for fear of increased violence toward them and their families. We discussed many options to ensure the anonymity of the guards, including those wearing sunglasses or riot masks.

In the end, Wilkinson had the final say, and we removed the media location outside the courtroom.

Phillips said keeping custody of Saddam was a sideshow; everyone wanted to see the captured dictator. Maj. Gen. Miller and I had a list of those who had access to #1. This was always changing. Miller would call daily and continually grant someone else on the access list. Phillips goes on to say that on the day of the arraignment, a field grade officer jumped on the bus and sat next to Saddam. Phillips told the officer he was not allowed on the bus and would have sent him back to the States if Miller hadn't interceded on his behalf.[17]

In addition, Phillips said, everyone wanted something of Saddam's. In the courtroom that day, Saddam had a ballpoint pen with him. Every day thereafter someone would ask they could have "that pen." Phillips sent his supply officer out and told him to buy three or four boxes of ballpoint pens. Every time Miller or one of his people would ask for Saddam's pen, he would pull a pen from one of these boxes and hand it to them. According to Phillips, there are probably at least forty people out there who think they have the pen Saddam wrote with the day of the arraignment. As a matter of fact, Maj. Gen. Miller probably thinks he has Saddam's pen from that day.[18] The actual pen Saddam used on the day of the arraignment was given to one of the young MP drivers that day. He had no idea what he had in his possession.[19] Saddam wrote poetry, and those books are now at the Carlisle Army Heritage Center at Carlisle War College.

Phillips had several conversations with Saddam. "He really thought the United States was going to reinstate him to power. He even invited me back once he was in control again. He would 'show me the real Iraq.' He never doubted he would be put back in power."[20]

PART 2

THE
ARRAIGNMENT

9

SADDAM HUSSEIN– A PRODUCT OF HIS ENVIRONMENT

THROUGHOUT SEVERAL CENTURIES, IRAQ HAS HAD A LONG tradition of violent conquest and occupation. Through repeated revolutions, many have sought to gain control of the wealthy country. Saddam was one of many in a long list of powerful leaders.

How did Saddam Hussein al-Majid al-Tikriti rise to such power? What influences shaped his life? How were his vision and style of leadership developed? Many factors would determine the change and direction Iraq would take once he ascended to power. If one were to look back on Iraq's history, it would soon become evident how the culture and Saddam's environment had shaped him as a man and the future leader of Iraq.

Throughout many centuries the "cradle of civilization," a geographical area that includes Iraq, was in endless conflict. By 1638, Iraq had become part of the fabled Ottoman Empire. During the subsequent two centuries, according to Phebe Marr, author of *The Modern History of Iraq* and a Middle East consultant, it was a fractured society, due to the many small communities being mostly tribal. It was the belief in Islam that held the country together.

Early in the nineteenth century, the area had to deal with foreign countries and their interests in the region's resources, specifically oil. This natural resource soon became a valued product that would be fought over for years to come.

In 1908, crude oil was discovered in Iran. Winston Churchill, Britain's then civilian head of the Royal Navy, was convinced that oil, not coal, was the fuel of the future. The British soon expanded their presence and investments in the region and plans were in place to conquer the southern portion of Iraq prior to World War I.

In August 1914, World War I began. In November 1914, the British Army occupied Basra to protect the oil fields and refineries in nearby Iran. In March 1917, under the leadership of Lt. Gen. Sir Frederick Stanley Maude, the British forces gained control of the city of Baghdad. More than 9,000 Turkish soldiers surrendered. Gen. Maude made the statement to Iraq and the world, "Our armies do not come into your cities or land as conquerors but as liberators." This was a statement the Iraqis would hear again some ninety years later.

The British Army continued to move north until it captured the northern city of Mosul. This gave them control of nearly all of Iraq. Before long, the Ottoman Turks in Northern Iraq were defeated by Gen. Maude. After his victory, he returned to Baghdad, where he died of cholera.

Iraqis and Arabs from other Ottoman provinces longed for self-rule. At the 1919 Paris Peace Conference, Arabs lobbied hard for independence and self-rule. However, the Iraqis' dream of self-rule was dashed when the League of Nations decided to divide the Ottoman provinces between the countries of France and Britain. Dina Khoury, a scholar at George Washington University, commented that Iraq was ready for independence, but Britain felt they needed their assistance and support in order to do so.

Iraq has experienced turmoil almost since its emergence as a modern state in the early 1920s. One clue to Iraq's difficulties can be found in a speech delivered to the British House of Commons by Winston Churchill in 1921. It was British policy, he explained, "to attempt to build around the ancient city of Baghdad, in a form friendly to Britain and her allies, an Arab state which can revive and embody the old culture and glories of the Arab race."[1] In the Kurdistan Region of Iraq, the Kurds lost their ancestral lands and were annexed to accommodate the interests of the British government.

Winston Churchill led the effort to remove direct British rule and install a British-friendly leader in Iraq. He invited Prince Faisal al Hussein as the ruler of the new state to install a new government. Although Faisal was not an Iraqi, he was a member of the ruling family of Mecca, and a decedent of the prophet Muhammad. In August 1921, he was elected king of Iraq in a referendum vote. At the time, the monarchy was foreign to Iraq.

In 1927, oil was discovered in Ottoman Iraq, in the city of Kirkuk. With this discovery, the Iraqi government now enjoyed a new source of wealth. Under King Faisal's rule, Iraq achieved greater freedom than in the past. At the urging of Faisal, Iraq was admitted as an independent state to the League of Nations in October 1932.

On April 28, 1937, in the small village of Al-Awja, eight miles from Tikrit, Iraq, in the Saladin Province and approximately 95 miles north of Baghdad, a woman named Subha Tulfah al-Mussallat bore a child. She named her new-born son Saddam Hussein al-Majid al-Tikriti. Saddam in Arabic means "one who confronts."[2] Saddam never knew his father, who disappeared six months before he was born.[3]

His mother remarried and Saddam gained three half-brothers (Watban Ibrahim Hasan, Barzan Ibrahim Hasan, and Sabawi Ibrahim al-Tikriti). His stepfather, Ibrahim al-Hasan, treated Saddam harshly, and at age ten Saddam fled and went to live with his uncle Khairallah Talfah in Baghdad. His uncle was a staunch Arab nationalist. Saddam had a difficult childhood. He retained the lessons of village life learned in his early years. He idolized his mother but was deeply marred by his shame about being fatherless. He looked to his mother's brother as a father figure, and it was his uncle who first introduced him to a life of crime and political rebellion.

Kenneth Pollack wrote about Saddam's life as a boy in his book *The Threatening Storm*. Saddam engaged in cruel activities. He would heat an iron poker until it was white-hot and then use it to impale cats and dogs. Years later, as a father with boys of his own, he would take his sons into prisons so they could watch and become accustomed to torture and executions.[4]

By the late 1940s, many Iraqis continued to oppose the pro-British monarchy. Throughout the country, the people lived in immense poverty and many economic issues arose, especially over land ownership. In May 1953, Faisal's son, Faisal II, ascended to the throne. In 1956, under his leadership, Iraq joined the Baghdad Pact, an anti-communism security alliance including Great Britain, Turkey, Pakistan, and Iran. That same year, King Faisal II reaffirmed his government's friendship and allegiance with Great Britain.

In 1957, at the age of twenty, Saddam joined the revolutionary pan-Arab Ba'ath Party, of which his uncle was a supporter and whose beliefs and attitudes shaped his political life. During this time, Saddam supported himself as a secondary school teacher. Later in his life, relatives from his native Tikrit became some of his closest advisors and supporters.[5]

Gen. Abdul Karim Qasim was the leader of the revolution and became prime minister of the newly formed Republic of Iraq. Because his progressive laws promoted women's rights and land reform, he was considered too radical by many Iraqis. As his tenure as Iraq's ruler continued, a movement to support the right-wing Ba'ath Party began to emerge and gain strength in Iraq. The Ba'ath Party was a mix of Arab nationalism and Arab socialism that was formed in the early 1950s. It grew stronger and extended its reach deep into the core of the elite army officers.

Later that year, the Ba'ath Party leadership was planning to assassinate Qasim. Saddam was a leading member of the operation. At the time, the Ba'ath Party was more of an ideological experiment than a strong anti-government fighting machine. Many of its members were either educated professionals or students, and Saddam fit the bill. The choice of Saddam as the leader was, according to historian Con Coughlin, "hardly surprising." The idea of assassinating Qasim may have been Egyptian president Gamal Abdel Nasser's, and there is speculation that some of those who participated in the operation received training in Damascus, Syria, which was then part of the United Arab Republic.[6]

The assassins planned to ambush Qasim in his car on Al-Rashid Street as he traveled in a caravan to a meeting on October 7, 1959. One man was to kill those sitting in the back of the car, the rest killing those in the front. During the ambush, it is claimed that Saddam began shooting prematurely, which disorganized the whole operation. Qasim's chauffeur was killed, and Qasim was hit in the arm and shoulder. The assassins believed they had killed him and quickly retreated to their headquarters. Qasim survived. At the time of the attack, the Ba'ath Party had fewer than 1,000 members.[7]

Following the botched assassination attempt in 1959, Saddam went into hiding before escaping to neighboring Syria and later to Egypt. He continued to live there until he returned to Iraq in 1963 when the Ba'ath Party seized power.[8]

Many foreign countries opposed Qasim, particularly after he threatened to invade Kuwait. In June 1961, six days after Kuwait received its independence from Britain, Gen. Qasim claimed Kuwait as Iraqi territory. A show of force by the British deterred Qasim from acting on his claims, but the Iraqi threat to Kuwait—sometimes explicit, always implicit—persisted throughout the next three decades.[9]

In February 1963, a coalition group of Ba'ath and Arab nationalist army officers staged another bloody coup to overthrow Qasim. After the coup ended,

Qasim was captured. He was executed in 24 hours.

Some members of the operation were arrested and taken into custody by the Iraqi government. At the show trial, six of the defendants were given the death sentence. However, for reasons unknown, the sentences were not carried out. Michel Aflaq was the leader of the Ba'ath movement. He organized the expulsion of leading Iraqi Ba'athist members, such as Fuad al-Rikabi, on the grounds that the party should not have initiated the attempt on Qasim's life. At the same time, Aflaq managed to secure seats in the Iraqi Ba'ath leadership for his supporters, one of them being Saddam. Saddam was given full membership in the Ba'ath Party.[10]

A former collaborator of Qasim in the 1958 revolution was Abdul Salam Arif. Ba'athist leaders were appointed to the cabinet, and Abdul Salam Arif became president. His nationalist supporters completely outmaneuvered the Ba'ath organization and took control of the government. The governments of the United States and the United Kingdom were complicit in the coup. Arif dismissed and arrested the Ba'athist leaders later that year in the November 1963 Iraqi coup d'état.[11]

Arif died in a helicopter crash in 1966. The crash may have been an act of sabotage by Ba'athist elements in the Iraqi military. Abd al-Rahman al-Bazzaz became acting president for three days, while a power struggle for the presidency occurred. In the first meeting of the Defense Council and cabinet to elect a president, al-Bazzaz needed a two-thirds majority to win the presidency. Al-Bazzaz was unsuccessful, and the brother of the late Abdul Salam Arif was elected president. He was viewed by army officers as weaker and easier to manipulate than his brother.[12] The Ba'ath Party took advantage of Arif's ineffective leadership and overthrew his government with a bloodless coup. He was sent into exile.

Saddam was a willing participant in the coup led by Ahmed Hassan al-Bakr. He was designated by al-Bakr as vice chair and second-in-command. Saddam Hussein was thirty-one years old and politically active. Saddam never forgot the tensions within the first Ba'athist government. Those formed the basis for his measures to promote Ba'ath Party unity, as well as his resolve to maintain power and programs to ensure social stability. Although Saddam was al-Bakr's deputy, he was a strong, behind-the-scenes party politician. Al-Bakr was the older and more prestigious of the two, but by 1969, Hussein clearly had become the moving force behind the party.[13]

In the early 1970s, there was a bitterness developing between Saddam and Ayatollah Ruhollah Khomeini. Khomeini had been exiled from Iran in 1964. He took up residence in Iraq, at the Shi'ite holy city of An Najaf. He became involved with Iraqi Shi'ites and developed a strong, worldwide religious and political following against the Iranian government, which Saddam tolerated. Khomeini began to urge the Shi'ites to overthrow Saddam's government, so Saddam decided to expel Khomeini in 1978 to France. This action would turn out to be a failure for Saddam and a political catalyst for Khomeini.

Saddam was reluctant to leave his safe haven of Iraq. His only visit to a Western country took place in September 1975, when he met with his friend, Prime Minister Jacques Chirac, in Paris, France.[14] Since Saddam rarely left Iraq, Tariq Aziz, one of Saddam's aides, traveled abroad extensively and represented Iraq at many diplomatic meetings. In foreign affairs, Saddam sought to have Iraq play a leading role in the Middle East. Iraq signed an aid pact with the Soviet Union in 1972, and arms were sent along with several thousand advisors. However, the 1978 crackdown on communists and a shift of trade toward the West strained Iraqi relations with the Soviet Union. Iraq then took on a more Western orientation until the Gulf War in 1991.[15]

In 1976, Saddam rose to the position of general in the Iraqi armed forces and rapidly became the strongman of the government. As the elderly, ailing al-Bakr became unable to execute his duties, Saddam took on an increasingly prominent role as the face of the government both internally and externally. He soon became the architect of Iraq's foreign policy and represented the nation in all diplomatic situations. He was the de facto leader of Iraq some years before he formally came to power in 1979. He slowly began to consolidate his power over Iraq's government and the Ba'ath Party. Relationships with fellow party members were carefully cultivated, and Saddam soon accumulated a powerful circle of support within the party.

In 1979, al-Bakr started to make treaties with Syria. Under Ba'athist leadership, he led Iraq to a union between the two countries. Syrian president Hafez al-Assad would become deputy leader in this union, and this would threaten to drive Saddam to obscurity.

Saddam acted to secure his grip on power and on July 17, 1979, al-Bakr resigned and stepped down from the presidency due to health problems. Saddam ascended to the top and proclaimed himself the new leader of Iraq.

Under Saddam's reign, the secret police spread an atmosphere of terror throughout all regions of Iraq. Everyone feared their neighbors and, more unsettling, parents feared their own children. Shortly after being declared the new ruler, Saddam convened an assembly of Ba'ath Party leaders on July 22, 1979. During the assembly, which he ordered videotaped, Saddam claimed to have uncovered traitors and conspirators within the Ba'ath Party. He directed Muhyi Abdel-Hussein to read out loud a confession and the names of sixty-eight alleged co-conspirators. These members were labeled "disloyal" and were removed from the room one by one and taken into custody. After the list was read, Saddam congratulated those still seated in the room for their past and future loyalty. The sixty-eight people arrested at the meeting were subsequently tried together and found guilty of treason. Twenty-two were sentenced to execution. Other high-ranking members of the party formed the firing squad. By August 1, 1979, hundreds of high-ranking Ba'ath Party members had been executed.[16]

Saddam's authority dominated. His decisions, whether arbitrating the promotion of a junior officer or the death of a rival or family member, were final. He was authoritarian and as brutal as the Soviet Union's Stalin, or China's Mao, or any among the regimes within the Arab world. His unilateral control and decision-making over a country that had been repeatedly raped and massacred allowed his power to grow along with his wealth.

Washington's first flirtation with Saddam came in the last years of the Carter administration. There were no illusions about the Iraqi dictator. The intelligence reports had shown a consistent analysis: Saddam was a thug and an assassin. However, he was the dictator of choice at a time when Washington was reeling from the twin setbacks of a Soviet invasion of Afghanistan and the Islamic Revolution in Iran. If Saddam was bad, it was thought, the Ayatollah was worse.[17]

On September 22, 1980, Kuwait was declared a new province of Iraq. Iraq had the support of the Arab states, the United States, and Europe, and was heavily financed by the Arab states of the Persian Gulf. Saddam Hussein had become "the defender of the Arab world" against a revolutionary Iran. The only exception was the Soviet Union, who initially refused to supply Iraq on the basis of neutrality in the conflict. Mikhail Gorbachev in his memoirs claimed that Leonid Brezhnev refused to aid Saddam due to Saddam's treatment of Iraqi communists.

Many viewed Iraq as "an agent of the civilized world." Iraq's blatant disregard of international law and violations of international borders were ignored. Instead, Iraq received economic and military support from its allies. The latter conveniently overlooked Saddam's use of chemical warfare against the Kurds and the Iranians and Iraq's efforts to develop nuclear weapons.[18]

In 1981, Saddam told a Kuwaiti newspaper that border adjustments between the two countries (Iraq and Kuwait) were necessary. Specifically, he asserted that Iraq needed access to the Arabian (Persian) Gulf, which might necessitate the transfer of the Kuwaiti islands of Warbah and Bubiyan to Iraqi sovereignty.[19] More threats and hostile acts followed. Iraqi extremists were implicated, for example, in the 1983 series of bombings in Kuwait, in the hijacking of a Kuwaiti airliner, and in a failed attempt to assassinate Kuwait's ruler in 1985.[20]

On November 26, 1984, Washington restored diplomatic relations with Iraq after a seventeen-year break. Saddam's new relations with Washington were matched by his relations with European governments. The research and development center for Saddam's missile program, known as Saad 16 near Mosul, was built by Germans, Austrians, Brazilians, and Egyptians. Saddam was an excellent arms customer for French companies. German companies sold him chemicals for his weapons program.[21]

Although the war between Iraq and Iran began in 1984, it wasn't until 1986 that the two countries had a significant battle in the city of Al-Faw, in the far southeast of the Basra province. Its oil facilities made it one of Iraq's major oil exporting ports prior to the 1984 war. Because of its strategic and geographic importance, it became a target for Iranian control. Iran was successful in capturing the port of Al-Faw with 85,000 Iranian soldiers. The following week, Saddam was so convinced that he could recapture Al-Faw that he invited foreign correspondents to the southern port city of Basra. One reporter was Deborah Amos, whom I met and worked with during the Gulf War, in Dhahran, Saudi Arabia.

Amos stated, "The capture of al-Faw showed a fundamental flaw in Saddam's military strategy. He insisted to his main financial backers, Saudi Arabia, and Kuwait, that Iran would eventually run out of steam and petition for peace. Saddam had ordered his generals to sit tight and keep the casualties to a minimum." But, Amos continued, "There is a darker side to this story. Western diplomats were told of the combat dead stored in giant freezers to be dispersed in small lots to dull the shock of loss. Saddam banned public funerals. Family gatherings for burials at Baghdad cemeteries were off-limits to reporters; to attend was an invitation for arrest by the local police as the government sought to downplay the death toll."[22]

In April 1988, the Iraqi military succeeded in regaining the Al-Faw Peninsula. The Al Faw Palace was built following the Gulf War in 1991 to honor the soldiers who freed Al-Faw from Iranian control. In addition, the Swords of Qadisiyah—also called the "Hands of Victory" or, as they are known by most soldiers in Baghdad, the "Crossed Swords"—were constructed to commemorate Iraq's victory in the Iran–Iraq War. The hands holding crossed swords mark the entrance to a parade ground. Saddam's design consisted of a pair of massive hands emerging at 45-degree angles from the ground, each holding a 140-foot sword. Each blade weighed 24 tons. The crossed swords are the most recognizable landmark in Baghdad. Of note, the helmets of more than 2,500 Iranian soldiers killed during the war are held in metal nets at the base of each hand.

In conjunction with the 1988 Anfal campaign, an attack occurred that was designed to reassert central control of the mostly Kurdish population of Northern Iraq and defeat the Kurdish peshmerga rebel forces. The United States then maintained that Saddam ordered the attack to terrorize the Kurdish population, but Saddam's regime claimed at the time that Iran was responsible for the attack. Some countries, including the US, supported the claim until several years later.[23]

The Anfal campaign took its name from Surah al-Anfal ("the Spoils of War") in the Qur'an, used as a code name by the former Iraqi Ba'athist administration. It represented a series of attacks against the peshmerga rebels and the mostly Kurdish civilian population of rural Northern Iraq between 1986 and 1989. This campaign also targeted Shabaks and Yazidis, Assyrians, Turkoman people, and Mandeans. Many villages belonging to these ethnic groups were destroyed. Human Rights Watch estimates that between 50,000 and 100,000 were killed. Some Kurdish sources put the number higher, estimating 182,000 Kurds were killed.[24]

On March 16, 1988, the Kurdish town of Halabja was attacked with a mix of mustard gas and nerve agents, immediately killing 5,000 civilians. Several thousand died later, and an estimated 10,000 were seriously affected.[25] Just prior to the launch of the spring 2003 offensive against Saddam and Iraq, the White House released the following, "The chemical attack on Halabja—just one of 40 targeted at Iraq's own people—provided a glimpse of the crimes Saddam Hussein is willing to commit, and the kind of threat he now presents to the entire world. He is among history's cruelest dictators, and he is arming himself with the world's most terrible weapons."[26]

Saddam harshly suppressed Shi'a and Kurdish movements during his reign. The Kurds had continually been subject to adversity since the end of World War I. They were denied their own homeland, splitting them among three countries: Turkey, Iran, and Iraq. The Kurds of Iraq were frequently under Saddam's knife of justice. Between 1987 and 1989, Saddam committed genocide, destroying more than 2,000 villages and murdering an estimated 50,000 Kurds.

Saddam was ruthless in disposing of his opponents. Many stories persist that claim he carried a pistol with him and even had killed someone when he was a child. Saddam was in charge of internal security. He eliminated any opposition to the Ba'ath government and to himself. Over a long period of time, the Ba'ath Party depended on the military to maintain their rule. Saddam developed a new and strong element for the party, the secret police. His powerful authoritarian regime was based on a system of violence, an extraordinary surveillance network, reward schemes, and incentives for supporters of the party.

Before Saddam's rise to power, Iraqis generally appended the name of their native village to their own names. Saddam was called Saddam Hussein al-Tikriti. He personally abolished this practice, reportedly to conceal the fact that all his high officials came from Tikrit.[27]

In April 1990, the US ambassador to Iraq joined Saddam for an emergency meeting. As Iraq–Kuwait relations rapidly deteriorated, Saddam was receiving conflicting information about how the US would respond to the prospects of an invasion. For one, Washington took measures to cultivate a constructive relationship with Iraq for roughly a decade. The Reagan administration gave Iraq roughly $4 billion in agricultural credits to bolster it against Iran. Saddam's Iraq became "the third-largest recipient of US assistance."[28]

Reacting to Western criticism in April 1990, Saddam threatened to annihilate half of Israel with chemical weapons if the latter moved against Iraq. In May 1990, he denounced US support for Israel, warning that "the United States cannot maintain such a policy while professing friendship towards the Arabs." In July 1990, he threatened force against Kuwait and the UAE, saying, "The policies of some Arab rulers are American. . . . They are inspired by America to undermine Arab interests and security." The US sent planes and combat ships to the Persian Gulf in response to those threats.[29]

After months of saber-rattling, on August 2, 1990, Saddam invaded Kuwait and within two days Kuwaiti Armed Forces were either overrun by Iraqi Republican Guard or had fled to neighboring Saudi Arabia or Bahrain. A few days later, Saddam announced that Kuwait was annexed and was now the 19th province of Iraq.

If one reflects back to Saddam's speech at the Royal Cultural Center in Amman, Jordan, on February 24, 1990, one might say that the invasion of Kuwait could have been predicted. In his speech, he asserted that the United States was both powerful and weak. According to Saddam, the US was "'potent after its Cold War victory but immobilized by Vietnam.' The marine withdrawal from Beirut after the 1983 terror bombing of the marine barracks loomed large in Saddam's perception. This US did not have the staying power." If there were "massive American casualties, fatigue and domestic self-recrimination would stall US military power."[30]

Saddam miscalculated the overwhelming international reaction to his decision to invade Kuwait. Around the first of September 1990, Molly Moore visited the Saudi Defense Ministry. The briefings she received provided her with a more complete understanding of the crisis at hand. According to Moore, "Despite the $3 trillion building of American military under President Ronald Reagan, distance and geography were hobbling the US military's ability to react quickly and effectively. And until a much larger force arrived, Saddam Hussein could march into Saudi Arabia virtually at will." The American consulate in Dhahran had already shredded all its sensitive papers and stocked up on water and food in preparation for an invasion.[31]

Gen. Schwarzkopf said, "I did not think Saddam would be reckless enough to start a war with the United States, but I was not prepared to bet my troops' lives on it. He was a tyrant surrounded by a bunch of yes-men, and since nobody on our side knew his intent, we had to assume that if he was militarily capable of something, he might do it."[32]

Moore said, "When I arrived in Dhahran in November, not much had changed. The fear of Iraqi invasion still loomed large. With the military forces Saddam had mounted at the Kuwaiti-Saudi border, Dhahran was less than 100 miles away and the roads were paved and open."[33]

By the middle of August, the US began sending troops to Saudi Arabia, and within three months I received orders to deploy to US Central Command (USCENTCOM) under the command of Gen. H. Norman Schwarzkopf. Upon arriving at the general's Saudi Arabia headquarters in the capital city of Riyadh, I was reassigned to the Joint Information Bureau (JIB) in the eastern city of Dhahran.

Once there I was assigned duties as the chief of the Navy News Desk where I had a staff of five including two officers and three enlisted personnel. Our mission was managing all media requests for US Navy interviews in the region, both ashore and afloat. In addition, our joint responsibilities included coordinating all Congressional Delegation (CODEL) visits arriving in theater and, once the war started, managing "combat correspondent pool" (CCP) assignments and deployments. Later, I found myself being the escort officer for four of these CCPs.

During the First Gulf War, I helped a journalist from *Newsweek* on numerous occasions to search for information for his magazine. His name was David "Hack" Hackworth. Hack was a retired US Army colonel and one of the most decorated soldiers the Army had produced. He earned two Distinguished Service Crosses (right below the Medal of Honor), nine Silver Stars, and eight Purple Hearts. He served from the end of World War II through the Vietnam War. He was a no-nonsense, outspoken, opinionated individual who was not liked by Army leadership. His twenty-six years of military service provided him many contacts who were serving on the front lines in Saudi Arabia, as we prepared to confront Saddam and his forces. With more than a quarter-century of military service to his credit, including tours in seven war zones, he spoke with the authority of experience.

Hack and I became friends and corresponded until his death in May 2005. The response to the invasion of Kuwait represents an opportunity the US did not capitalize on, and Hack made an interesting comment about Desert Storm: "It worries me that the Pentagon will conclude that Desert Storm should be the model for future wars. Any such conclusion would be incorrect. From the beginning to the end, Desert Shield and Desert Storm were freaks of nature. In Saddam Hussein, we fought a rank amateur, who did everything wrong. What other opponents will ever grant us six months to build an overwhelming force right in front of his foxholes?"[34]

It was his position that the US government and military "should have been searching for a way to finish off Saddam Hussein once and for all so that the United States would never have to go back to those battlefields. Instead, they left him in power with enough strength to drag us around by the nose."[35]

It was Hack's contention that one possible reason we stopped short was that "President Bush and his advisors felt squeamish about images they were seeing on TV from the so-called Highway of Death. [This was the road leading out of Kuwait City, and the Iraqi military was driving everything they could get their hands on—jeeps, trucks, transports, and tanks, all stuffed with loot—to vacate the city.] The US bombings of the highway made it miles of a huge mess with burned-up vehicles and a few Iraqis killed along the way. They worried the United States might wind up looking like a barbarian eager for the great bloodbath."[36]

Hack said, "But you must never go to war unless you clearly intend to win. War is like marriage: It's unconditional." He continued, "President Bush, Gen. Powell, and Gen. Schwarzkopf should have delivered the KO punch as we did with Hitler and Tojo. Gen. [George] Catlett Marshall didn't stop simply because he had succeeded in kicking the Germans out of France. He went in and destroyed Adolf Hitler. We haven't really won a war since World War II."[37]

The American view of Saddam's seizure of Kuwait had not been troubled by shades of gray. The deed soon equated with the German invasion of Belgium in 1914, the Japanese occupation of Manchuria in 1931, and the German conquest of Poland in 1939. By the standards of modern sovereignty, the invasion was unpardonable.[38] Under Saddam, Iraq had great potential with many resources at its disposal. It was forced to be underdeveloped because of the Gulf War and the leadership of its president. Saddam remained defiant.

Of concern for the coalition forces was the number of Scud missile batteries Saddam had and whether they could be knocked out in the early stages of the Gulf War. US intelligence estimated Saddam had at least sixty-five fixed and mobile Scud launchers and showed that most of the launchers had been destroyed. The assessments were vastly underestimated. Saddam had converted a fleet of flatbed trucks into mobile missile launchers. While I was in Dhahran, during the early stages of the war, nightly Scud attacks would occur from about 10 p.m. until 4 a.m. The Scud is not an accurate weapon; aware of this, the Saudi Arabian population was terrorized by the Scuds' unpredictability.[39]

According to Norman Schwarzkopf, "On December 6 [1990], Saddam suddenly announced that Iraq would immediately free all its remaining foreign hostages; he called this a humanitarian gesture to promote peace—and added that Iraq had built up its defenses to the point where human shields were no longer necessary. As soon as the Americans were released the following week, Washington pulled the rest of its personnel out of the embassy in Kuwait City. These moves did little to defuse the crisis, but they simplified our war planning; we no longer had to worry about bombing human shields or mounting risky rescue operations in Iraq or Kuwait."[40]

The war ended in defeat for Saddam and Iraq in February 1991. For the next twelve years, Iraq endured international sanctions, weapons' inspections, and air strikes. The Iraqis continued to suffer. Saddam increasingly portrayed himself as a devout Muslim, to co-opt the conservative religious segments of society. Some elements of Shari'a law were reinstated, and the ritual phrase "Allahu Akbar" (God is great), in Saddam's handwriting, was added to the national flag. Saddam also commissioned the production of a "Blood Qur'an." It was written using twenty-seven liters of his own blood, to thank God for saving him from various dangers and conspiracies.[41]

Bob Woodward notes in his book, *Plan of Attack*, that as early as 1991, the US government was secretly asking to have Saddam removed from power. Woodward writes, "After the 1991 Gulf War, President George H. W. Bush signed a presidential finding authorizing the CIA to topple Saddam. But, leading up to the run-up to the Iraq War, the CIA concluded [that] . . . covert action is not going to remove Saddam." Woodward summarized the then-prevailing view: "The CIA had to face the reality . . . the only way to succeed was for the CIA to support a full military invasion of Iraq."[42]

Saddam was providing direct and material support to the Taliban while the Taliban was supporting the al-Qaeda plot of September 11, 2001. Members of al-Qaeda had direct relationships with the Iraqi government. The international community, especially the US, continued to view Saddam as a bellicose tyrant who was a threat to the stability of the region. After the September 11, 2001, attacks, Vladimir Putin began to tell the United States that Iraq was preparing terrorist attacks against the United States. In his January 2002 State of the Union Address to Congress, President George W. Bush spoke of an "axis of evil" consisting of Iran, North Korea, and Iraq. Moreover, Bush announced that he would possibly take action to topple the Iraqi government, because of the threat of its weapons of mass destruction. Bush stated, "The Iraqi regime has plotted to develop anthrax, and nerve gas, and nuclear weapons for over a decade. . . . Iraq continues to flaunt its hostility toward America and to support terror."[43]

By 2002, many in the international community felt Iraq had hidden weapons of mass destruction (WMD). Richard Engel, NBC News, stated, "I visited Iraq in October 2002, to cover Saddam Hussein's referendum, the election in which not a single Iraqi supposedly voted against Saddam's continued, unchallenged and brutal rule." He went on to say, "I made several contacts during my initial visit and left $200 'facilitation fees' with low-level officials of the Information Ministry's press center, which I hoped would assure success with future visa applications. As tension mounted, however, the money I'd left proved worthless. And by January 2003, the front door to Iraq was closed."[44]

After the passing of United Nations Security Council Resolution 1441, which demanded that Iraq give "immediate, unconditional and active cooperation" with UN and International Atomic Energy Agency (IAEA) inspections, Hussein allowed UN weapons inspectors led by Hans Blix to return to Iraq. During the renewed inspections beginning in November 2002, Blix found no stockpiles of WMD and noted Iraqi officials were generally "active" but not always "immediate" in their cooperation, as called for by UN Security Council Resolution 1441.[45]

With the war still looming, on February 24, 2003, Saddam Hussein gave an interview to CBS News reporter Dan Rather. Talking for more than three hours, he denied possessing weapons of mass destruction or any other weapons prohibited by UN guidelines. He also expressed a wish to have a live televised debate with George W. Bush, which was declined. The interview with Dan Rather was Saddam's first with a US reporter in more than a decade. CBS aired the taped interview later that week. Saddam appeared to contradict himself when he later told an FBI interviewer that he had once left open the possibility that Iraq possessed WMD to appear strong against Iran.[46]

The Iraqi government and military collapsed within three weeks of the beginning of the US-led invasion of Iraq on March 20, 2003. By the beginning of April, US-led forces occupied much of Iraq. The resistance of the much-weakened Iraqi Army either crumbled or shifted to guerrilla tactics, and it appeared that Saddam had lost control of Iraq.

Before his detention, Saddam was last seen in a video that purported to show him in the Baghdad suburbs surrounded by supporters. When Baghdad fell to US-led forces on April 9, marked symbolically by the toppling of his statue by iconoclasts, Saddam was nowhere to be found. The Iraqi president was on the run and would be captured eight months later. With Saddam Hussein removed, an opportunity emerged for change in Iraq in June 2004.[47]

Iraq had gone through a significant transition not seen by many other countries in the region. It was shaped over centuries, but one can certainly see how the culture shaped the man who would become its leader for twenty-nine years.

(Note: Transcript translation was a long and laborious process. Finding individuals who were fluent in Arabic and willing to translate the arraignment material was a challenge. No one person I found had the time to review all twelve DVDs, which contained the individual court proceedings. I traveled to area high schools with foreign language departments as well as colleges and universities with political science or foreign language departments. Because there are several different Arabic dialects and six different individuals were involved in the translation process, some words/phrases may have been given different interpretations. Although I offered to list the translators' names in the acknowledgments, they declined, fearing for the safety of themselves and their families.)

TRANSCRIPT OF SADDAM HUSSEIN DIALOGUE WITH JUDGE RA'ID

JUDGE: Please state your full name and tribal name.

SADDAM: Saddam Hussein, the president of Iraq.

JUDGE: Please state your full name and tribal name.

SADDAM: Saddam Hussein al-Majid, president of the Republic of Iraq.

JUDGE: Is it right that you were born in 1937?

SADDAM: It is right.

JUDGE: April 1937.

JUDGE: The occupation is the former president of Iraq.

SADDAM: I'm the current president of Iraq; this is the will of the people.

JUDGE: In addition to the post of the leader of the dissolved Ba'ath Party, leader of the dissolved revolution leadership council, Secretary General of the dissolved Iraqi Ba'ath leadership, and General Commander of the dissolved Iraqi armed forces.

JUDGE: What is your address; would you like us to write Iraq?

SADDAM: Every Iraqi house is my home.

JUDGE: Iraq. What's your mother's name?

SADDAM: Subha Tulfah.

SADDAM: May I ask something?

JUDGE: Please do.

SADDAM: You should introduce yourself first.

JUDGE: I will do that.

SADDAM: Please do.

JUDGE: Mr. Saddam, I am the investigating judge of the Iraqi central court . . .

SADDAM (INTERRUPTING): According to what resolution was it formed?

JUDGE: It was formed by the coalition authorities.

SADDAM: Coalition authorities? This means that you are an Iraqi representing the forces occupying your country.

JUDGE: I'm Iraqi, representing Iraq.

SADDAM: But you have said that . . .

JUDGE (INTERRUPTING): I have been appointed as a judge according to a decree issued by the previous government.

SADDAM: Isn't that right?

JUDGE: Yes, and I'm still practicing my job till now.

SADDAM: The purpose behind my question is to establish that the Iraqi law existed from the beginning, and it represents the people's demands in rightness, so you shouldn't be working according to what you call coalition forces. These forces are invasion forces.

JUDGE: I would like to clarify something; I am an Iraqi judge appointed during the previous regime . . .

SADDAM (INTERRUPTING): I respect all judges and you know so.

JUDGE: I know that you respect the judiciary process, and when you, like any other Iraqi citizen, face charges, you . . .

SADDAM (INTERRUPTING): I am proud to abide by the Iraqi laws.

JUDGE: You are submitted to the new Iraqi law . . .

SADDAM (INTERRUPTING): That is right.

JUDGE: So if these charges are proven against you, you will be convicted; if they are not proven with evidence, then you will be released. So, the role of the court is to ensure that justice is applied. If evidence exists, then the defendant will be convicted; if not, then he will not. So right now, you are charged according to the Iraqi law . . .

SADDAM (INTERRUPTING): Excuse me, please, I don't mean to complicate matters, but you are a judge, aren't you?

JUDGE: Yes.

SADDAM: The most important thing for judges is to respect the law, and to judge according to the law. Isn't this correct?

JUDGE: Absolutely, according to law and [justice] . . .

SADDAM: [Justice] is a relative thing. To us, [justice] is represented in our immortal heritage and in our holy Qur'an and is the prophet's Shari'a. Isn't this right?

JUDGE: Yes.

SADDAM: I say this, I am not talking about Saddam Hussein, whether as a citizen or in any other description when I mentioned my post, I am holding on to any position, but I do respect the will of the people, where they decided in a semi-unanimous vote, so . . .

JUDGE (INTERRUPTING): Please . . .

SADDAM (INTERRUPTING): Please allow me to continue. So when I mention that I am the president of Iraq, I am not trying to present formal aspect or to hold onto a position, but I am trying to show the Iraqi people that I respect their will. This is one thing; the second thing is that you summoned me here today to direct accusations against me.

JUDGE: No, you are here to be informed about the crimes referred to you.

SADDAM: Crimes. See, you called them crimes . . .

JUDGE (INTERRUPTING): The crimes referred to you . . .

SADDAM: Referred to me, good.

JUDGE: Pardon, when we finish the investigation process, the judge according to the law decides whether there is evidence or not; if there are pieces of evidence the defendant referred to the court and court referred the charges.

SADDAM (INTERRUPTING): No, please, I just want to understand the judicial aspect of this. Any accused when he appears in court should be investigated first.

JUDGE: This is not a court; this is an investigation.

SADDAM: An investigation, your honor.

SADDAM: I just want you to keep in mind that you are a judge empowered by the people.

JUDGE: If God wills.

SADDAM: It is not that you are going to sentence me or not, this is not important to me. The key things for you to keep in mind is that you are a judge. Therefore . . .

JUDGE (INTERRUPTING): I'm always a judge in the name of the people.

SADDAM: Don't mention the occupation forces that your people consider a shameful state.

JUDGE: I judge in the name of people and my authorities . . .

SADDAM: That's it: "I judge and investigate in the name of the people as an Iraqi judge."

JUDGE: Mr. Saddam, in order to go into the investigation process, it is one of your rights to know the crimes referred to you.

SADDAM (INTERRUPTING): Before that, if you don't mind, in relation to the judicial aspect . . .

JUDGE (INTERRUPTING): If you want me to clarify for you, I will.

SADDAM: You have been notified that I've got lawyers.

JUDGE: Yes.

SADDAM: Isn't it supposed that I should meet these lawyers before attending before you?

JUDGE: If you would be patient with me for ten minutes and let me finish the mechanism of formalities . . .

SADDAM: Take it easy.

JUDGE: . . . then you would hear your rights and guarantees, and we would have been finished with the mechanism of calling your lawyers. According to the law, Mr. Saddam, the investigating judge should make it clear for the defendant who has been presented before him the types of charges leveled against him. Later then he would read out the rights pertaining to each Iraqi defendant that is stipulated by the panel code in the article nos. 123, 124 and 125. So, the first process . . .

SADDAM (INTERRUPTING): Pardon, these items have been signed by Saddam Hussein?

JUDGE (INTERRUPTING): Still valid.

SADDAM: So you are now using the laws issued by us in the name of the Iraqi people.

JUDGE: Not Saddam, the Iraqi people issued these laws. The constitutional mechanisms issue these laws . . .

SADDAM (INTERRUPTING): Please allow me to talk; I am a man of law.

JUDGE: I know that.

SADDAM: It's true that I practiced law neither as a judge nor a lawyer, but originally, I am a man of the law. So, is it possible to summon the president of a country elected by the people and charge him with a law he issued by his own free will and the will of his people? There is a contradiction in this.

JUDGE: Let me clarify the legal framework, I will explain the legal mechanisms of this process and after that, you have the right to ask questions and the court will answer you. First, I will not try you . . .

SADDAM (INTERRUPTING): You are interrogating me according to the law issued by myself.

JUDGE: A while ago, I said that I'm only investigating you, I am not trying you. Secondly, the post of the president is only a quality, an occupation. According to law and constitution, when committing a violation or when charges are directed against them, they should appear in the court, and according to our history, the [Imam Ali] who was Iman of the Muslims appeared in court himself. So, it is not shameful for a previous president to appear in court.

JUDGE: You are an Iraqi citizen.

SADDAM: According to the Iraqi law, which constitutes this, there are procedures to be followed when charging a president, so you can't take only parts of the law and assume the former president to be an ordinary citizen and neglect all the procedures regarding how to charge a president.

JUDGE: What you have said is right, and for this process to be an honest one . . .

SADDAM (INTERRUPTING): I am only discussing this legally.

JUDGE: I respect a legal discussion, and what you just said is true, where there are certain procedures, formalities, and even immunities granted to certain positions, but all these have been canceled . . .

SADDAM (INTERRUPTING): Canceled by whom?

JUDGE: By Geneva Conventions, which Iraq has signed on because of Iraq's being an occupied country. So according to item 27 from the 4th agreement, which authorized the UN Security Council to declare that the party governing the country, which is the coalition, has the right to issue decisions and suspend the legal text which might oppose the legal process.

SADDAM: So, this means that the Americans can try Saddam Hussein if Geneva Conventions allow them to do so? But my question is about an Iraqi judge representing them even if it is against his will. This is what I object to.

JUDGE: No, this is not the case, the processes are like that. According to the Geneva Conventions it talks about prisoners of war and criminals. Of course, in the previous time you were considered a prisoner of war, hence according to the complaints made against you by which you were accused, you became a defendant according to the Iraqi judiciary, so the Iraqi judiciary has got the right to proceed.

SADDAM (INTERRUPTING): I don't want to embarrass you, this subject you know very well in the depth of your heart, and I don't want to embarrass you; all the world and the Iraqi community are aware and know the fact that this is a theater scene, that you don't want it.

JUDGE: No, this is a judicial process.

SADDAM: Please, this is a process Bush wants, Bush the criminal who came to occupy Iraq.

JUDGE: No, this is the Iraqi people who are represented by the Iraqi judiciary.

SADDAM: No, Bush wants this before the election . . .

JUDGE (INTERRUPTING): When you listen . . .

SADDAM (INTERRUPTING): When this broadcasts, he tells the universal public opinion that "we as an occupying country have nothing to do with Saddam Hussein," but he was referred to the Iraqi judicial system which referred the charges to him.

JUDGE: There is no need for this . . .

SADDAM (INTERRUPTING): This is the outcome.

JUDGE: The most important things are the crimes referred to you. The first one is the premeditated killing using chemical weapons in Northern Iraq, in Halabja.

SADDAM: Yes.

JUDGE: Second, the premeditated killing of many Iraqi Barzanian [the family of Barzani] in 1983. Third, the premeditated killing of members of political Iraqi parties without lawful trials. Fourth, the premeditated killing of large numbers of Iraqi cleric in 1994. Fifth, the premeditated killing of Iraqi citizens and destruction of villages and their own houses in Northern Iraq in the Anfal attacks. Sixth, the premeditated killing of large numbers of Iraqis in 1991 events. Seventh, the invasion of Kuwait, the lawful article . . .

SADDAM (INTERRUPTING): Please, the seventh is what?

JUDGE: The invasion of Kuwait.

SADDAM: Oh, no, for God's sake . . .

JUDGE (INTERRUPTING): Article 406 . . .

SADDAM (INTERRUPTING): You are Iraqi. Kuwait is an Iraqi city.

JUDGE: The lawful article applied on the act is 406/1/A of the modified Iraqi Penal code No. 111 of 1969; this court, Mr. Saddam Hussein, wants to inform of your rights and guarantees according to the Iraqi law system. First, you have the right to assign a lawyer to defend yourself; this is one. Second, if you don't have the capability to assign a lawyer or can't afford to pay his fees . . .

SADDAM (INTERRUPTING): How come I don't have . . .

JUDGE (INTERRUPTING): Let me continue . . .

SADDAM: Please, the American government said that Saddam has funds in Geneva's banks . . .

JUDGE: Just in case you don't have . . .

SADDAM: You have the knowledge, as a citizen you know.

JUDGE: If God wills. Third, you have the right to remain silent and not to answer any questions or argue and that won't be used as evidence against you. Four, you have the right to discuss all evidence and argue witnesses. These guarantees are rights for every Iraqi defendant. For the current time, we reach a key matter, you have listened to the crimes—do you have any complaints about them?

SADDAM: I have a comment on this matter.

JUDGE (INTERRUPTING): Let me continue. The second thing, you have listened to the guarantees. In the beginning, you mentioned that you want to meet a lawyer during the investigation process, which means you request to adjourn the investigation until you meet your lawyer?

SADDAM: Yes.

JUDGE (TO THE COURT REPORTER): Put down that the court has leveled the charges against the accused, Saddam Hussein al-Majid, and clarified the lawful article applied on the act; then the court read out all the rights and guarantees to the defendant represented by his rights to assign a lawyer, to remain silent and not to answer any questions referred to him, his right to discuss the evidence and argue the witnesses. The defendant requested to meet the defense lawyer . . .

SADDAM (INTERRUPTING): The defense lawyers . . .

JUDGE: His own defense lawyers to attend with him the investigation proceedings. Considering what has been said, the minutes have been closed up and the investigation adjourned with the defendant till he gets the opportunity to meet his defense lawyers and set another date for the next proceedings.

JUDGE (TO THE COURT REPORTER): Give it to me, please.

SADDAM: A legal comment, if you don't mind.

JUDGE: A legal comment! Yes, go ahead.

SADDAM: The charges are leveled to Saddam Hussein.

JUDGE: Yes. Go ahead.

SADDAM: How can I speak? Finish what you are signing in order [for me] to talk to you, you are the judge . . .

JUDGE: Then sign and we will talk to each other.

SADDAM: No, before I sign, if you don't mind, I want you to listen.

JUDGE: Yes.

SADDAM: Your honor, as a judge you leveled charges against me in cases you mentioned in this meeting, in this hearing, and I talk to you as a judge.

JUDGE: We don't have personal relations.

SADDAM: I meet you as a judge, but you leveled charges against me as President of the Republic of Iraq, the talk concerning Halabja I also heard about it in the news, the talk about attacking Halabja in a region that President Saddam was in office . . .

JUDGE: You are now going into lawful details that we should answer, and a while ago you requested to adjourn talking in this matter until the defense [lawyer] meets you and now you are answering these charges, this is a lawful talk.

SADDAM: No. This is a subject about previous knowledge. If we are going to repeat what is going to be said now next time with the presence of the lawyer without signing, then yes, I'll adjourn. But if you want me to sign and then the lawyers come, no, you should listen to me.

JUDGE: I'm listening.

SADDAM: The invasion of Kuwait, the seventh charge, what a pity! That to be mentioned by an Iraqi, but you are . . . I know . . .

JUDGE: The law . . .

SADDAM: Yes, the law tries Saddam Hussein because the Kuwaitis said that would make the Iraqi women's honor equal to ten dinars in the street and he acted in his capacity as an honored Iraqi to defend Iraq and revive the historic rights towards these dogs.

JUDGE: Don't be rash on anybody, you are in lawful proceedings.

SADDAM: Yes, I'm in a lawful proceeding, and it's my right, and I bear all responsibilities of what I'm saying . . .

JUDGE (INTERRUPTING): Any words exceeding the proper bounds of politeness aren't allowed.

SADDAM: Please, then the seventh charge that Saddam Hussein, who is the president of the Republic of Iraq, the General Commander of Armed Forces—and the armed forces went to Kuwait, right? In a formal way, then is it right to level charges in a formal way and the defendant treated apart from the formal guarantees that are stated in the constitution and the law, including this law that you conduct the investigation according to it? This is the whole essential matter that revolved around the charges because they happened during the reign of its president Saddam Hussein without the presidential immunity. Is this possible, from the lawful aspect, I mean?

JUDGE: If I answer you, that means I'll go into the core of the investigation. This is—we adjourned the investigation—a mere charge. If you're able to answer, then answer it formally with the presence of your lawyer; then you can, if you read the papers' case—and I think that you are a good reader—if you read the papers' case, which says that we adjourned the case and not to start it.

SADDAM: Then please, if you don't mind, I won't sign until the defense [lawyer] is present.

JUDGE: This is one of your rights; it's law, you are free to sign or not, but the guarantees . . .

SADDAM: No, I don't want to interfere with your rights, I'm talking about myself.

JUDGE: Yeah, yeah, your rights as a human being, as a defendant—but you should sign your rights because they have been referred to you.

SADDAM: Yes, they have been referred to me, but it is part of the whole process, we should wait.

JUDGE: No, they are not.

SADDAM: Yes, they are; why do we argue with each other?

JUDGE: No . . .

SADDAM: As a result, I'll stand before you again and all these papers will be submitted to me with the presence of the defense lawyers.

JUDGE: Yes.

SADDAM: We don't want to do something that would be happened [by] rushing, and I don't want you to be accused as an Iraqi judge of being rushed.

JUDGE: There is no rush. If you don't like to sign, you have the right to do so, and we will write down this in the papers' case. These are your rights.

SADDAM: I didn't say I don't want to sign, I said I'll sign the papers with the presence of the defense lawyers.

JUDGE: There is no problem with that. That means you are going to sign the papers with the presence of the defense lawyers.

SADDAM: Yes.

JUDGE: You may leave.
SADDAM: That's it.
JUDGE: Thank you very much.

10

ABID HAMID MAHMUD AL-TIKRITI

"ACE OF DIAMONDS" (#4 ON IRAQ'S MOST-WANTED LIST)

Abid Hamid Mahmud, a distant cousin of Saddam, was born in 1957 near Tikrit, Iraq. Saddam's al-Tikriti tribe, of which Mahmud was a member, is concentrated around the town of Tikrit in the north-central area of Iraq approximately 90 miles northwest of Baghdad.

Not much information is available about his childhood or early life. Mahmud began his military career as a non-commissioned officer and rose through the ranks to become a lieutenant general. Saddam would select him as his right-hand man, and Mahmud, with his signature beret and mustache, was frequently seen at his side. He was a trusted advisor, acting as gatekeeper for access to the Iraqi leader.

According to the British dossier "Iraq—Its Infrastructure of Concealment, Deception, and Intimidation," Abid Hamid Mahmud al-Tikriti oversaw the presidential secretariat. The secretariat reportedly had around 100 staff and was responsible for Saddam's personal security, as well as defense, security, and intelligence issues. Mahmud's official title was presidential secretary.[1] "He was

Abid Hamid Mahmud al-Tikriti listens as the judge reads charges. (Photo from Combat Camera)

right at the center. He was present at so many meetings and decision-making events where nobody else was at—and he had Hussein's trust," said Judith Yaphe, a former Iraq analyst for the CIA and now a senior fellow at the National Defense University.[2]

Some observers placed him as high as second-in-command. An unnamed US official told the French news agency Agence France-Presse (AFP), "He was Saddam's key advisor, and his responsibility included overseeing basically any issue of importance to Saddam, particularly regime security." Others believed he was third in power in Iraq behind Saddam's sons, Qusay and Uday Hussein. A powerful figure in Saddam's regime, Mahmud controlled all access to Saddam and had the ability to override government decisions. He is said to have directed matters of state and handed down many of the regime's repressive orders. He also headed the Iraq Special Security Organization.

Steven Emerson, an expert on Middle East terrorism, offered another perspective on the general in an interview with MSNBC on April 24, 2003. The interview took place shortly after attempts to kill Mr. Hussein. Mr. Emerson said, "This is a guy that really knew exactly where entire operational secrecy was for Saddam Hussein, where the palaces were, where the bunkers were, where his hideouts were, where exactly he would go in case there was an attack." According to Emerson, "The No. 1 bodyguard and was responsible for tracking Saddam Hussein 24 hours a day. If he got any word that there was going to be an attack, he would wake him up 15 minutes before, oust him and bring him to someplace else."

Another indication of Gen. Mahmud's status was given by Ahmad Chalabi. He reflected on the hunt for Saddam Hussein and whether Saddam might be in hiding with his sons. Mr. Chalabi said, "He is not traveling with Uday or Qusay." Rather, Mr. Chalabi surmised, the deposed dictator, if still alive, would be traveling with General Mahmud. This would later prove not to be the case.

US officials believed Mahmud might have had information about Saddam Hussein's fate following the end of the US-led war in April. They also believed that he might have had knowledge of Saddam's alleged weapons of mass destruction program.[3]

Gen. Mahmud was captured in a joint raid by special operations forces and the 1st Battalion, 22nd Infantry Regiment of the 1st Brigade, 4th Infantry Division, in June 2003. At the time, his capture was recognized as the "greatest success" since the end of major hostilities. It was a sign that Saddam Hussein might soon be found. US officials said they wanted to put Mahmud on trial for war crimes or crimes against humanity, allegedly committed during the period of Saddam Hussein's rule.[4]

ARRAIGNMENT

Mahmud entered the outer room with two guards escorting him to his chair. After having removed the handcuffs in the outer room, the three entered the courtroom. The chains to hold the handcuffs in place were still visible under the detainee's jacket. Mahmud was seated and the guards assumed their posts on either side of the entry to the room. Mahmud had a very notable long gray-black beard, and his black hair was balding. He wore a brown suit, white shirt, and dark shoes. His arraignment in front of Judge Ra'id lasted approximately nine minutes.

Mahmud was accused of "crimes against the Iraqi people" in the brutal repression of the Shi'ite uprising in 1991. Tens of thousands of people were killed. According to the transcript, at one point Mahmud requested that Malik Dohan al-Hassan be his lawyer. His request elicited some chuckles from the courtroom members, and this seemed to puzzle Mahmud. Unknown to him was the fact that the lawyer had recently been named justice minister in Iraq's new interim government.

He sat back in his chair and rested his right hand on the armrest. He was composed during the proceedings. Periodically, he would lean forward and adjust his suit jacket as if it might have been a little snug. The assigned court clerks were writing feverishly to record all ongoing discussions between the judge and Mahmud. This defendant, like the previous ones, occasionally looked to his right to view the group seated in the jurors' box. The charges against him were read aloud, recorded by the court clerk, and signed by the judge. The clerk delivered the papers to Mahmud. He quickly reviewed, signed, and returned them to the clerk. Once he handed the documents back to the clerk, the security guards approached, and one on either arm turned him around and escorted him out the door and into a waiting room with the other HVDs.

TRANSCRIPT OF ABID HAMID MAHMUD AL-TIKRITI DIALOGUE WITH JUDGE RA'ID

JUDGE: Your full name?

MAHMUD: Abid Hamid Mahmud al-Tikriti.

JUDGE: Date of birth?

MAHMUD: 1957.

JUDGE: Positions you assumed?

MAHMUD: First, bodyguard for the Republic president, escort, and secretary. In 1980, I became an escort. In April 1991, I became the Republic president's secretary.

JUDGE: The secretary of the previous Republic president.

JUDGE: Your address?

MAHMUD: I am originally from Tikrit/Al-Oja, but now I live in Baghdad.

JUDGE: Where in Baghdad?

MAHMUD: Al-Jadriyah.

JUDGE (TO THE CLERK): Write Tikrit/Al-Oja and now Baghdad/al-Jadriyah.

JUDGE: Your mother's name?

MAHMUD: Thuria Abid Allah.

JUDGE (TO THE CLERK): After I introduced myself as the investigation judge.

JUDGE: Mr. Abid Hamid Mahmud al-Tikriti.

MAHMUD: Yes.

JUDGE: Today is your first session with the investigating judge, which means not a trial, to show you the crime complained against you and the appropriate law applied to it. We will clarify your full rights. After we clarify your rights, you have the right to hire a lawyer.

MAHMUD: Yes.

JUDGE: The crime you are accused of is participation in the operations of the murder of a number of Iraqi people in the events of 1991 in Iraq, which conforms with the provisions of law 406/1/A from the Iraqi penal code.

MAHMUD: Can I speak now or after?

JUDGE: Let me finish first, and then you can speak. This court would like to inform you, Mr. Abid Hamid Mahmud, in your guarantees a right as a defendant before the Iraqi judiciary.

JUDGE: First, you have the right to appoint a lawyer to defend you. Second, in case you cannot appoint a lawyer, you should inform the court and it will appoint a lawyer to defend you.

MAHMUD: Is it okay Iraqi or Arabic lawyer? [Note: "Arabic" in this context means from an Arabic country other than Iraq.]

JUDGE: Iraqi is okay; if Arabic, there must be a judicial agreement between Iraq and that country.

JUDGE: Third, you have the right to refuse to speak or answer any question and that will not be used against you.

JUDGE: Fourth, you have the right to discuss the witnesses and the evidence. These are your rights.

MAHMUD: It is excellent if it is like this.

JUDGE: Would you like to wait for a lawyer to be present with you during the investigation?

MAHMUD: Yes, sure, I can answer these questions, but I need a lawyer to be present with me.

JUDGE: The court informed the defendant about the crime he is charged with, and the law applied to it; then, the court informed him about the rights and the guarantees that are related to him. Therefore, the defendant requests to postpone the investigation session until he gets a lawyer.

MAHMUD: Can I give the lawyer's name now or not?

JUDGE: It is up to you.

MAHMUD: Tallal Fahad Alfaisal and Malik Dohan al-Hassan.

JUDGE (TO THE CLERK): He requested to have lawyer Tallal Fahad Alfaisal and the lawyer Dr. Malik Dohan al-Hassan to be present with him at the investigation session. Therefore, the investigation session is postponed until the mentioned lawyers are informed about his interest in hiring them.

MAHMUD: If Arabic, the lawyer Dr. Hani Alkhosami if it is possible.

JUDGE: Hani the Jordanian lawyer?

MAHMUD: Yes.

JUDGE: Yes, it is okay.

MAHMUD: His wife is from Iraq.

JUDGE: No problem.

JUDGE (TO THE CLERK): Also, inform the Jordanian lawyer Hani Alkhosami of the will of the defendant to hire him; therefore, the investigation is postponed until the defense lawyers are contacted and able to be present with the defendant in the investigation.

MAHMUD: If you would let me contact my family just in case they hired another lawyer, because I do not know what they have done.

JUDGE: We will allow you, Inshallah [God willing].

MAHMUD: Inshallah.

JUDGE: You need to sign with me.

MAHMUD: Can I speak about this issue now?

JUDGE: You requested to postpone the investigation.

MAHMUD: This is just for you.

JUDGE: If it is just for me, no.

MAHMUD: Will you let me speak later?

JUDGE: Sure, we will listen to everything you have in a formal session.

MAHMUD: Okay.

MAHMUD: If this crime is proved against me, I would accept that.

JUDGE: Did you attend law school? Is that right?

MAHMUD: No, I have a PhD in political science.

JUDGE: So, you know this is just an investigation.

MAHMUD: Yes.

JUDGE: After the investigation is finished, the court will see if there is evidence against you or not.

MAHMUD: Thank God there are a court and justice.

JUDGE (TO MAHMUD): Thank you so much.

MAHMUD: You are welcome.

11
ALI HASSAN AL-MAJID AL-TIKRITI ("CHEMICAL ALI")

"KING OF SPADES" (#5 ON IRAQ'S MOST-WANTED LIST)

Ali Hassan al-Majid was born November 30, 1941, in al-Awja near Tikrit, Iraq. Like Saddam, he was a member of the Bejat clan of the al-Bu Nasir tribe. He was Saddam's first cousin. Also like Saddam, Ali Hassan was a Sunni Muslim who came from a poor family and had very little formal education. He worked as a motorcycle messenger and driver in the Iraqi Army until the Ba'ath Party seized power in 1968.[1]

Ali Hassan's rise through the government was accelerated due to his relationship with his cousin Saddam. He initially became an aide to Iraqi defense minister Hammad Shihab in the early 1970s after joining the Ba'ath Party.[2] He became head of the government's Security Office, serving as an enforcer for the increasingly powerful Saddam.

In 1979, Saddam seized power by pushing aside President Ahmed Hassan al-Bakr. Ali Hassan would soon hold many key positions during Saddam's reign. These included: Ba'athist Iraqi Defense Minister, interior minister, military commander, chief of the Iraqi Intelligence Service (Iraqi secret police known as the Mukhabarat), and the governor of annexed Kuwait during the Persian Gulf War. He became one of Saddam's closest and most highly regarded military advisors.[3]

Following an unsuccessful assassination attempt on Saddam in 1982, in the town of Dujail, north of Baghdad, Ali Hassan directed the subsequent collective punishment operations. Scores of local men were killed, thousands of inhabitants were deported, and the entire town was razed to the ground.[4]

Ali Hassan's signature event—and the one that established his legacy throughout the country of Iraq and his nickname, "Chemical Ali" (Ali Kimyawi)—was the Anfal campaign. According to Iraqi Kurdish sources, Ali Hassan openly boasted of this nickname.[5] Others dubbed him the "Butcher of Kurdistan."

During the late stages of the Iran–Iraq War, Ali Hassan was given the post of Secretary General of the Northern Bureau of the Ba'ath Party. He served in this capacity from March 1987 to April 1989. He effectively commanded all state agencies in the rebellious Kurdish-populated region located in northeast Iraq. He was known for his ruthlessness, ordering the indiscriminate use of chemical weapons such as mustard gas, sarin, tabun, and VX against Kurdish targets during a genocidal campaign dubbed Al-Anfal or "The Spoils of War."[6] The first such attacks occurred as early as April 1987 and continued into 1988, culminating in the notorious attack on Halabja in which more than 5,000 people were killed.[7]

With Kurdish resistance continuing, Ali decided to cripple the rebellion by eradicating the civilian population of the Kurdish regions. His forces embarked on a systematic campaign of mass killings, property destruction, and forced population transfer ("Arabization"). Thousands of Kurdish villages were razed, and their inhabitants were either killed or deported to the south of Iraq. Ali signed a decree in June 1987 stating that, "Within their jurisdiction, the armed forces must kill any human being or animal present in these areas."[8] By 1988, some 4,000 villages had been destroyed, an estimated 180,000 Kurds had been killed, and some 1.5 million had been deported.[9]

Two years later, after the invasion of Kuwait in August 1990, Ali Hassan became the military governor of the occupied emirate or the "19th Province of Iraq."[10] He instituted a violent regime under which Kuwait was systematically looted and purged of "disloyal elements." In November 1990, he was recalled to Baghdad and was appointed interior minister in March 1991. Following the Iraqi defeat in the war, he was given the task of quelling the uprisings of

Ali Hassan al-Majid al-Tikriti ("Chemical Ali") arriving to the outer waiting area. (Photo from Combat Camera)

the Shi'ites in southern Iraq as well as the Kurdish north. Both revolts were crushed with great brutality, with many thousands killed.[11] Saddam ordered Iraq divided into sections and he put his most trusted relatives and aides in charge of them. Ali Hassan was put in command of the Shi'ite-dominated south.[12]

The Ba'ath Party commissioned a film of Ali Hassan, the newly appointed interior minister, conducting operations against Shi'ites. On one occasion in the film, Ali Hassan can be heard giving instructions to an Iraqi helicopter pilot on his way to attack a group of rebels holding a bridge. He says, "Don't come back until you are able to tell me that you have burnt them; and if you haven't burnt them don't come back." Later in the film, which was distributed to Ba'ath Party activists after the revolt had been suppressed, he is joined by another senior Ba'athist, Muhammad Hamza al-Zubaydi. The two men slapped and kicked some of the prisoners as they lay defenseless on the ground.[13]

Ali Hassan was subsequently given the post of Minister of Defense. He briefly fell from grace in 1995, when Saddam dismissed him after it was discovered that Ali Hassan was involved in illegally smuggling grain to Iran. In December 1998, Saddam recalled him and appointed him commander of the southern region of Iraq. The United States was carrying out an increasing number of air strikes in the southern no-fly zone. He was reappointed to this post in March 2003, immediately before the start of the Iraq war.[14]

Ali Hassan based himself in the southern port city of Basra, and in April 2003, he was mistakenly reported to have been killed in a US airstrike.[15] At the Pentagon, officials released video of the strike on Chemical Ali's house. The official went on to say, "We believe that the reign of terror of 'Chemical Ali' has come to an end."[16] US Intelligence later discovered Ali Hassan survived the attack and escaped the city, but he was arrested by American forces on August 17, 2003. At the time he was captured, he was in control of the network of Ba'ath militia and Fedayeen operating out of Basra in southern Iraq.[17]

ARRAIGNMENT
Ali Hassan al-Majid was once the most feared man in Iraq after Saddam. Two guards removed his handcuffs in the outer room before they escorted him into the courtroom and directed him to his chair. He walked with a cane. Once he was seated, he placed the cane to the right of his chair. The two guards took their customary positions on either side of the entry door.

He was wearing a brown suit, white shirt, and dark shoes. He had a full head of hair crew-cut style. His hair was once jet black but now was salt-and-pepper. He had dark brown eyes and a well-trimmed mustache that was the same color as his hair. According to John Burns, "He certainly looked much more subdued than when he was filmed many times directing summary executions, during the 1991 Shi'ite uprising, where he was laughingly congratulating the men who carried them out."[18] Half of the time, he sat slumped in the chair with his hands folded in his lap. The other half of the time, his elbows were on the armrests with his hands interlocked below his chin.

During his eleven-minute arraignment, Ali Hassan politely answered

Chemical Ali listens to the charges against him. (Photo from Combat Camera)

questions from Judge Ra'id and listened intently as the charges against
him were read. He was sometimes animated, moving his hands about while

CHAPTER 11

Chemical Ali signing arraignment documents. (Photo by Combat Camera)

responding during the process. At one point, he reached into his coat pocket and retrieved his glasses before responding to a question.

The judge told Ali Hassan that he stood accused of crimes in the Halabja attack, in the Kuwait invasion, and in the suppression of the Shi'ite uprising after the Gulf War. When the judge read the charge for the defendant's alleged role in overseeing the Halabja attack, Ali Hassan seemed pleased. He smiled broadly at the judge after the charges were read and said, "Thank you and thank you. I'm happy with the accusations, because I'm innocent of them, and as you will see, justice will prevail." According to the transcript, he asked if the judge could help him track down his counsel. He said, "If you don't mind, I'm going to give you a piece of paper with the telephone number of the lawyer."

The assigned court clerks were carefully recording the discussion going on between the judge and Ali Hassan. He would occasionally glance to his right to see who was seated in the jurors' box.

The charges against him—having been read aloud, recorded by the court clerk, and signed by the judge—were delivered by the clerk to Ali Hassan. To sign the documents presented by the court clerk, he brought his cane around from the chair and placed it between his legs.

The clerk needed to show him where to sign. He returned the signed papers to the clerk. Almost routinely, the security guards came and assisted him up from the chair and escorted him out of the courtroom. As he rose to leave, steadying himself with his cane, he invoked God's help, as had Saddam and several others. "In the name of God, the most Merciful and Compassionate," he said, quoting from the Qur'an.

Burns observed, "Ali spoke in an even tone that had something of the quality of a man concerned that he has been overcharged for his car repair but is unwilling to make much of it."[19] Then, the defendant remarked audibly to a courtroom guard as he left that he was surprised that the charges had not been worse. As I stood off to the side, fifteen feet from Chemical Ali, I thought to myself, here was one of the most feared men in Iraq for the past twenty years. He had killed thousands of men, women, and children, and he looked like someone's elderly grandfather.

TRANSCRIPT OF ALI HASSAN AL-MAJID DIALOGUE WITH JUDGE RA'ID

JUDGE: Your name?

ALI HASSAN: Ali Hassan al-Majid.

JUDGE: al-Majid or Majid?

ALI HASSAN: al-Majid.

JUDGE: Date of birth?

ALI HASSAN: 1941.

JUDGE: What positions did you assume?

ALI HASSAN: The highest position was a member of the Iraqi revolutionary council.

JUDGE: This is one.

ALI HASSAN: Member of the Iraq Ba'ath Party branch leadership.

JUDGE: And?

ALI HASSAN: Minister of Defense.

JUDGE: What year?

ALI HASSAN: From 1991 to 1995. Minister of Interior from March 1991 to October or November 1991. Minister of self-governance from 1989 to 1991. [Note from the translator: this position was in Kurdistan.]

JUDGE: Any other high positions?

ALI HASSAN: No. These are the leadership positions I assumed.

JUDGE (TO THE CLERK): Between parentheses write in the former regime.

JUDGE: Address?

ALI HASSAN: I lived in Baghdad, in a government-owned house in the Dijla compound because I don't own any house in Iraq.

JUDGE: What about Salahuddin?

ALI HASSAN: I don't own a house. I don't own a house in any of Iraq's municipalities. Thank God.

JUDGE: Mother's name?

ALI HASSAN: Amouna Sultan.

JUDGE (TO THE CLERK): He stated the following after I introduced myself as the investigation judge.

JUDGE: Mr. Ali, this is an investigation, it is not a trial. Some think it's a trial. First, the investigation court will charge you of the crimes and complaints against you and the appropriate laws will be applied. Then it will move to clarify your guarantees and rights as an Iraqi defendant. The crimes you are accused of are: First: Manslaughter during the events in the north, in the Halabja incidents. Second: Manslaughter in Kuwait in 1990. Third: Participating in manslaughter against Iraqis during the events of 1991 in Dhi Qar province.

ALI HASSAN: Thank you.

JUDGE: As for your guarantees and rights, this court would like to inform you, Mr. Ali Hassan al-Majid, of the guarantees and rights you have as a defendant before the Iraqi judicial system.

ALI HASSAN: Yes.

JUDGE: You have the right to appoint a lawyer to defend you. In case you cannot, you should inform the court and it will appoint a lawyer to defend you and will bear the expenses. You have the right to stay silent and not answer any questions.

ALI HASSAN: No. There is no need for that.

JUDGE: This will not be used against you. You have the right to respond to witnesses and evidence.

ALI HASSAN: Yes. Thank you.

JUDGE: I think you need a lawyer to be present with you during the investigation?

ALI HASSAN: Now, no. But in the future, we will need a lawyer.

JUDGE: So you will need a lawyer to defend you.

ALI HASSAN: I am happy with the crimes you accused me of. It looks like, thank God, it's an easy case.

JUDGE: Inshallah. The judiciary system is just.

ALI HASSAN: You will see how the truth will prevail.

JUDGE: Inshallah.

ALI HASSAN: Yes. Thank you.

JUDGE: The court informed the defendant of the crimes he's charged with based on the complaints it received and the laws applied. The court also informed the defendant of all the rights and guarantees. Do you have a specific lawyer?

ALI HASSAN: I would like to contact lawyer Hamid Salih al-Rawi. He was the head of the lawyer's union in Iraq before.

JUDGE: The defendant requested to contact lawyer Hamid Salih al-Rawi.

ALI HASSAN: Is it possible to contact an Arab lawyer?

JUDGE: If we have an international treaty with them, yes. For instance, a judicial coordination treaty.

ALI HASSAN: He's Jordanian.

JUDGE: Jordanian is ok.

ALI HASSAN: Then write lawyer Hani al-Khasawna. I want them both.

JUDGE: Inshallah.

JUDGE (TO THE CLERK): He requested to contact lawyer Hamid Salih al-Rawi and lawyer Hani al-Khasawna. The lawyers should be informed to be present during the investigation. Therefore, the investigation is postponed.

ALI HASSAN: No. There is no need. I'll not ask for them to be present.

JUDGE: These are guarantees. We will ask them. If they're willing to take the task, okay. If not . . .

ALI HASSAN: If they are not.

JUDGE: We will contact you again.

ALI HASSAN: No. I authorize you now, any lawyer appointed by the court will do.

JUDGE: The defendant added in case the lawyers rejected the task.

ALI HASSAN: Can I give you the phone number of the Iraqi lawyer?

JUDGE: Give it to this man.

ALI HASSAN: No. I have other numbers here. I don't want to give them.

JUDGE: Okay. We will contact the lawyers officially. I'm sure his name is in the records.

ALI HASSAN: Yes. But to make it easier for you. If you don't want that, it's up to you. It's 5555681.

JUDGE (TO THE CLERK): He authorized the court to appoint a lawyer. Therefore, the investigation has been postponed until the lawyers mentioned before being informed of his will to hire them.

JUDGE (HANDING HIM THE FILE): This is what we just said. My signature and yours at the end.

ALI HASSAN: Yes. Thank you.

12
AZIZ SALEH AL-NUMAN

"KING OF DIAMONDS" (#8 ON IRAQ'S MOST-WANTED LIST)

There is conflicting information concerning when Aziz Saleh al-Numan was born. The date most often given is 1941, in Nasiriyah, Iraq. He was a Sunni and first cousin of Saddam Hussein.

While he was governor of Karbala and al-Najaf, there were numerous press reports that he ordered the destruction of Shi'ite holy sites. In addition, other reports during this time state that while he was governor of Najaf, al-Numan arrested, tortured, and killed Shi'ite clerics during the 1980–1988 Iraq–Iran War.

Saddam appointed al-Numan as Iraqi Governor of Kuwait during the 1991 Gulf War. He was a member of the "dirty dozen." This group was responsible for the torture and murder of many Iraqis. Prior to the US coalition forces invasion in March 2003, al-Numan was the Ba'ath Party's regional commander, responsible for West Baghdad.

He was captured and taken into custody by US coalition forces on May 22, 2003. At the time of his capture, al-Numan was #8 on the US Central Command's list of the fifty-five most-wanted Iraqis.[1] He was the highest-ranking person on that list to have been taken into custody at that time. He was one of the nine Iraqi leaders that the United States wished to see tried for either war crimes or crimes against humanity.[2]

151

Aziz Saleh al-Numan preparing to enter courtroom. (Photo by Combat Camera)

ARRAIGNMENT

Al-Numan entered the room with two guards escorting him and directing him to his chair. The guards were large men. They appeared to weigh at least 250 pounds each and looked like NFL offensive linemen. The guards had removed his hand-cuffs in the outer room before he entered the courtroom. After seating al-Numan, the guards stood like sentries on military watch at their positions by the door.

Al-Numan was wearing a dark brown jacket with light brown pants, white shirt, and dark shoes. He was balding, and his black-and-gray hair was cut extremely short. He had a mustache that appeared not to have been shaved for the afternoon event. He sat with his hands on his lap, and his fingers were interlocked during his eleven-minute arraignment in front of Judge Ra'id.

Periodically, he would use hand gestures to emphasize his replies to the judge. At some points in his testimony, he displayed a nervous twitch in his right leg as he bounced it up and down. He listened intently as the charges against him were read aloud and answered all the questions that he was asked.

The court was not equipped with court recording machines. That made it necessary for the clerks to record longhand all the proceedings, questions by the judge, and the defendants' answers. Those seated in the jurors' box caught the attention of al-Numan. All the defendants were very observant of anyone in the courtroom. The charges against al-Numan were read, recorded by the court clerk, and signed by the judge. The clerk delivered the papers to al-Numan. He immediately signed the documents and was escorted out of the courtroom.

TRANSCRIPT OF AZIZ SALEH AL-NUMAN DIALOGUE WITH JUDGE RA'ID

JUDGE: What is your name?

AL-NUMAN: Aziz Saleh al-Numan.

JUDGE: What's your occupation?

AL-NUMAN: In 1976, I was the governor of the province of Karbala.

JUDGE: Did you have any leading position?

AL-NUMAN: I was Minister of Agriculture in 1987. I was in the leadership in 1992. I was governor of Kuwait but with no authoritative powers. That was in 1991.

JUDGE: Where did you live?

AL-NUMAN: In Baghdad, Nasiriyah neighborhood, Province of Hofaz, tribe of Khafaja in the village of Naaman.

JUDGE: Where were you in Baghdad?

AL-NUMAN: In the Hafia.

JUDGE: Mother's name?

AL-NUMAN: Najma.

JUDGE: Mr. Aziz, you are accused of participating in intentional killing in the events of 1991 and the violent and ferocious acts committed in Kuwait. And that applies to section 400/1 of the Iraqi laws issued in 1969. In what concerns your guarantees . . .

AL-NUMAN (INTERRUPTING): May I?

JUDGE: Mr. al-Numan, based on the evidence you are accused of, you have the following special rights: You have the right to a lawyer to defend you. In case you are not able to appoint a lawyer, the court will appoint one for you. You have the right to be silent and not answer any questions, and this will not be held against you or be part of the evidence.

AL-NUMAN: May I have your permission to talk?

JUDGE: Hold on. In regard to the guarantees, do you have anyone in mind to appoint to defend you?

AL-NUMAN: No, sir, I've been incarcerated for over a year and a month and fifteen days, and I have not seen or talked to anyone, therefore I have no idea who I'm going to consider for a lawyer. And who is going to allow me to search for someone to defend me?

JUDGE: If you have a lawyer that you want to represent you, of course we will consider him. If you do not like the lawyer we appoint for you, we can consider another person.

AL-NUMAN: I have confidence in the Iraqi legal system.

JUDGE: Listing for the courts records that the accused was informed of having the right to hire a lawyer, and in case he cannot hire one the court will appoint one for him. And we'll let the accused get in touch with his relatives and appoint a lawyer if he so wishes.

AL-NUMAN: Let me point out I did not work as a policeman or anything directly on the street. I was a governor, and my job was administrative work. I did not have any relation to killings or crimes.

(Judge talks to an associate; words are inaudible.)

AL-NUMAN: Can you repeat the charges I'm accused of?

JUDGE: You are accused of participating in the intentional killing of citizens in 1991.

AL-NUMAN: Your honor, I think there is only one person accusing me of that.

JUDGE: You are accused of the crimes committed in Kuwait.

AL-NUMAN: I went to Kuwait in August 1990. I was an administrator only, and I did not have an official title to participate in any criminal activities. Again, I am an administrator only. You know the governor, or vice governor, for a province is an administrative function. I worked as a governor and as Minister of Agriculture. And in 1992 I was responsible for supplies.

JUDGE: We read the accused his rights and guarantees, and now we are going to give him the papers to sign.

(The defendant signs the paper documents and was able to read them.)

AL-NUMAN: Is that all?

JUDGE: Yes, you are dismissed.

13
MUHAMMAD HAMZA AL-ZUBAYDI

"QUEEN OF SPADES" (#9 ON IRAQ'S MOST-WANTED LIST)

Muhammad Hamza al-Zubaydi was born in Babylon, Iraq, in 1938. There is not much known about his childhood. His political career began in early 1987 when he appeared in press reports as Iraq's Minister of Communications.[1]

Between 1986 and 1992, Muhammad was the secretary of the Ba'ath Party's Northern Bureau. As such, he allegedly had command responsibility for the acts of genocide carried out against the Kurds, including the Anfal operation in 1988. He was another on "Saddam's dirty dozen" list of people responsible for torture and murder in Iraq.[2]

In 1991, Muhammad was named the fifty-ninth prime minister of Iraq. At this time, he violently suppressed the 1991 Shi'a uprisings after the Gulf War. Tens of thousands of Shi'a were killed. He was featured in Iraqi news video kicking and beating captured Shi'a dissidents. He became known as Saddam's "Shi'a thug." From 1992 to 1998, he presided over the destruction of the southern marsh region. He was seen in videotape giving instructions in the field as the Iraqi prime minister to army generals to "wipe out" specific marsh Arab tribes.[3] It has also been reported that he ordered mass executions, torture, and destruction in the Iraqi cities of Samawa, Nasiriyah, Basra, Amara, and Kut.

As commander of the Central Euphrates Region from 1998 to 2000, Hamza al-Zubaydi allegedly continued to repress Shi'a political-religious activities and unrest. In early February 1999, there was a serious indication of deteriorating relations between Iraqi Shi'ites and the Baghdad government. The Special Republican Guards and the Special Security Organizations stepped up their attacks against Shi'ites in the south of Iraq, especially in Nasiriyah, Kufa, and Najaf, as well as in Baghdad itself. These attacks resulted in numerous deaths. Grand Ayatollah al-Sadr had defied Saddam's authority over the previous few months. At the same time, the regime increased measures to harass him and his followers throughout Iraq. Baghdad sent a team under the command of Hamza al-Zubaydi to the mosque in Kufa to prevent the faithful from conducting their prayers under the direction of al-Sadr. The cleric still insisted on leading the prayers and delivering the Friday sermon on February 12. Hamza al-Zubaydi was said to have been directly involved in the assassination of al-Sadr and two of his sons, which occurred in the Shi'ite center of al-Najaf on February 18, 1999.[4]

Muhammad was relieved in May 2001 of his positions as Deputy Prime Minister and member of the Ba'ath Party Regional Command. At the time Iraq was attacked, he was the country's fifty-ninth prime minister. He was arrested April 21, 2003, by Iraqi opposition forces in the town of Hillah, south of Baghdad, and turned over to coalition forces.[5] US forces transferred custody of him and other HVDs to Iraq's Interim Government (IIG) on June 30, 2004, in order for him to be arraigned on July 1, 2004. On July 20, 2004, it was reported that he was willing to be a prosecution witness against Saddam concerning the 1998 orders he received to assassinate Grand Ayatollah al-Sadr and the repression of the Shi'a upheaval in 1991.[6]

ARRAIGNMENT

The next defendant to be escorted by the two guards was the former prime minister, Muhammad Hamza al-Zubaydi. The guards, per their routine, had removed his handcuffs before they entered the courtroom. The defendant's waist chains that held the handcuffs in place were visible under his jacket. After assisting Muhammad to his chair, the guards took their positions of sentry on either side of the entrance to the courtroom.

Muhammad was wearing a brown suit, white shirt, and dark shoes. He was balding with very short gray hair, dark brown eyes, and a gray mustache. He looked quite old and weathered. He politely answered all the questions from the judge and listened intently as the charges against him were read aloud. In a similar fashion as for previous HVDs, he glanced several times to his right and

Muhammad Hamza al-Zubaydi arrives in the courtroom. (Photo by Combat Camera)

studied those seated in the jurors' box. He placed his hand on his chest when answering some of the questions from the judge, and even smiled during the conversation. He was animated at times during his responses, moving his hands about. At one point during his eleven-minute arraignment, he asked the judge's assistance in recalling and testifying to the years in which he held various posts.

The assigned court clerks recorded the discussion between the judge and Muhammad in longhand. The charges against him, having been read aloud and recorded by the court clerk, were signed by the judge. The clerk then delivered the papers to the defendant for his signature. The defendant signed the papers as instructed by the clerk. The documents were now in the hands of the clerk. The security guards came and assisted Muhammad from the chair. He stood with a hand on his chest, said "Inshallah," and was escorted out of the courtroom.

TRANSCRIPT OF MUHAMMAD HAMZA AL-ZUBAYDI DIALOGUE WITH JUDGE RA'ID

JUDGE: Your full name?

MUHAMMAD: Muhammad Hamza al-Zubaydi.

JUDGE: Your grandfather?

MUHAMMAD: Muhammad Hamza Getan al-Zubaydi.

JUDGE: Date of birth?

MUHAMMAD: 1938.

JUDGE: Positions you assumed in the previous regime?

MUHAMMAD: I served as governor of Kirkuk.

JUDGE: In which year?

MUHAMMAD: I do not remember, but I will mention the sequence: governor of Kirkuk; Minister of Transport and Communications for three-and-a-half years; deputy prime minister. I served as prime minister until I retired, and now I am retired.

JUDGE: And at the level of the Revolutionary Command Council?

MUHAMMAD: I served as a member of the Revolutionary Command Council.

JUDGE (TO THE CLERK): A member of the dissolved Revolutionary Command Council.

JUDGE: And at the party level?

MUHAMMAD: I served as a member, then a member of the leadership band, then a member of the leadership of the country.

JUDGE: Did you assume the position of member of the leadership of the country?

MUHAMAD: Yes.

JUDGE (TO THE CLERK): A member of the leadership of the country in Iraq in the disbanded Ba'ath Party.

JUDGE: In which year?

MUHAMAD: From 1968, I am not sure, it is written in your documents.

JUDGE: How many years did you stay?

MUHAMMAD: Approximately three years.

JUDGE: That means from 1968 to 1971. Is that right?

MUHAMMAD: Yes, approximately.

JUDGE: After that?

MUHAMMAD: I retired.

JUDGE: You retired.

MUHAMMAD: Yes, just make sure from the right dates because I got dizzy from the plane, so I am not sure about the dates.

JUDGE: You were the official of the North Office in 1987.

MUHAMMAD: Yes, I think.

JUDGE: You were a member of the leadership of the country from 1991 to 2001?

MUHAMMAD: Yes.

JUDGE: You were the deputy prime minister from 1991 to 2001. And in the 1990s, you served as the official of the Middle Euphrates Office regulations.

MUHAMMAD: In fact, I was the official of the Middle Euphrates Office regulations before the revolution of 1968.

JUDGE: Good.

JUDGE (TO THE CLERK): Official of North Office regulations.

MUHAMMAD: And the South as well.

JUDGE (TO THE CLERK): And the South.

JUDGE: Your recent address?

MUHAMMAD: Baghdad.

JUDGE: Where in Baghdad?

MUHAMMAD: Baghdad, Karada outside, home #15.

JUDGE: In the complex?

MUHAMMAD: No, on the coast.

JUDGE (TO THE CLERK): Write Baghdad/Karada outside, home #15, adjacent to the Tigris River.

JUDGE: Your mother's name?

MUHAMMAD: Athia Hamza.

JUDGE (TO THE CLERK): After I introduced myself as the investigation judge.

JUDGE: Mr. Muhammad, this is the first session for the investigation and not a trial in the court, but it is an investigational process with the investigating judge. First, I would like to show you the crimes complained against you and the appropriate law applied to them. Then we clarify your full rights as a defendant and Iraqi citizen before the Iraqi judiciary. The crimes you are accused of so far based on the report and the complaints are these: murder of a number of Iraqi people in 1991; murder of a number of Iraqi people in al-Najaf Province at the end of 1991.

JUDGE: This is what relates to the crimes that you are accused of so far, and this court would like to inform you, Mr. Muhammad Hamza al-Zubaydi, what is related to your rights and guarantees as a defendant before the Iraqi judiciary. First: You have the right to appoint a lawyer to defend you. Second: In case you cannot appoint a lawyer or pay the attorney's fee, you should inform the court and it will appoint a lawyer to defend you and the court will pay the lawyer's fee. Third: You have the right to refuse to speak or answer any question and that will not be used against you. Fourth: You have the right to discuss the witnesses and the evidence. These are your rights and the crimes you are accused of. Do you have a lawyer?

MUHAMMAD: You know I don't.

JUDGE: We do not need your comments about the crimes for now; just tell me, do you have a lawyer?

MUHAMAD: My son is a lawyer, and he can hire a lawyer because I am in prison and I do not know a lawyer.

JUDGE: You can contact your family, there is no problem.

MUHAMAD: If the court can contact my home and request from my son, he is a lawyer and he will hire an appropriate lawyer.

JUDGE: You mean, you want to hire your son or whom your son sees appropriate?

MUHAMMAD: Yes, but he is a lawyer, and he can defend me. His name is Muthana Muhammad Hamza.

JUDGE (TO THE CLERK): The court informed the defendant about the crimes he is charged with, and the law applied to it; then, the court informed him about the rights and the guarantees that are related to him as a defendant before the Iraqi judiciary that is stipulated by law.

JUDGE: How about if we cannot contact your son, in case he is traveling. Do you want us to contact your family to hire a lawyer?

MUHAMMAD: Yes, contact with my family is better, anyone from my family.

JUDGE (TO THE CLERK): The defendant requests to allow him to contact his relatives to hire a lawyer to defend him and be present with him in the investigation sessions. Based on that and the defendant's interest to have his legal rights to hire someone who can defend him legally, the investigation is postponed until contact is made with the defendant's relatives.

JUDGE: Do you have something to add?

MUHAMMAD: No.

JUDGE: This document has the guarantees that we have informed you about and they have my and your signatures, so we can contact your family.

MUHAMMAD: If you do not facilitate the contact, I won't be able to contact my family.

JUDGE: No, no, we are going to facilitate the contact process based on the law.

JUDGE: Thank you.

14

BARZAN IBRAHIM HASAN AL-TIKRITI

"FIVE OF CLUBS" (#38 ON IRAQ'S MOST-WANTED LIST)

Barzan Ibrahim Hasan al-Tikriti was born February 17, 1951. He was one of three half-brothers (Barzan, Sabawi, and Watban) of Saddam Hussein. His wife was the sister of Saddam's first wife, Sajeda Kheit Allah. Barzan was a leader of the Mukhabarat, the Iraqi intelligence service, from 1974 to 1983.

According to historians and former CIA staff, Barzan, who was barely 18, joined his brothers, Sabawi and Watban, and elder half-brother, Saddam, along with their cousin Ali Hassan al-Majid (Chemical Ali), at the gates of the presidential palace in Baghdad. In the early hours of July 17, 1968, they gained admittance by using military passes provided by a member of the Iraqi military intelligence, who just happened to be on the CIA payroll.

Their clansman, Brig. Gen. Ahmed Hassan al-Bakr, had joined other officers from differing political affiliations in an attempted coup. The coup was headed by the military intelligence chief Abdul Razzaq al-Nayef designed to oust President Abdul Rahman Aref. Saddam and his Ba'athist gang hijacked the coup, giving al-Bakr stronger bargaining chips. Barzan was calculating and managed to stop Saddam from killing al-Nayef. Barzan found a use for al-Nayef. Later, al-Nayef was helpful in negotiating better deals with the American oil companies. However, al-Nayef was assassinated ten years later by Barzan's men in London.

In the early 1970s, Barzan was a frequent hunting companion of Saddam. Their favorite locations were Kut, Swaika, Samara, al-Dour, and Tikrit. These hunting parties helped Saddam identify any possible future rivals and bring any different ideologies to the surface.[1]

Saddam took Joseph Stalin as his model. As head of intelligence, however, Barzan suggested Saddam obtain books on Nazi Germany. Barzan was impressed by the Nazi political/bureaucratic experiment, and he believed that Saddam might be interested in the subject. Saddam and his gang did not focus on the elements of racism or anti-Semitism (the Ba'ath had no need for tutors or models in this respect), but Barzan believed the Nazis were a good example of a successful organization of an entire society by the state for the achievement of national goals.[2]

In 1973, there was a plot to assassinate Saddam. A man by the name of Hamdani had taken charge of Saddam's personal office and worked on a range of key issues, including helping establish Iraq's unconventional weapons program. He was a Shi'ite, of which there were very few in Saddam's inner circle. The plot was exposed and included fifty-five Ba'athists who were convicted. Hamdani was one of twenty-two sentenced to death through "democratic executions." The form of capital punishment devised by Saddam required loyal Ba'athists to participate by carrying out the death sentence of their treacherous former colleagues. Each was personally provided a handgun by Saddam. It has been reported that the execution of Hamdani was botched. He was left writhing on the ground after the first bullet failed to kill him. Barzan, who had been responsible for Hamdani's denunciation in the first place, finished him off by firing two bullets into his head.[3]

In 1979, Barzan instructed his elder brother Sabawi Ibrahim—his deputy in the intelligence service—to establish a network of European front companies to import unconventional weapons. They also sought to hire hit teams to assassinate opponents or former officials who knew too much.[4]

In 1980, there was an assassination plot to kill Tariq Aziz, Saddam's deputy prime minister in Najaf. The leading suspect was Mohammed Bak al-Sadr. He was the head of the Iranians' anti-Saddam party called the Shi'ite Muslim Dawa Party. Iraq's Special Forces were sent to the city, al-Najaf, located about 60 miles south of Baghdad. Al-Sadr and other militants were rounded up. Al-Sadr and his sister were among those arrested. All were executed; however, it was reported that the cleric and his sister were allegedly tortured by Barzan before being hanged in secret after a summary trial. No record of the trial has ever been produced.[5]

On July 8, 1982, an assassination attempt on Saddam in the town of Dujail thrust Barzan into the Iraqi spotlight. Saddam's presidential convoy was proceeding to a new government-funded clinic where he would make remarks to a gathered crowd. Suddenly, over a dozen shots rang out from behind a wall of thick foliage on the left side of the road. Saddam's Mercedes with bulletproof windows skidded to a halt. Neither Saddam nor his guards suffered any injuries.[6]

The assassins escaped, and hundreds of Dujailis gathered to beg Saddam not to punish them. Saddam immediately sent for Barzan, head of the Mukhabarat (secret police). Barzan arrived with scores of tanks and helicopter gunships. Iraqi army units sealed the entrances and exits to the town; civilians could not flee. Helicopters strafed civilians working the farms. Artillery shelled the neighborhoods. In the next few days, Iraqi forces began to arrest entire families. Meanwhile, at his temporary headquarters on the outskirts of town, the thuggish Barzan spent several days personally interrogating more than 500 townspeople. More than 300 were implicated in the attack and received a one-way ticket to the dreaded Hakimiya detention facility in Baghdad. The facility was run by the detested Mukhabarat. In some cases, entire families, including young children, were sent to Hakimiya. Many of the Dujailis perished during the interrogation. Other Dujailis were transported to a compound known as Liya, in the Samawah desert. They were held there for years.[7] This event would show the rest of Iraq the power wielded by Barzan and the price Iraqis would pay for such an act.

In the summer of 1983, the most serious challenge to Saddam's position came from within his own family. Saddam was forced to place his three half-brothers—Barzan, Watban, and Sabawi—under house arrest. Precisely what caused this family fallout has never been adequately explained. It has been suggested that Barzan was involved in a coup attempt against his half-brother. Barzan was approached by a group of military officers and offered the presidency if he would support a takeover against Saddam. Another version blames the failure of Barzan to detect a plot against Saddam. It is ironic, given that the previous year Barzan had published a book entitled *Attempts to Assassinate Saddam Hussein*. In this book, he provided details of seven alleged plots against Saddam. Some of those attempts took place before Saddam became a leader and accused such disparate forces as Syria, Israel, and the United States of being the masterminds behind the schemes. A more likely explanation was that Saddam and his half-brothers became embroiled in a family feud. It is probably no coincidence that these tensions developed soon after the death of Saddam's beloved mother, in August 1983. She was fiercely protective of her sons from her second marriage. The rivalry between the al-Majids, Saddam's blood relatives through his natural father, and the al-Ibrahim, his relatives through his mother's second marriage, became one of the key causes of tension within his regime.[8]

These disputes between Saddam and Barzan surfaced in 1983 when Barzan was Chief of Intelligence. Saddam relieved Barzan of his Intelligence responsibilities and appointed Barzan as Iraq's representative at the UN in Geneva, where he served until 1988. As one journalist noted, "Half-brother Barzan, the diplomat/conspirator, was in Geneva overseeing what money remained in Swiss banks from the now-defunct Committee for Strategic Development. These funds were used to take care of the family and perpetuate its hold on power."[9]

In late 1984, Saddam arranged for his son Uday to marry his cousin Saja, the daughter of Barzan. It was not uncommon for Iraqi men to marry close relatives. The previous year, Saddam had refused to allow Barzan's son to marry Saddam's eldest daughter, Raghad, which caused a family feud. By allowing one of Barzan's daughters to marry his eldest son, Saddam clearly hoped to settle the feud. Saddam had hoped that the marriage would persuade Barzan to return home to Iraq from Geneva.[10]

The marriage between Uday and Saja took place, and everything appeared set for formal reconciliation. But both of Saddam's sons aspired to playboy lifestyles, and Uday's marriage collapsed after less than three months. The failed marriage was truly scandalous even by the low moral standards of the Hussein clan.[11]

As the Iraqi ambassador to the UN in Geneva, Barzan had responsibility for the regime's finances abroad. By 1993, it was estimated that Barzan was taking full advantage of the closed world of Swiss banking. He controlled a web of undercover investments worth $20 billion.[12]

After the Gulf War ended, the US was searching for a suitable replacement for Saddam. In his book, *Saddam Hussein: The Politics of Revenge*, Said Aburish made the statement: "[T]hey wanted someone they could control." America's first move consisted of direct contacts with Barzan. Aburish continued, "The CIA was now considering promoting him as a replacement for Saddam. The American who contacted Barzan was an Arabic-speaking agent, operating under the cover of a business consultant, who was related to a highly placed US official—high enough for copies of his reports to reach the White House."[13]

Barzan had a complex personality, charming in civilized conversation, showing knowledge of culture and art as he dined with international

Barzan Ibrahim Hasan al-Tikriti reacts to the judge's comments. (Photo by Combat Camera)

diplomats and financiers, but he could also be violent, tough, and vengeful. He even exchanged gunfire with his nephew, Saddam's son Uday.[14]

His evident reluctance to return to Iraq at the end of 1998 put him under the spotlight of suspicion, and he was interrogated at length by Qusay. By

Barzan pleading with the judge. (Photo by Combat Camera)

mid-1999, the tide had turned against Barzan, as Saddam's immediate family accused him of plotting to overthrow the regime. Those charges may have caused Barzan to briefly flee abroad before returning to Baghdad.

On December 27, 1999, Iraqi President Saddam Hussein granted high medals to his three half-brothers in their first public meeting in two years. Barzan, Iraq's former permanent delegate in the European headquarters of the UN in Geneva, was granted five bravery medals and two high medals of merit. Watban Ibrahim Hasan al-Tikriti, the former minister of interior, was granted the bravery medal and the high medal of merit, and the third half-brother, Sabawi Ibrahim al-Hasan al-Tikriti, was granted the bravery medal.

In March 2003, Saddam placed Barzan under house arrest in the Radwaniya presidential palace when Barzan contested Saddam's wish for his younger son, Qusay, to succeed him should Saddam be killed. When US troops entered Baghdad, Barzan fled to his farm in Ramadi, 60 miles northwest of the capital. He made the mistake of telephoning his family in Switzerland to tell them he was "safe and sound." The Americans traced his call, but by the time they dropped six "bunker buster" bombs on the farm, Barzan had fled. Only a week later, with the help of information from Iraqi citizens, Barzan was arrested in Baghdad.[15]

Barzan was captured by coalition forces during a raid as he was preparing to flee to Syria. He was taken into custody on April 16, 2003.

ARRAIGNMENT

The guards removed the detainee's handcuffs in the outer room. As the two guards were escorting Barzan Ibrahim al-Hasan al-Tikriti to the courtroom, he shouted angrily and threatened to strike one of the guards for holding him too tightly. The guards were not intimidated by this defendant's outburst. As he was being escorted to his seat, Barzan pushed one of the guards' hands away from his right arm. After Barzan was seated, the guards turned around and walked to their posts.

Barzan was wearing a brown suit, white shirt, and dark shoes. He had dark thinning hair, a graying mustache, dark brown eyes, and dark eyebrows touched with a bit of gray. Barzan spent about half the amount of time in front of the judge as had his half-brother, Saddam Hussein. Barzan's arraignment lasted a little more than fifteen minutes; Saddam's lasted twenty-eight minutes.

Barzan was more animated than some of the other defendants, but he did listen intently as the charges against him were read aloud, and he answered all the questions he was asked. The proceedings were recorded by the court clerks. Once all court requirements were met and all signatures were obtained and the documents were secured, Barzan's hand came across the wooden rail and he pointed his finger, making gestures at the judge. Then the security guards approached and escorted him out of the courtroom.

TRANSCRIPT OF BARZAN IBRAHIM AL-TIKRITI DIALOGUE WITH JUDGE RA'ID

JUDGE: Come in. Please be seated.

BARZAN (TO THE GUARD): Do not hold me!

JUDGE: Please be seated.

SECURITY GUARD: Please be seated.

JUDGE: You are in front of the judiciary.

BARZAN: It is okay that I'm in front of the judiciary, but he is humiliating me.

JUDGE: You've got to respect yourself.

BARZAN: He is humiliating me. I always respect myself, Mr. Judge.

BARZAN (ADDRESSING THE GUARD): Get to the back!

BARZAN: But he is humiliating me. This is humiliation!

JUDGE: There is no humiliation.

BARZAN: What am I, a kid?

JUDGE: He holds your hand just in case. This is his duty.

BARZAN: I do not want to do anything.

JUDGE: This is his duty.

BARZAN: Well, this is an insult. It's against human rights.

JUDGE: Mr. Barzan, your full name.

BARZAN: Barzan Ibrahim al-Tikriti.

JUDGE: And the name of your grandfather?

BARZAN: I do not have a grandfather.

JUDGE: You do not have a grandfather?

BARZAN: No.

JUDGE: Didn't your brother say that he had a grandfather, his name is Hasan?

BARZAN: No, that's it . . . what is known by that name.

JUDGE: Barzan Ibrahim.

BARZAN: al-Tikriti.

JUDGE: Hasan or al-Tikriti?

BARZAN: No, al-Tikriti! Don't you know? Have you ever heard one day that someone referred to me as al-Hasan?

JUDGE: What is your name in your ID?

BARZAN: Barzan Ibrahim al-Tikriti, and in the passport and in the profession and the ID.

JUDGE: What is the name in the passport?

BARZAN: al-Tikriti.

JUDGE: Okay. (dictating) Barzan Ibrahim al-Tikriti.

JUDGE: When were you born?

BARZAN: '51.

JUDGE: Born in 1951?

BARZAN: Yes.

JUDGE: The positions you occupied in the Mukhabarat [intelligence service]? Which years? And what were they?

BARZAN: Mr. Judge, I worked in the Mukhabarat from '77 till '83.

JUDGE: What were your positions?

BARZAN: From '77 till '79, late '79, Assistant Director of the Mukhabarat.

JUDGE: And from '79 until when as Director of the Service?

BARZAN: Until '83.

JUDGE: From the year 1979 until . . . ?

BARZAN: The first half of '83.

JUDGE: That means June?

BARZAN: Before June in '83; in May I submitted my resignation and stopped working and remained not attending until in October they accepted my resignation by retiring me.

JUDGE: I served as Chief of the Intelligence Service from 1974 to 1983.

JUDGE: Your address?

BARZAN: I live in Baghdad, but since '88.

JUDGE: Where in Baghdad?

BARZAN: Up until now, I was not in Iraq.

JUDGE: Yes, but where in Baghdad?

JUDGE: In Jadriyah.

JUDGE: Baghdad—al-Jadriyah.

JUDGE: The name of your mother?

BARZAN: Subha.

JUDGE: Tulfah?

BARZAN: Subha Tulfah.

JUDGE: The name of the mother is Subha Tulfah.

JUDGE: Mr. Barzan.

BARZAN: Yes.

JUDGE: This is the first session of the investigation with you, not a trial. In the investigations, in the first session, the defendant would be informed of the crimes he is accused of according to suits submitted against him. Then the court would move to make him understand his rights and guarantees as a defendant before the court. To begin, the crimes that are attributed to you:

- Deliberate killing of several Iraqis in 1979.
- Deliberate killing, by using chemical and biological agents, of prisoners at the Intelligence service.
- Deliberate killing of several Iraqis from the al-Barzani tribe.
- Destroying the villages of Dujail and Jizani.

This is regarding the crimes. The article of the law, which is applicable to those crimes, is article 406/1/A of the penalty law. Those are the crimes, and this is the article of law that is applicable to them. As for your rights, they are as follows. This court would like to inform you, Mr. Barzan Ibrahim al-Tikriti, of your rights and guarantees as a defendant before the Iraqi judiciary.

- You have the right to appoint a lawyer to defend you.
- In case you are not able to appoint a lawyer to defend you, the court will mandate a lawyer, the fees of whom the court will pay, and he will accordingly defend you.

- You have the right to keep silent and not answer any question, and this will not be considered evidence against you at the court.
- You have the right to debate the evidence and the witnesses.

This is the crime; this is an article of the law, and those are your guarantees as a defendant before the Iraqi judiciary. Do you have a lawyer that you would like to appoint?

BARZAN: Well, your honor, since I was imprisoned until now, I have not seen anyone.

JUDGE: We will take care of this.

BARZAN: So how can I assign a lawyer?

JUDGE: You may take the time to contact your family.

BARZAN: No, I . . . if you can order for me to meet a person whose name I will provide.

JUDGE: Okay. Who?

BARZAN: So that he comes to me, and I explain the issue to him. I have a guy; his name is Abdul Karim Ali.

JUDGE: Abdul Karim what?

BARZAN: Ali.

JUDGE: Does he live in a specific known place?

BARZAN: Well, he lives in Baghdad, al-Jadida [the new Baghdad].

JUDGE: Is there anything else? His job?

BARZAN: Well, I do not even know his phone number.

JUDGE: What is his job so that we can reach him?

BARZAN: He does not do anything. He is not a government employee.

JUDGE: Not an employee. Not a merchant?

BARZAN: Not a merchant or anything.

JUDGE: How can we reach him?

BARZAN: Well, it must be . . . if the administration would allow me to use the phone so that I can get his phone number.

JUDGE: So, we should contact someone for you? Whom should we contact for you so that we get the number of this man?

BARZAN: All the people's names I will give to you, I do not have their numbers, and it would be difficult for you.

JUDGE: Well, your brother asked to appoint Talal Al Jassim; do you want us to add you to him?

BARZAN: No, I've got other lawyers.

JUDGE: Other lawyers.

BARZAN: I have Iraqi lawyers . . . Arab lawyers.

JUDGE: Good.

BARZAN: And even probably foreign lawyers.

JUDGE: No problem. Do you want us to contact a specific lawyer?

BARZAN: Like, for example, Nazar al-Tabakchali.

JUDGE: Would you like us to contact Nazar al-Tabakchali?

BARZAN: If it is [possible], Nazar al-Tabakchali. But I ask your honor that you order for me to meet with . . .

JUDGE: Abdul Karim Ali?

BARZAN: Yes.

JUDGE: Just give me a way that we can reach this man.

BARZAN: If you just give your order, I will try from the prison camp. I can call someone and get his phone number.

JUDGE: Okay, give me the number of that person.

BARZAN: I do not have it on me, your honor.

JUDGE: Oh, you do not have it on you.

BARZAN: Yes, I do not have it. I do not have it. If you can order someone to pass by me, I will give him the phone number.

JUDGE: Inshallah, we will solve it.

BARZAN: God bless you.

JUDGE: Okay, write [speaking to the court reporter] the court recited to the defendant the crimes attributed to him indicated now, and it stated the article of law related. I beg your pardon . . . the article of law, which is applicable to this act, and the court recited the guarantees of the defendant and his rights, and he asked to enable him to contact one of his acquaintances to appoint a lawyer to defend him. As a guarantee to the right of the defendant to get someone to defend him and attend with him the investigation sessions, he is allowed to appoint a lawyer and the investigation is postponed until the defendant gets someone who represents him in front of this court.

BARZAN: If you would allow me, your honor.

JUDGE: Go ahead.

BARZAN: Your honor, regarding the accusations . . .

JUDGE: No, you respond to the accusations while the lawyer is present, in a fully legal session. Now you have requested to contact Abdul Karim Ali.

BARZAN: Yes.

JUDGE: So that you appoint a lawyer. This is a guarantee for you.

BARZAN: I thank you, but those accusations, I mean . . . if such things

171

did happen . . . the Jizani and Al Dujail, those should be addressed to another establishment. I do not now know whether or not the Intelligence Service is involved in such issues.

JUDGE: When the investigation starts, you will see the process of being involved.

BARZAN: And then, the Jizani is an area, is that right?

JUDGE: Right.

BARZAN: I mean, it is not an abandoned house and so is Dujail . . . isn't that right? There are people in it and inhabitants and maybe 50,000.

JUDGE: There could be a witness or there might not; this is what the investigation process would prove.

BARZAN: And there are the procedures of the State.

JUDGE: If there is a witness, so it would be; if not, then the investigation will take its due process. Isn't that right?

BARZAN: And also in the same respect . . . regarding the mass killings with . . . medicines, you said, your honor?

JUDGE: Yes, by using chemical agents.

BARZAN: Yes, the same thing here, the Intelligence Service is not a research center. So that you . . . you have probably seen the Intelligence Service. Inshallah.

BARZAN: The Intelligence Service is a building, and even the buildings and its garden are open to the main street and people can see.

JUDGE: When we get into the investigation there will be a debate.

BARZAN: And regarding the issue of Kurds, this establishment is not involved.

JUDGE: You are now answering . . . we are getting into the answers now.

BARZAN: No, I will also repeat the response; let Mr. Masoud al-Barazani speak for himself.

JUDGE: Just sign this so that accordingly we can contact Abdul Karim Ali.

JUDGE: Then you ask the testimony of Mr. Masoud. We would summon him to testify.

BARZAN: If Mr. Masoud says that I have a relation to this thing, Mr. Masoud and Mr. Jalal when they wanted to contact the government would send me a word. They would come to Geneva when I used to be an ambassador; they would send me a delegation so that I would contact Baghdad and they would come here and negotiate.

JUDGE: Inshallah.

BARZAN: One time Mr. Jalal sent me a person, and he said, "I want to see you." I sent a word to Baghdad, and they said, "See him." He left the north and went to Ankara and he saw politicians there. Once he was done, he held a press conference. They asked him, "Where are you going now?" He said, "I'm heading to Europe, to Geneva." They asked him, "What would you be doing in Geneva?" He said he had a friend there, and this friend was Barzan al-Tikriti, and that unfortunately for us, he left the government because this is the only person that can understand us, and we understand him, and we could get to something with him. At night . . . he said that during the day before noon . . . at night I received a cable from Baghdad saying to cancel the meeting with him. I said to him, "Abu Shalal [Father of Waterfall], why did you have to say that word? You should have let us see you, so that we find a word that benefits you, or benefits us." The government here said, "How could he say that Barzan al-Tikriti is good, and we could reach an understanding with him and that he is the only one in the government that we can talk to?" so they said to cancel . . . [he laughs] they said to cancel the meeting.

JUDGE: God willing, we will contact Abdul Karim Ali. And we will arrange it.

BARZAN: Sir, I have one thing.

JUDGE: Go ahead.

BARZAN: I hope you accept my apology.

JUDGE: No. No, there is no need.

BARZAN: I apologize very much to you and to all the folks here . . . but the guard treated me a bit rough.

JUDGE: Not at all. No one treats you in any way; you are respected in front of the judiciary.

BARZAN: I apologize to you and to all the attendance.

JUDGE: God bless you.

BARZAN: I thank you, sir, and we will see you [again] well.

JUDGE (ADDRESSING THE GUARDS): Let him be.

BARZAN: Sir, your instructions to the camp.

JUDGE: Yes, it will happen, inshallah.

BARZAN: We became pickles inside.

JUDGE: No, inshallah it will be good.

15

SABIR ABDUL AZIZ AL-DOURI

SABIR ABDUL AZIZ AL-DOURI WAS BORN IN EITHER BAGHDAD or Mosul. He came from Ad-Dawr and was a member of the Albu Haidar tribe in Saladin Governorate. There is very little known about his early childhood or early life. During his career, he held several cabinet-level positions.

Sabir graduated from the Iraqi Military Academy in March 1967 and later from the Staff College. During his career he held numerous military positions: Commander of the 14th Tank battalion; Commander of the 10th Armored Brigade; Commander of the 17th Armored Division; Director of military strategy in the Iraqi Ministry of Defense; member of the General Command of the Armed Forces in July 1985; Director of General Military Intelligence in April 1986; and promoted to the rank of lieutenant general in 1989.

He was governor of Karbala Province from 1996 to 2001, then served as governor of Baghdad Province from 2001 to 2003.

ARRAIGNMENT
Two guards flanked Sabir and escorted him into the courtroom. The guards directed the defendant to the chair. Following their routine, they removed the

175

Sabir Abdul Aziz al-Douri enters the courtroom. (Photo by Combat Camera)

handcuffs from the defendant's wrists in the outer room before they entered. Sabir's jacket did not completely hide the heavy chains that were about his waist holding the handcuffs in place. Once the defendant was seated, the guards assumed their watch positions on either side of the courtroom door. Sabir was wearing a brown suit with a white shirt and dark shoes. He had a full head of

Sabir Abdul Aziz al-Douri listens to the judge. (Photo by Combat Camera)

graying hair that was somewhat adrift, a graying mustache, and dark black eyebrows. He had brown eyes and drooping eyelids. He looked tired, and the edges of his lower eyelids were reddish in color.

The arraignment was brief, lasting ten to twelve minutes. This defendant was composed during the entire proceeding and showed no hostility to the judge as the charges against him were read. Most of the time he stared straight ahead. Occasionally, he glanced toward the jurors' box. His hands were interlocked, resting on his lap. He answered all the questions that were asked of him by the judge while the combat camera photographer moved about the room, cognizant not to go beyond the judge's desk.

The assigned court clerks recorded all testimony between the judge and Sabir. Once all the charges against him were read and recorded by the court clerk, they were signed by the judge.

One of the clerks delivered the papers to the defendant. The defendant was given instructions regarding where to sign the document and once he did, he returned it to the clerk. The security guards approached Sabir to assist him from his chair. As they approached him, they stepped back, to allow the judge and Sabir to engage in additional conversation. The conversation concluded and the guards continued assisting him and escorted him out of the courtroom.

TRANSCRIPT OF SABIR ABDUL AZIZ AL-DOURI DIALOGUE WITH JUDGE RA'ID

(Sabir enters the courtroom.)

JUDGE: Have a seat.

SABIR: Thank you.

JUDGE: State your full name.

SABIR: Sabir Abdel Aziz.

JUDGE: Birth year?

SABIR: 1949.

JUDGE: Positions held from 1986, 1987 until now.

SABIR: 1986 until 1991 I was the head of the army intelligence unit. I was Head of Intelligence from 1991 to 1994.

JUDGE: Can you repeat the first one?

SABIR: From 1986 to 1991, I was the Head of Army Intelligence. 1991 to 1994, again I was head of the country's intelligence. 1994 to 1996 I was retired. 1996 to 2001 I was the governor of Karbala Province. I was the governor of Baghdad until the war started [2001–2003].

JUDGE: Place of residence?

SABIR: My birth town, el-Dorr.

JUDGE: Your recent address?

SABIR: Baghdad, Al Yarmuk.

JUDGE: Mother's full name?

SABIR: Amina Makhlif.

JUDGE (TO THE CLERK): Therefore, after I introduced myself as the judge in charge of the investigation.

JUDGE (TO SABIR): Mr. Sabir, this is day one of the investigation. I informed you of the crimes you are accused of and the articles under which these crimes fall in the Iraqi judicial system and after that your rights and guarantees. After that, you can comment. The crimes you are accused of are the intentional killing of Iraqi citizens in 1991 and the intentional killing of Iraqi citizens without proper prosecution in 1987. You are accused of being a part of the assassination of Taleb el

Silaa in 1994. These are the crimes of which you are accused. The article that relays to these crimes falls under the judicial court 406/1/Y under the laws of punishment. Next, I would like to inform you of your rights and guarantees under the judicial system. First, you have the right to appoint an attorney to defend you. Second, if you cannot afford an attorney the court will appoint one for you and pay the fees. Third, you have the right to remain silent and it will not be held against you. Fourth, you have the right to question evidence and witnesses. So, you are informed of the crimes of which you are accused, the articles related to your crimes under the judicial system, and your rights and guarantees as an Iraqi citizen. My question to you now is do you have an attorney to defend you? Do you have one or would you like to appoint one to defend you?

SABIR: I would like to hire an attorney to defend me, but first let me meet with a member of my family because I cannot remember the name of an attorney to defend me.

JUDGE (TO THE CLERK): The accused was informed of the crimes of which he is accused and the articles of law which they lay under and his rights and guarantees. The accused asked to be given time to contact a family member to be able to hire an attorney who will be able to defend him and represent him in future investigative sessions. For that reason, the investigative session will be postponed until a defense attorney is present. I am signing the document relating to your accusations, rights and guarantees, and the articles from the punishment codes.

JUDGE (TO SABIR): I have signed and stamped, and I would like for you to sign under your name.

SABIR: Thank you very much.

JUDGE: Do you have anything to say before you leave?

SABIR: Yes, I would like to comment on a few things related to the crimes I am accused of.

JUDGE: These comments you cannot make now. You need to wait until the next sessions where your attorney is present.

SABIR: I just want to clarify some of these accusations. There are plenty of witnesses who know that I was in Baghdad from 1987 to 1991 doing my job and I was not in the northern part of the country. The person in charge of the northern part of the country, everyone knows, was a member of the elite guard in charge of that region. Even all the intelligence personnel and army personnel were under his control due to the conflict in that region during that time. Secondly, regarding the assignation of Taleb al-Silaa . . .

JUDGE (INTERRUPTING): Please stop. This is for your protection. Do not say anything further without your attorney present.

SABIR: Okay, I agree with you, but there is one more thing I would like to discuss. I am sure you know that my family, my education, and my reputation do not allow me to commit such crimes.

JUDGE (INTERRUPTING): Once again, let me clarify, legally this is an investigation, not a trial; investigations often start one way and end up another. You were the party of the former regime. Often once we investigate and we determine a person is innocent for all charges, they will be released. We provide evidence and the accuser can provide evidence, and whatever evidence presented can tip the scale of the court to your favor. We guarantee you a fair trial as we guarantee any Iraqi citizen. (Sabir nods and departs courtroom.)

16
SULTAN HASHIM AHMAD AL-TAI

"EIGHT OF HEARTS" (#27 ON IRAQ'S MOST-WANTED LIST)

Sultan Hashim Ahmad was born in Mosul in 1944. While not much is known about his early life, Ahmad graduated from Baghdad's National Security Institute in 1975. He became an expert on military intelligence and rose to prominence serving Saddam during the 1980–1988 Iran–Iraq War.

He became the highest-ranking general in the Iraqi Army. In 1988, he was commander of the Iraqi Army's First Corps. He played a direct role in the genocidal Anfal campaign against rural Kurds. He was, however, regarded largely as a figurehead in the Iraqi armed forces.

During the First Iraq War, then-Lt. Gen. Hashim was the deputy chief of staff of the Ministry of Defense. This senior Iraqi military leader met with Army Gen. Norman Schwarzkopf, Commander, US Central Command, on March 3, 1991. The two convened in a tent at the desert village of Safwan, located in southern Iraq, near the Iraq–Kuwait border.[1]

Schwarzkopf "announced through an interpreter that all delegates and observers would be searched." Gen. Hashim balked, protesting that the Iraqis had left their weapons behind. Only when Schwarzkopf agreed to be frisked himself did Ahmad yield.

Schwarzkopf had demanded the formal ceasefire negotiations be held in Iraqi territory.[2] The historic meeting opened at 11:34 a.m. (local time), and Schwarzkopf reminded Gen. Hashim the agenda had been set by Washington and sent to Baghdad.[3]

Sultan nodded, smiling slightly. "We are authorized to make this meeting a very successful one in an atmosphere of cooperation."

Schwarzkopf went through the agenda, unveiling a "map marked with the proposed ceasefire boundary."[4] Sultan and other Iraqis in attendance seemed stunned at the extent of the allied occupation. Schwarzkopf assured them this was not a permanent line and had nothing to do with the borders.

There was only one request by Sultan: "We have a point, one point. You might very well know the situation of our roads and bridges and communications. We would like to agree helicopter flight is sometimes needed to carry officials from one place to another because the roads and bridges are out." Since the talks went so well, Schwarzkopf felt this was an acceptable request and stated, "As long as flights are not over the part we are in, that is absolutely no problem."

Ahmad looked skeptical. "So you mean even armed helicopters can fly in Iraqi skies!"[5]

Schwarzkopf assured them, "I will instruct our Air Force not to shoot at any helicopters that are flying over the territory of Iraq."[6]

Schwarzkopf and Lt. Gen. Hashim signed the Safwan Agreement, a document that initiated a ceasefire and ended the First Gulf War.

Gen. Hashim was one of the most admired officers in the Iraqi officer corps. Junior generals looked to him to speak up as the most knowledgeable about warfare. But, once in his position as Defense Minister, he held unswervingly to the party line.[7]

Gen. Hashim once said, "I effectively became an assistant to Qusay, only collecting and passing information." He went on, "Qusay knew nothing, and his understanding of general things was like a civilian."[8] He acknowledged after the Gulf War, "Only Saddam's relatives would dare to present him with even mildly opposing views."

During his thirty-year military career, Gen. Hashim commanded two brigades, three divisions, and two corps of regular army corps before assuming responsibilities as Minister of Defense. He held that position until the US overthrew Saddam in the spring of 2003.

As the invasion of Iraq loomed, it was reported in *The Guardian* in February 2003 that Hashim had been placed under house arrest by Saddam Hussein. It was a move that was designed to prevent a coup. Nevertheless, he continued to appear on Iraqi state television, to preserve a sense of normality.

On September 19, 2003, after nearly a week of negotiations, Gen. Hashim gave himself up in Mosul to the 101st Airborne Division (Air Assault). Dawood Baghistani was the Iraqi Kurdish editor in chief of *Israel-Kurd* and former Minister of Defense. Baghistani was also the former chief of the autonomous northern region's human rights commission. He arranged the general's surrender to Maj. Gen. David Petraeus. Dawood said Gen. Hashim was handed over "with great respect" and was with his family at the time. He also said the US military had promised to remove Hashim's name from the list of Iraq's fifty-five most wanted, meaning he would not face indefinite confinement and possible prosecution. "We trust the promise," Baghistani said.

Special treatment for Ahmad could have been an effort to defuse the guerrilla-style attacks that were taking a toll on American soldiers. Many of the attackers were thought to be former soldiers in Saddam's army. Seeing their former military leader well-treated by the Americans might have encouraged them to lay down their arms.

After his capture, Ahmad shared with his interrogators that many of the generals were stunned by the news of the fall of Baghdad. Iraq had relied on chemical weapons to fend off the Iranians during their long war with Tehran. Saddam had propagated the notion that Iraq's arsenal of chemical and biological weapons had enabled him to deter US forces from marching on Baghdad after the 1991 Persian Gulf War. The Iraqis had also used the threat of WMD to keep Shi'ites in line. The disclosure that the cupboard was empty sent morale plummeting.[9]

In addition, for more than a year, Rick Francona, then an Air Force lieutenant colonel, was part of a secret CIA task force working to overthrow Saddam Hussein. The efforts were the Clinton administration's failed attempt at regime change in Iraq.[10] Now an NBC News analyst, Francona was talking for the first time about his role in recruiting generals for that mission seven years before the US invasion. He laid out why he thought the US should try to stop the hanging of former Iraqi Defense Minister Sultan Hashim Ahmad, one of the generals recruited in that effort.

Hashim had been convicted of war crimes by an Iraqi court and was scheduled to hang in the next few days unless the US military could quietly get the Iraqi government to commute his sentence. "I moved in and out of Northern Iraq, as well as the countries bordering Iraq," said Francona. "We were involved in what was known inside the Agency as 'DBACHILLES,'" a code name for an

Sultan Hashim Ahmad al-Tai arriving in the waiting room. (Photo by Combat Camera)

effort to support a coup to overthrow of Saddam Hussein in 1995. It was initiated on what the agency thought was the dictator's Achilles' heel: a military whose loyalty even Saddam questioned.[11] "We at CIA had tried to contact and co-opt as many Iraqi military officers as we could, hoping to convince them that they should not fight when and if an invasion or coup attempt occurred. That program had some successes."

Sultan Hashim Ahmad al-Tai ponders charges the judge reads to him. (Photo by Combat Camera)

Francona said that he did not know what help Gen. Hashim had provided but noted that there was ample evidence he offered to help. He was told that Hashim even volunteered to have communications gear hidden at his estate north of Baghdad in preparation for a coup attempt. Moreover, Jalal Talabani, president of Iraq from 2005 to 2014 and the man who brought Hashim to the CIA's attention, said publicly that the defense minister "cooperated" in the effort. The recruiting of Hashim was kept separate from the recruiting of lesser

Iraqi generals. Still, at one point, Hashim's name was entered into a CIA database as an "agent of influence."[12]

ARRAIGNMENT

Escorted by two Iraqi security guards, Sultan entered the courtroom. His handcuffs were removed in the outer room before entering the courtroom. Once again, the two guards positioned themselves on either side of the entry door after the defendant was seated in his chair. Sultan was a thick, heavyset individual who was wearing a brown jacket, gray slacks, white shirt, and dark shoes. He had dark black hair that was barely showing some silver streaks, as was his bushy mustache. He had black eyebrows and dark eyes with bold dark circles under them. John Burns observed, "He was like many of the other leaders: he appeared suddenly ordinary in his ill-fitting jacket and trousers."[13]

Gen. Hashim occasionally rubbed his face and chin during the proceedings that lasted a little more than twelve minutes. He sat slouched in his chair and listened to the charges against him being read aloud into the court records. He leaned forward to address the judge and answer his questions.

According to the transcript, he argued that he should not be held accountable for crimes committed under Mr. Hussein. The crimes he was told he would be investigated for included the use of chemical weapons against Halabja and other atrocities committed during the Anfal campaign. This campaign was a horrific act against Iraqi Kurds in the late 1980s, and evidence of the campaign was presented at the arraignment.

Ahmed did not protest that there had been an atrocity at Halabja, only that he had not been responsible for it. He told the judge he had arrived in Northern Iraq, as the corps commander in the area, a month after the Halabja attack. He said that in nearly forty years in the Iraqi Army he had "never hurt anybody." He then added: "As an army commander, there is a certain procedure. You must follow orders, unlike an ordinary citizen. It's a little bit different when you get an order; you carry it out. Sometimes, when you do it, you ask yourself if this can really be true."

Burns commented, "Like Nazi leaders at Nuremberg, Mr. Hashim claimed that at times when he alleged to have participated in mass killings, he was only taking orders."[14] As Tariq Aziz had stated during his time in front of the judge, Sultan suggested that he should seek to save himself at trial by arguing that all the blame should be shifted to Hussein, or at least to a small group around him.

The assigned court clerks were recording the questions and answers between the judge and the defendant. Hashim often stared at those seated in the jurors' box. All the proceedings followed a routine and were kept on track and moving along. The charges against the defendant were read aloud, recorded by the court clerk, and signed by the judge. The clerk delivered the papers to the defendant and once he read them, he signed them and returned the documents to the clerk. At that point, Ahmad had another brief discussion with the judge. Then, keeping to their routine, the security guards came and assisted the HVD up from the chair and escorted him out of the courtroom.

A side note: In the courtroom to the right of where the HVDs were seated were two unidentified Iraqi women and one Iraqi male. All three were taking notes and listening to all the proceedings. I never was able to determine who they were with or who was their sponsor to allow them into the courtroom.

The still photographer, Karen Ballard, moved around the courtroom, first to the left of the judge and then to the right, taking photographs and looking at the images taken on the preview finder to ensure the quality of the photos.[15]

TRANSCRIPT OF SULTAN HASHIM AHMAD AL-TAI DIALOGUE WITH JUDGE RA'ID

JUDGE: What is your full name?

SULTAN: Sultan Hashim Ahmad Muhammed al-Hamadi.

JUDGE: Date of birth?

SULTAN: 1944.

JUDGE: What positions did you occupy from 1988 until the present?

SULTAN: I was commander of the Sixth Army division [Iraq], then the First Army division.

JUDGE: Where were you located?

SULTAN: I was there for a year in the north. Then, I was commander of the first division, from January 14, 1988, to October 6, 1989. I was for the same duration assistant to the Army Chief of Staff.

JUDGE: In what area?

SULTAN: In the Mira, and a year and a half after that I was in operations in 1995, and in 1995 I became Army Chief of Staff. And in July 1995 I became a minister.

JUDGE (REPEATING TO THE CLERK): He became chief of staff in 1995, and in July became a minister.

JUDGE: What location were you in then?

SULTAN: Mosul/Jeddah.

JUDGE: What's your mother's name?

SULTAN: Nasma Jasser Al-Hamad.

JUDGE: Mr. Sultan, today we are going to interrogate you.

SULTAN: Welcome.

JUDGE: I will list your special guarantees, and we go on from there.

SULTAN: Yes.

JUDGE: You are accused of activities in Northern Iraq, in Haj, and in killing activities in the Anbar province. That is stated in section 406/1 of the penal code. Special guarantees for you, Mr. Hashim, are as follows:

1. You have the right to appoint a lawyer to defend you. In case you are not able to retain a lawyer, the court will appoint a lawyer to defend you.
2. You have the right to be silent, and not answer any questions you are asked, and this will not be held against you.
3. You have the right to contest the witnesses.

JUDGE: Those are the guarantees and accusations. Do you have a lawyer?

SULTAN: I was surprised by this situation, and I must call my folks to let them know what we need to do.

JUDGE: Do you have anyone in mind?

SULTAN: I will hope one of my brothers will come to see me, and I have an important point I would like to say that will not affect the outcome of this trial.

JUDGE: Hold on.

SULTAN: I just want to say that I never hurt anyone, and I refused to take orders that would hurt anyone. And that is my point.

JUDGE (TO THE CLERK): The accused was given his rights and his guarantees of the Iraqi legal system, and the laws listed accordingly. And the accused has asked to get in touch with his relatives so he can retain a lawyer to defend him who will be present with him in the interrogation sessions, and to guarantee his rights. So, the interrogation was postponed until then; it will proceed when a defense attorney is present. The documents were signed by the judge and given to the defendant to sign.

SULTAN: May I say that the best way to get this information is from the governor of the province of Mosul [defendant reading and signing the document papers]. I would like to point out something, the date is not right: it's January 4 in Khalabja.

(Notes and documents were returned to the judge, who corrected and initialed that change and returned to the defendant to sign.)

SULTAN: I would just like to say that commands between military personnel may not be interpreted the same as between military and civilian people.

JUDGE: This is not the forum for this statement, and you are dismissed now.

17
KAMAL MUSTAFA SULTAN AL-TIKRITI

"QUEEN OF CLUBS" (#10 ON IRAQ'S MOST-WANTED LIST)

Kamal Mustafa Sultan al-Tikriti was born May 4, 1955, in Tikrit, Iraq. Even though Kamal was one of the top ten most-wanted Iraqis, there was not much known about him. He was a cousin of Saddam Hussein, and he served as Secretary General of the Republican Guard and held the rank of general.

To ensure loyalty, Saddam surrounded himself with fellow members of his al-Tikriti clan, all from his hometown of Tikrit in northern Iraq. Kamal was Saddam's son-in-law, marrying one of his daughters, allegedly his favorite—Hala, the third daughter, born in 1972. In 1998, Saddam arranged her marriage with Kamal. She fled with her two children to Jordan the day Baghdad fell.

US Central Command issued a statement from MacDill Air Force Base that Kamal surrendered on Saturday, May 17, 2003, in Baghdad.[1]

ARRAIGNMENT

Kamal Mustafa Sultan al-Tikriti entered the room. He was escorted by the two imposing guards who directed him to his chair. The guards had removed

191

Kamal Mustafa Sultan al-Tikriti has chains removed upon arriving in the waiting area. (Photo by Combat Camera)

the defendant's handcuffs in the outer room before he entered the courtroom. Although the handcuffs were removed, the large weighty chain that held the handcuffs was visible under the defendant's jacket and was a reminder of the seriousness of the proceedings. Once Kamal was seated, the guards automatically turned and walked back to their positions on either side of the entry door.

Kamal was wearing clothing similar to that of the other defendants who had appeared in the courtroom before him: brown suit, white shirt, and dark shoes. His black-and-gray hair was cut short. His mustache was trimmed and the same color as his hair. He had dark heavy eyebrows and brown eyes. His nine-minute arraignment in front of Judge Ra'id was a bit shorter than others. Kamal was composed during the entire proceeding. As those before him had done, he occasionally looked toward the jurors' box. The charges against the defendant were read aloud and he appeared to listen intently. Without displaying any emotion, he answered the questions he was asked by the judge. The dialogue between the judge and Kamal was in low tones. The judge looked to his right and addressed the court clerks who were recording all that had transpired during the hearing. Once the charges against Kamal were read, they were recorded by the court clerk and signed by the judge. The court clerk reached over the wooden rail and handed Kamal the papers to sign. Once he signed the documents, they were returned to the clerk. The security guards came and assisted Kamal up from the chair and escorted him out of the courtroom.

TRANSCRIPT OF KAMAL MUSTAFA SULTAN DIALOGUE WITH JUDGE RA'ID

JUDGE: Have a seat here. How are you?

KAMAL: Great, and you?

JUDGE: State your full name.

KAMAL: Kamal Mustafa Abdullah al-Sultan.

JUDGE: Birth year?

KAMAL: 1955.

JUDGE: Officer in the army?

KAMAL: Yes.

JUDGE: Rank?

KAMAL: Major general.

JUDGE: Since when? Last position held? I need your ranking in 1990, 1991, and 2003.

KAMAL: 1990 thru 1991, I was head of the Republican Guard with a rank of major general. In 2003, I was Assistant of the Joint Chief of Staff for the northern region of the country in the ranking of major general.

JUDGE: Place of Residence?

KAMAL: Baghdad el-Haretheya.

JUDGE: Where in the Haretheya?

KAMAL: El Kende Street.

JUDGE: Where in el-Kende Street?

KAMAL: Not sure . . . I am not sure what you are asking.

JUDGE: Do you recall a landmark, a school or restaurant that you lived by?

KAMAL: There were a bunch of restaurants, but I don't recall.

JUDGE: So, don't you recall?

KAMAL: No, I don't.

JUDGE: Mother's full name?

KAMAL: Hadlah Hasan.

JUDGE (TO THE CLERK): Moving forward, after we get the personal information of the suspect in front of the presiding judge of the investigation.

JUDGE (TO KAMAL): Mr. Kamal, this is the first session of the investigation. You are in front of the Iraqi judicial court. I am the presiding judge of the investigation. I want to discuss with you what you have been accused of based on the information we have received. I want to clarify the crimes that we are investigating and after that, we will discuss your rights, then I will allow commentary. You are accused of being part of the intentional killing of civilians in 1991. Under article number 406/1/Y of the Iraqi criminal punishment, you have rights and guarantees related to your case. The court would like to advise you of your rights and guarantees under the Iraqi judiciary laws. First, you have the right to hire an attorney to defend you. Second, if you cannot afford an attorney, the court will appoint one and pay the fees. Third, you have the right to remain silent and not answer any questions and that will not be held against you. Fourth, you have the right to question the witnesses and the evidence. These are your rights. Now, do you have an attorney?

KAMAL: Not now.

JUDGE: Would you like time to contact your family so that they can retain an attorney for you? Or would you like us to call your family for that reason?

KAMAL: I would rather I call them myself.

JUDGE (TO THE CLERK): The accused was informed of the crimes of which he is accused and the article from the Iraqi law that applies to his case and the court informed him of all his rights and guarantees under Iraqi judiciary law.

KAMAL (INTERRUPTING): As an accused before Iraqi justice, I would like to ask something if you will allow.

JUDGE: Please let me finish and then you can ask. The accused asked to give him time so he could contact his family so they can appoint an attorney to be present with him for further investigative sessions.

KAMAL (INTERRUPTING): I want to make a statement.

JUDGE: I will not allow statements without an attorney present.

KAMAL: I just want to ask a question then, not make a statement. I want to ask that the investigation and the trial to be fair and unbiased since I am an Iraqi citizen and whoever has accused me of these crimes are Iraqi citizens too.

JUDGE: If it wasn't for the fairness and non-bias of the Iraqi judicial system, we would not inform you of your rights and guarantees or give you an attorney to defend you. You know you stand before the Iraqi judiciary system, and you should know better of what Iraqi laws are.

KAMAL: I did not mean to offend you.

JUDGE: I am not offended. I am just clarifying for you how the law and judicial system work in Iraq.

KAMAL: I was just trying to say that I am an Iraqi citizen.

JUDGE (INTERRUPTING): Yes, and you have all the rights and guarantees of such, and the court will guarantee you and every Iraqi citizen a fair trial.

KAMAL: God willing. I am an Iraqi citizen, proud of my nationality, and I have fought defending this country and I will continue to defend this country. Whoever accused me of these crimes, if there is no proof, I expect an apology from these accusers in front of all the citizens of this country.

JUDGE: Inshallah.

KAMAL: Inshallah.

JUDGE (TO THE CLERK): For this reason, the investigation will be postponed until the defendant has an attorney appointed to defend him. [Judge signs and stamps paperwork.] This is the documentation of what we have discussed that shows your guarantees and rights signed and stamped by me. It requires your signature under your name. Do you need a pen?

KAMAL: Yes. I don't have one.

(The clerk gives Kamal a pen. He signs the paperwork and leaves the courtroom.)

18

TAHA YASSIN RAMADAN

"TEN OF DIAMONDS" (#20 ON IRAQ'S MOST-WANTED LIST)

Taha Yassin Ramadan was born February 22, 1938, in Mosul, Iraq. Located in Northern Iraq, Mosul is a mixed Arab-Kurdish city.

Ramadan was of Kurdish origin; this was unusual for Saddam's clique. Ramadan seemed to want to disguise that part of his identity. Not much is known about his early childhood. As a youth, he detested social disparities and the pro-British government of King Faisal, the Harrow-educated cousin of Jordan's King Hussein. He worked as a bank clerk before he became a junior army officer.[1]

In 1956, Ramadan joined the Ba'ath Party. He joined the Ba'ath leadership in 1966 and in 1968 he entered the Revolutionary Command Council. He immediately began purging perceived enemies.[2] In the 1970s, Ramadan was designated as the Minister of Industry. He reportedly admitted, "I don't know anything about the industry. All I know is that anyone who doesn't work hard will be executed." A book he wrote listed Shi'a Muslims, Jews, and flies as three things Allah should not have created. In 1970, he ordered the summary execution of forty-two people accused of plotting to overthrow the government.[3] In 1974, he took command of a 250,000-strong paramilitary Iraq army that protected the regime. Ramadan pushed for war against Iran.

Five years after his inauguration as president in July 1979, Saddam convened an extraordinary conference of senior Ba'ath Party members.[4] There, Ramadan stage-managed a gruesome meeting where he denounced an "atrocious Syrian plot." Fellow members of the 21-member Revolutionary Command Council were forced to confess. They were led out and shot.[5] Thereafter, among Saddam's first orders of business was to create several new offices. One of these was Deputy Prime Minister. Ramadan was the first named to the new position.[6]

In 1983, Iraqi oil exports were at their lowest. Saddam called on Iraqi civilians to donate their jewelry and savings to the nation. Ramadan, as the Iraqi Deputy Prime Minister, said, "This is a referendum in favor of the party . . . in favor of the revolution and the leadership of Saddam Hussein." Iraqi citizens were told they would be handed back the items in the future. However, Iraqis received nothing in return for their generosity.[7]

In January 1991, Ramadan was named Deputy President and threatened to mutilate anyone investigating human rights abuses in Iraqi-annexed Kuwait.[8] While Ramadan deserved credit for funneling oil money into social services, it was his brutality that won him Saddam's gratitude. After the First Gulf War, Shi'as died by the thousands when he crushed their southern revolt. He was promoted to vice president of Iraq in March 1991 and served in that capacity until the fall of Saddam Hussein in April 2003. In 1997, he condemned UN weapons inspectors as American stooges. The next year, he infuriated the Arab League when he questioned the validity of the UN-demarcated Iraq-Kuwaiti border.[9]

Ramadan spearheaded Iraq's reconciliation with Russia, India, Iran, and regional neighbors. According to Middle East analyst Amir Taheri, "Ramadan also headed a Mafia-style crime syndicate that controlled imports from France and Germany." In 2000 and 2001, Ramadan signed free trade agreements with Jordan, Egypt, and Syria, thus eroding US attempts to isolate Iraq.

In October 2002, four months before the United States invaded Iraq, Ramadan suggested US President George W. Bush and Saddam Hussein settle their differences in a duel.[10] He reasoned this would not only serve as an alternative to a war that was certain to damage Iraq's infrastructure but would also reduce the suffering of both the Iraqi and American people. Ramadan's offer included the possibility that a group of US officials would face off with a group of Iraqi officials of same or similar rank (president vs. president, vice president vs. vice president, etc.). Ramadan proposed that the duel be held in a neutral land, with each party using the same weapons, and with UN Secretary-General Kofi Annan presiding as the supervisor. On behalf of President Bush, White House Press Secretary Ari Fleischer declined the offer.[11]

As US threats mounted, Ramadan called on Muslims to become "human bombs." He failed to negotiate a way out of the impasse in February 2003, via Syria and Turkey. On March 20, 2003, the Americans and British invaded Iraq. Two days later Ramadan's career literally crumbled around him when US missiles destroyed his villa. That same day he damned Kofi Annan as a "colonialist high commissioner" pushing the despot oppressors in Washington and London towards eliminating Iraq. He predicted the US would "suffer the biggest losses of human life in their history."[12]

I had the opportunity to work with a journalist during my time in Iraq named Richard Engel. He was a reporter with NBC News and had written a book titled *A Fist in the Hornet's Nest*. In his book, he shared an encounter with Ramadan in late March 2003. Ramadan was holding a press briefing. When Engel arrived, Ramadan was bragging that the Iraqi forces had captured several American soldiers. He went on to say that Iraqi television would broadcast their pictures later that day. He also made what Engel believed the first direct call from a senior Iraqi official for a global jihad against America. Ramadan stated, "Every Arab and Muslim around the world should be a bullet directed at the chest of the enemy until the aggressors leave the lands of the Arabs and Islam." Ramadan was calling for a holy war along the lines of what Osama bin Laden supported.[13]

After the fall of Baghdad, Ramadan was captured on August 19, 2003, in Mosul, by fighters of the Patriotic Union of Kurdistan (PUK) and handed over to US forces.[14]

ARRAIGNMENT

Taha Yassin Ramadan was escorted into the courtroom by the imposing guards. They removed the handcuffs from his wrists in the outer room prior to entering the courtroom. After Ramadan was escorted to his seat, the guards returned to their sentry positions on either side of the door that led into the courtroom.

Ramadan wore a brown suit, white shirt, and dark shoes. He was short in stature, balding, and his black-and-gray hair was cut extremely short. He had a black-and-gray mustache. His eyebrows were very dark, and he had dark circles under his eyes.

His arraignment in front of Judge Ra'id was again a brief one, lasting a little more than ten minutes. The charges against him were read aloud. Ramadan was calm and composed. The proceedings followed the same pattern of events as the previous ones, with all conversations and questions and answers being written in longhand by the court clerks. All the charges against Ramadan were recorded by the court clerk, then stamped and signed by the judge. The

Taha Yassin Ramadan responds to a question from the judge. (Photo by Combat Camera)

defendant signed the documents, and they were returned to the clerk. To complete the process, the security guards came and assisted him up from the chair and escorted him out of the courtroom.

TRANSCRIPT OF TAHA YASSIN RAMADAN DIALOGUE WITH JUDGE RA'ID

JUDGE: What is your full name?
TAHA: Taha Yassin Ramadan al-Hasan.
JUDGE: What is your date of birth?

TAHA: 1938.

JUDGE: What occupations did you have, the positions you occupied?

TAHA: I was Minister of Housing and then I was First Deputy to the Prime Minister. In addition, I was also the Industrial Minister.

JUDGE: What year was that?

TAHA: In 1979, and I was vice president in 1991.

JUDGE: Until when?

TAHA: 2003.

JUDGE: Accused was a Deputy Prime Minister and Vice President and a regional Ba'ath Party leader; what year?

TAHA: I became a vice president in 1991, and that was in April approximately.

JUDGE: Were you a popular community commander?

TAHA: Yes, in 1988.

JUDGE: Where are you living?

TAHA: Currently?

JUDGE: Yes.

TAHA: Baghdad, Al Yarmuk.

JUDGE: Is that an apartment?

TAHA: No, it is my house.

JUDGE (TO THE COURT REPORTER): "Baghdad, Al Yarmuk neighborhood."

TAHA: I have another house on Zeitoun Street where I have my family.

JUDGE: What is your mother's name?

TAHA: Fatma Ahmad Al Jabouri.

JUDGE: Mr. Taha, today we are only discussing what you are accused of, and we'll list all your guarantees and rights. Then we can listen to your comments. What was presented to us is that you are accused of the killing of Iraqi people in the provinces of Najaf and Babel in 1991. As far as the guarantees, the court will state what you are entitled to within the Iraqi legal system. You have the right to retain a lawyer to defend you. If you are not able to retain a lawyer one will be appointed by the court. You have the right to be silent, and that will not be held against you. You have the right to discuss the evidence and the witness statements as they relate to section 406/1 of the penalty codes. Do you have a lawyer to represent you?

TAHA: First I must get in touch with my family. I have been in here for ten months and they will find me a lawyer. I'd like to ask if I can have more than one lawyer?

JUDGE: Yes, you can if you have someone to represent you.

TAHA: Can they be Iraqis or Arabs?

JUDGE: Iraqis, yes, but Arabs must be agreed upon with the legal cooperation with our government.

TAHA: What about Egypt?

JUDGE: If there is a legal agreement with them.

JUDGE: (to the court clerk): The court has recited the accusation to the defendant and the legal section to which it applies. And the court informed the accused of his rights and guarantees. In addition, the accused asked permission to get in touch with his relatives for the purpose of having a lawyer to defend him and to be present with him in the interrogation sessions, and for that and to guarantee the rights of the defendant. Therefore, the court is adjourned in order to allow the defendant to retain a lawyer and to get in touch with his relatives for the purpose of having a lawyer.

(Paper documents signed by the judge and given to the defendant to read and sign.)

JUDGE: Here are your documents for you to sign.

(Documents signed by the defendant and the court adjourned.)

19
TARIQ AZIZ

"EIGHT OF SPADES" (#43 ON IRAQ'S MOST-WANTED LIST)

Tariq Aziz was born on April 28, 1936, in the Assyrian Christian town of Tel Keppe in Northern Iraq. He was an Arab nationalist, ethnic Assyrian, and a member of the Chaldean Catholic Church. He was baptized Manuel Christo. He changed his Assyrian Christian name to a more Arabic-sounding one to gain acceptance among the Arab and Muslim majority; he took the name Tariq Aziz.

His association with Saddam began in the 1950s when both were activists for the then-banned Arab Socialist Ba'ath Party. Tariq studied English literature at Baghdad University, and he obtained a Master of Arts degree in English. He started his professional life as a schoolteacher. In the 1960s, he joined and then left the Ba'ath Party. He rejoined the party in 1968.[1]

In 1969, Aziz was appointed an editor of the Ba'ath newspaper, *Al-Thawra*. In November 1974, he became Minister of Information. He proved himself an ally of Saddam, penning helpful editorials in support of Saddam's policies. When Tariq Aziz's son was born a few years later, he paid his mentor the ultimate tribute by naming the child Saddam.[2]

He began to rise through the ranks of Iraqi politics after the Ba'ath Party came into power in 1968. Outside of his own minority Sunni sect, Saddam trusted only a certain number of Iraqi Christians (excluding Assyrian nationalists) in his government. As a result, Aziz became close to Saddam who rapidly promoted him, especially after the Ba'ath Party purged prominent Shi'as in the mid-1970s. He served as a member of the Regional Command, the Ba'ath Party's highest governing organization, from 1974 to 1977, and in 1977 became a member of Hussein's Revolutionary Command Council. In 1979, Aziz became Deputy Prime Minister of Iraq. He worked as a diplomat to promote Iraq's policies to the world.

In early April 1980, Dawa Party members who were Iranian supporters tried to assassinate senior Iraqi officials, including Aziz. On April 1, a grenade was thrown at Aziz at a public gathering in central Baghdad. He was only slightly wounded. A few days later a second attempt occurred where there was an unknown number of dead and wounded.[3]

In 1981, Iraqi officials affirmed their willingness to accept a negotiated settlement that was satisfactory to the Palestinians. In August 1982, in an interview with US congressman Stephen Solarz, Saddam went even further, stating that a condition of security for Israel was necessary for a resolution of the Arab-Israeli conflict. This unprecedented statement was followed by a declaration by Aziz, the foreign minister, that Iraq "was not opposed to a peaceful settlement of the problem, and therefore negotiations with Israel."[4]

In April 1983, during a meeting of the CIA's station chiefs in the Middle East, a bombing of the American embassy and the US Marine compound in Beirut wiped out most of the CIA's best Middle East experts. Within weeks, satellite intercepts of telephone conversations confirmed American suspicions. The terrorist responsible for the bombing had been guided by Tehran.

Washington thereafter began to build bridges with Baghdad. The US moved quickly, and the following month Secretary of State George Shultz met secretly with Aziz during a trip to Paris. Shultz and Aziz both saw the logic of pooling resources in the fight against the ayatollahs. The US was still wary of normalizing relations with Saddam as long as he harbored Abu Nidal. The previous year Abu Nidal had masterminded the attempted assassination of Shlomo Argov, the Israeli ambassador to London. Shultz insisted that Saddam must first get rid of Abu Nidal. The Iraqi leader duly obliged but in a bizarre way. Soon after the Schultz–Aziz meeting, the government-owned media solemnly announced that Abu Nidal had died of a heart attack. A month later, just as the report was starting to acquire credence in the international intelligence community, Libya's Colonel Gaddafi announced that Abu Nidal was alive and living in Tripoli, thereby undermining Saddam's rather disingenuous attempt to wash his hands of the Abu Nidal issue.[5]

In November 1984, Saddam sent Aziz to Washington, DC. The latter delivered a message from Saddam to President Ronald Reagan and other leading members of the administration that the US might be able to quietly maintain a CIA office in Baghdad.[6] During the 1980s, Saddam required all new ambassadors to present their credentials not to Saddam but to Aziz at the Presidential Palace. This practice continued into the 1990s.[7]

In early July 1990, Kuwait and the United Arab Emirates promised to engage in over-producing oil. On July 16, Aziz sent a letter to the Arab League reiterating the accusation that the two countries were involved in an American-inspired scheme to lower oil prices. The letter also said that Kuwait had illegally extracted oil from the Rumaila oil field, which lay under both sides of the Iraq-Kuwait border. To make amends for these acts and to help the Iraqi economy recover from its defense of Arab homelands against Iran, Aziz demanded that Kuwait raise oil prices; cease the "theft" of oil from the Rumaila field and pay Iraq $2.4 billion to compensate for the "stolen" barrels; begin a moratorium on Iraq's wartime loans; and create a "Marshall Plan" to reconstruct Iraq.[8]

The next day, July 17, Saddam made these demands public in a speech broadcast on Iraqi television. "If words fail," he concluded, "we will have no choice but to resort to effective action."[9]

The encounters between the Kuwaiti and Iraqi delegations were electric. A day before a summit in Iraq, Saddam announced the annexation of Kuwait as its nineteenth province. In one encounter, Foreign Minister Aziz confronted the Kuwaiti prime minister and told him he had "the tapes." Apparently, these were personal videotapes that Iraqi soldiers had collected at the prime minister's private quarters in Kuwait. Prime Minister Sheikh Saad al-Sabah was known to have exotic tastes, and news of the tapes made him apoplectic.[10] Saad al-Sabah responded by making a reference to the fact that Aziz was a Christian, a remark intended as a slur. Aziz heaved an ashtray at him. The atmosphere was too much for Kuwait's foreign minister, who fainted.[11]

A last-ditch effort to resolve the conflict by diplomacy was undertaken by the US at the end of November 1990. Having secured UN approval for military action, President Bush offered to send James Baker, his secretary of state, to Baghdad and in turn to receive Aziz in Washington, DC. Saddam mistook Washington's offer of talks as a sign of weakness. He was wrong.[12]

On January 9, 1991, Secretary Baker met with Aziz for nearly seven hours in Geneva. Baker presented a three-page letter from President Bush to Saddam in which the US president warned, "There can be no reward for aggression. Nor will there be any negotiation. A principle cannot be compromised." Aziz refused to accept the message and repeated Baghdad's intransigent stand. "Perhaps," Aziz told Baker, "it will just come down to fate."[13] Baker also stated at this meeting, and cautioned Aziz, that a chemical attack could cause the allies to amend their war aims and put the Ba'athist regime's existence at risk.[14] Aziz returned to Baghdad with the news.

The allied attack was launched on January 16, 1991, and subjected Iraq to one of the most intensive aerial bombardments known to the modern world.[15] After a thirty-eight-day air campaign, President Bush's patience had run out. Soviet President Mikhail Gorbachev, however, was still hoping to broker a last-minute ceasefire with Aziz, using a more generous peace proposal.[16]

On February 17 and 18, with the land invasion just days away, Saddam again sent Aziz on a mission. This time he went to Moscow. Saddam instructed him to accept any plan that would stop allied forces from waging war.[17] On February 19, after lengthy meetings with Aziz, Soviet President Mikhail Gorbachev announced a revised plan that took into consideration all American objections to previous Soviet's suggestions. It called for an unconditional Iraqi withdrawal from Kuwait based on United Nations Security Council (UNSC) Resolution 660, with a ceasefire to begin immediately.[18]

Aziz continued to suggest that six weeks might be required to dismantle the Iraqi occupation. He said that two divisions initially entered Kuwait; several hundred thousand entered the emirate since. Aziz promised that Saddam was ready to leave Kuwait unconditionally, but more time was needed to work out the details.[19]

Aziz returned to Iraq and Saddam accepted the plan on February 21. Saddam asked for one week to pull out of Kuwait City. President Bush demanded that all Iraqi forces withdraw by noon on February 23 or face a ground war.[20] Aziz did his best to save the plan, but Saddam was gripped by anger and despair and determined to preserve the appearance of doing something. So, Saddam set the Kuwaiti oil fields on fire and began an oil spill of unprecedented size.[21]

The ground war commenced on February 24.[22] On March 2, Aziz accepted all United Nations resolutions, and on March 5, the Revolutionary Command Council formally rescinded all laws on Kuwait's annexation and agreed to pay reparations and return all Kuwaiti property.

In April, an emergency committee was set up under Aziz to decide how best to defy the UN, with orders from Saddam to save as much of Iraq's weapons of mass destruction capability as possible.[23] Saddam was determined not to declare any aspect of his nuclear weapons program, code-named PC-3, which he had successfully concealed from inspectors working for the International

Atomic Energy Agency (IAEA) for more than a decade.[24] Aziz did his best, but Baghdad was put on notice. Saddam formed another committee, this time controlled by his second son, Qusay.[25]

In October 2000, the junior minister for Foreign Affairs from Britain, Peter Hain, set up a secret war-avoidance team to carry messages back and forth between himself and Aziz. After initial cooperation, Aziz rebuffed the delegations.[26]

On February 14, 2003, Aziz reportedly had an audience with Pope John Paul II and other officials in Vatican City. According to a Vatican statement, Aziz communicated "the wish of the Iraqi government to cooperate with the international community, notably on disarmament." The same statement said that the Pope "insisted on the necessity for Iraq to faithfully respect and give concrete commitments to resolutions of the United Nations Security Council, which is the guarantor of international law."[27]

On March 19, 2003, reports surfaced from Iraq that Aziz had been shot dead while trying to enter the Kurdish part of the country. The rumor was quashed rather quickly when Aziz held a press conference assuring the world that he was still alive and well.[28]

In early April, with US forces fast approaching Baghdad, Iraqis would soon be liberated from Saddam's rule. Men like Aziz who were very close to the former dictator and had been one of his most effective apologists since the mid-1970s were left to make their own arrangements for escape. They were given no information about Saddam's intentions. Aziz and several other prominent former Ba'athists found that they had no alternative other than to surrender.[29]

Tariq Aziz voluntarily surrendered to American forces on April 24, 2003, after negotiations had been mediated by his son. His chief concern at the time was for the welfare of his family. At the time of his surrender, Aziz was ranked number forty-three out of fifty-five on the American list of most-wanted Iraqis, despite a belief that "he probably would not know answers to questions like where weapons of mass destruction might have been hidden and where Saddam Hussein might be."[30]

The allies were still interested when Aziz negotiated his surrender. They believed that he would be able to shed light on Saddam's whereabouts, but they were disappointed because Aziz, although he was more than happy to talk, indeed knew little about what Saddam had been up to or where he might be hiding. Paranoia was deeply entrenched in Saddam's regime. Even senior officials such as Aziz were kept in the dark about Saddam's innermost secrets.[31]

Aziz was forthcoming about Saddam's leadership. Even the most capable

Tariq Aziz listening to Judge Ra'id. (Photo by Combat Camera)

subordinates could challenge the official wisdom at their peril. Aziz stated, "It was not allowed to raise your hand above anyone around you; it was

Tariq Aziz disputes the charges against him. (Photo by Combat Camera)

dangerous." Aziz did share with his interrogators, "If a military leader disappeared, we did not know how it happened, but he was probably dealt with by security service."[32] Aziz went on to state, "Saddam thought they would not fight a ground war, because it would be too costly to the Americans. He was overconfident."[33]

ARRAIGNMENT

The two guards escorted Tariq Aziz to his chair, after the removal of his handcuffs before he entered the courtroom. The heavy waist chains were visible under his jacket. After the defendant was seated, the guards walked to their positions on either side of the entry door.

John Burns observed, "Mr. Aziz cut a figure of unshakable self-confidence in power, stalking the marble halls of Baghdad's palaces pulling on a cigar, boasting until the last weeks before the Americans attacked in March 2003 that he and other government leaders would be 'shadows' by the time American troops arrived in Baghdad, uncatchable. In fact, he gave himself up shortly after Hussein's government was toppled."[34]

Aziz, like many others, was a shadow of his former self. His once jet-black hair, visible for years, was now gray and thinning. His eyebrows were gray, and his full bushy mustache was gray. His dark brown eyes were accentuated by his large, black-framed glasses. He was wearing a brown suit with a white dress shirt and dark shoes. His shoulders were bowed, and he wiped his forehead and blew his nose. His hands were interlocked, and he periodically placed his right hand in his right jacket pocket.

According to Burns, "He sat through the hearing with the chain used to manacle him dangling at his wrist. Once a man who prided himself on his well-cut suits, he did not seem to notice the chain nestling against his ill-fitting, American-bought suit."[35] Under Hussein, even high-ranking civilian leaders like Aziz liked to wear olive drab military-style uniforms signifying their rank in the Ba'ath Party. But in the courtroom, stripped of any inhibiting effect the uniforms lent them, they appeared commonplace.

Aziz's arraignment in front of Judge Ra'id lasted approximately fourteen minutes. He adjusted his glasses on occasion, and his responses to the judge were accompanied by hand gestures. His discussion with Judge Ra'id was lively. He only looked at those in the jurors' box twice. The way he looked at them suggested that he knew those seated.[36]

As with other defendants, the charges against Aziz were presented to him. According to the transcript, charges included "deliberate killing of innocent Iraqis in 1979, when Hussein began his presidency with the executions of dozens of senior Ba'ath Party officials who opposed his seizure of power, and in 1991, when tens of thousands of Shi'ites in southern Iraq were killed after an abortive uprising that followed the Gulf War."

Aziz claimed that being a member of Hussein's Revolutionary Command Council should not be taken as proof that he had anything to do with decisions leading to the deaths of innocents that were made by the "leadership," meaning Mr. Hussein.[37]

"What I want to know is, are these charges personal?" Aziz asked. "Is it Tariq Aziz carrying out these killings? If I am a member of a government that makes the mistake of killing someone, then there can't justifiably be an accusation against me personally. Where there is a crime committed by the leadership, the moral responsibility rests there, and there shouldn't be a personal case just because somebody belongs to the leadership." He added, "I never killed anybody by the acts of my own hand."

Aziz, Iraq's former Deputy Prime Minister, who headed crucial diplomatic negotiations, suggested in court that he might seek to save himself at trial by arguing that all blame should be shifted to Hussein, or at least to a small group around him.[38] The judge cut off Aziz, telling him brusquely that he would proceed with an investigation of the charges. Aziz slumped back in his chair. According to the transcript, Aziz was told, like most of the defendants, that his case would be considered under Article 406 of the Iraqi criminal code. The code provided the death penalty for premeditated killing. Legal executions in

Iraq, under Hussein, were usually carried out by hanging or firing squad in cases involving military offices or some high-ranking officials.[39]

Once the charges against him were read, recorded by the court clerk, and signed by the judge, the clerk delivered the papers to Aziz. He quickly reviewed, signed, and returned them to the clerk. Once the documents had been handed back to the clerk, the security guards approached the defendant and one on either arm turned him around and escorted him out the door and into the waiting room with the other HVDs.

TRANSCRIPT OF TARIQ AZIZ DIALOGUE WITH JUDGE RA'ID

JUDGE: Please sit down. Good day.

AZIZ: Good day.

JUDGE: State your full name, year of birth, and positions held.

AZIZ: Tariq Aziz Issa. Born 1936. Positions held: 1969, I was editor-in-chief for the *Al-Thawra* newspaper. 1974, I was Minister of Education and Press Secretary. 1977, I was a member of the Thawra Council. 1979, I was the vice prime minister. 1983, I was still the vice prime minister and Secretary of State. I was in that position until 1991 and I stayed after that as the vice prime minister until 2002 and was no longer Secretary of State.

JUDGE: What positions did you hold in the Ba'ath Party?

AZIZ: I was a member of the national and local Ba'ath parties.

JUDGE: What is your place of residence?

AZIZ: Baghdad, al-Jadriyah.

JUDGE: Mother's name?

AZIZ: Zakia Yacoub.

JUDGE: This is the first session of many related to the investigations of the crimes of which you are accused. In the first session, usually we tell the suspect what crimes he is accused of and then after this, we discuss the legal process. Then we will read you your rights. In relation to your position, you are accused of committing mass murder in 1979 against Iraqi civilians.

AZIZ: What? 1979?

JUDGE: Yes, 1979. Your second charge is the participation in the intentional killing of Iraqi citizens between 1991 and 1997. The legal article according to the Iraqi constitution that is related to the charges made against you is 406/1/A from the laws of punishment. This is according to the crimes of which you are accused based on the documents we have been given as of today. The court would like to clarify what your rights and guarantees are.

AZIZ: Can I comment on that?

JUDGE: As soon as I finish you have the right to comment on what you want. As a suspect in the Iraqi court, you have rights that you need to be made aware. You have the right to an attorney to defend you. If you cannot afford an attorney, the court will appoint one and will pay all expenses.

AZIZ: Allow me one question.

JUDGE: Let me finish and you can ask your question. You have the right to stay silent and not answer any question and this will not be held against you. You have the right to question any witness and evidence presented to the court. At the present time, do you have an attorney to represent you, or do you need to contact your family?

AZIZ: At the present time I do not have an attorney, but I need to ask you since you stated it is my right, I just want to make sure if I must hire any Arab attorney or whether I can hire a foreign attorney who would be willing to defend me.

JUDGE: You can hire an attorney if the attorney is from a country with which we have a judiciary reciprocation between us, such as Jordan.

AZIZ: I have Jordanian lawyers, Lebanese lawyers, French, and even American lawyers.

JUDGE: There is no problem if there are judicial agreements between the countries.

AZIZ: I don't know if you have agreements with these countries or not. We are accused of political crimes.

JUDGE: No, right now it has nothing to do with politics; it is criminal. I told you if you paid attention to what I said that you are accused in front of me with criminal, not political, crimes.

AZIZ: You are talking about 1979 and 1991? Allow me to ask you a question—accusations for which I am accused: am I accused personally for these crimes or because I am a member of the Ba'ath Party, or because I am a member of the cabinet?

JUDGE: For my answer to be completely legal this answer will be part of the investigation and then you just must tell me that you have an attorney that represents you and, as I stated, bring him here and you will get your answers. This is part of the investigation, not a court session.

AZIZ: Even without an attorney, I am an educated man.

JUDGE: Inshallah.

AZIZ: Someone is accusing me of killing people in 1979 and 1991. Is he saying that I personally killed these people, that Tariq Aziz killed so and so, or just because I am a member of the ruling party and part of the government that I am being accused? According to political life, it is a group responsibility when there is a ruling government. To give an example, if the interior cabinet, that branch of the government committed a crime that does not mean that everyone in the government committed the crime. The secretary in charge of that cabinet, if he does not resign from his position, is considered responsible for ethical reasons that do not mean he committed the crime himself. When you say I am accused as a criminal, as a judge you know that means that you committed the crime yourself or you were part of the crime. You kill someone, you assassinate someone. That is criminal. Not just for being a member of the government.

JUDGE: You were accused of killing several people in 1979.

AZIZ: Personally, I killed these people, you are saying? Personally, I did not kill anyone.

JUDGE: The answer to that should be made with your attorney present.

AZIZ: This is an accusation made against Tariq Aziz? That person who is making the accusation does not know the truth.

JUDGE: Do you have a specific attorney you wish to appoint?

AZIZ: Yes, I have a specific attorney.

JUDGE: Do you want to call your family?

AZIZ: Yes, I want to call my family because I don't know where my attorneys are. Some are in Iraq; some are outside of Iraq. Most of the famous attorneys in Iraq are my friends.

JUDGE: Would you like to call your family?

AZIZ: I have attorneys from western countries and Europe. I can defend myself too if these are the only two crimes of which I am accused.

JUDGE: These are the only two crimes we have presented in front of us as of now.

AZIZ: Are there any other things?

JUDGE: No, these are the only things we have in front of us now.

AZIZ: If these are the only two, I need an attorney for technicalities, but I can defend myself. I am a politician; I know the laws and the justice system.

JUDGE (TO THE COURT REPORTER): The court has addressed the accused for the crimes set forth and informed him of the judicial articles as applicable by law. The court has also addressed the personal rights of the accused and asked to give him the means to contact his family to obtain an attorney to be with him during the investigative process and protect him and his rights. To allow the accused time to obtain legal representation, this investigation will be postponed until such is obtained.

JUDGE: Mr. Tariq, these rights that were just reviewed with you, we need you to sign an acknowledgment of receiving these charges on this document.

AZIZ: Is this part of the Iraqi law?

JUDGE: Yes, it is part of the Iraqi law revised.

AZIZ: Do you mind reading it for me?

JUDGE: I do not have a copy of the revised law. Here is the article: Punishment is the death penalty for anyone who committed the following crimes: Murder according to these conditions as apply to you if it was premeditated.

AZIZ: Is this the article?

JUDGE: Yes, this is the article. We just need your signature on the affidavit.

AZIZ: Thank you.

JUDGE: Thank you very much. Go in peace.

20

WATBAN IBRAHIM HASAN AL-TIKRITI

"FIVE OF SPADES" (#37 ON IRAQ'S MOST-WANTED LIST)

Watban Ibrahim Hasan al-Tikriti was born in Tikrit, Iraq, in 1952. Like several other HVDs, not much is known about Watban's early life. He was a half-brother of Saddam Hussein; they shared the same mother. Saddam kept on good terms with his half-brothers, even though he clearly had a difficult relationship with them during his childhood.[1]

In 1963, during the early shaping of the Ba'ath Party, Saddam had many family members, including Watban, experience the Palace of the End and passed through training camps, learning skills such as firing machine guns and abducting opponents.[2] The Palace of the End was located at Qasr al-Nihayah, so called because it was the site where the monarchy had been wiped out in 1958. One of the notorious practitioners of the torturer's art was Nadhim Kazzar, who later became Saddam's head of national security. Kazzar's reputation for sadism stood out.[3]

In 1978, everything was running smoothly under Saddam. He named Watban as governor of the expanded province of Tikrit, which was renamed

Salaheddine in honor of the Muslim warrior Saladin.⁴ A few years later, however, family feuds were beginning to surface between the Ibrahims and the
al-Tikrits. In early 1982, Saddam was trying to normalize and rehabilitate these
family issues. As a result, he gave Watban a high-ranking job in the regime and
made him head of State of Internal Security.

Watban was linked by his position as head of State of Internal Security to
the fate of more than 180,000 Kurds who went missing in the 1980s Anfal campaign. All those within Saddam's inner circle were said to have been involved
when the ethnic cleansing operations against the Kurds were launched.

Watban also was reportedly involved in the brutal repression of the uprising
that followed the Gulf War in 1991. This included mass executions, torture, and
destruction, particularly in the Baghdad suburbs of Thawra, Shu'la, Hurriya'
Bayya', the village of Yousiffiya, and the nearby districts of Mahmoudiya.
Some of those executions were reportedly videotaped, with copies kept at the
ministry.

Watban was allegedly responsible for repression of religious and ethnic
minorities including forced deportation, disappearances, and murder committed by troops under his control. He reportedly permitted and encouraged the
systematic use of torture, including rape and the threat of rape, by his troops.⁵
Firsthand accounts exist of his personal lethally brutal behavior towards at least
one person.

Family feuds began to be more commonplace. After several open attacks
on Watban in the newspaper, *Babel*, in May 1995, he was forced to resign as
Minister of Interior. One evening, his nephew, Uday (Saddam's son) and
Watban had an argument during one of Uday's many drunken fits. Uday shot
Watban nine times and seriously wounded him in the leg. At the same time,
three of Watban's companions were killed. Fearing for his life, Watban claimed
the shooting was an accident. Later, Watban's leg had to be amputated.⁶

In 1996, there was an assassination attempt on Uday. There was no short-
age of suspects, and in the next few days, some 2,000 people were questioned,
including Watban. He was still recovering from the injuries he sustained when
Uday shot him. The assassination attempt was later attributed to a group that
called itself al-Nahda (the Awakening). A few days after the shooting, Saddam
summoned his family for an emergency summit around Uday's bed. Present
were his son Qusay, half-brothers Watban and Sabawi, and Chemical Ali.
Saddam delivered a scathing denunciation of their general conduct. All those
present were given a dressing-down for being either incompetent or corrupt.⁷

After the Gulf War in 1992, Saddam was aware of the danger of his position. He decided to bridge the gap between the Special Republican Guard,

whose responsibility it was to protect him, and his Special Security detail. Together they became the Organization of Special Security (OSS). In addition, with the expanded OSS he imposed greater family control on various elements of the army and security. Watban was made Minister of Interior. Despite his family ties to Saddam, Watban Ibrahim was not thought to be fully trusted by Saddam Hussein. Nevertheless, he served afterward as presidential advisor.[8]

Within days of the fall of Baghdad, US forces detained Watban while he was trying to flee Iraq to the country of Syria.

ARRAIGNMENT

Watban entered the room with the two guards assigned to escort him and direct him to his chair. The guards were tasked with removing the defendant's handcuffs in the outer room before they escorted him into the courtroom. His jacket did not hide the chains around the waist that held the handcuffs. Once the defendant was seated, the guards assumed their positions at the entry of the room. Watban's brown suit jacket had visible tags that were sewn on the left arm. He wore a white shirt and dark shoes. He had jet black hair and eyebrows and a bushy dark brown mustache. The shadow of a dark brown beard was just beginning to show. His arraignment in front of Judge Ra'id lasted almost ten minutes. He would periodically run his fingers through his hair as though he were attempting to fix it. Other times his hands were interlocked, resting at his waist. He appeared composed during the entire process. He listened as the charges against him were read aloud and answered all the questions he was asked by the judge. The court clerks were diligently recording all the testimony, questions, and answers between the judge and Watban. The defendant at times gazed at the occupants of the jurors' box.

Watban signed the required documents presented to him after all charges were read and recorded. Without hesitation, the security guards came and assisted him up from the chair and escorted him out of the courtroom.

TRANSCRIPT OF WATBAN IBRAHIM HASAN AL-TIKRITI DIALOGUE WITH JUDGE RA'ID

(Watban enters the courtroom.)

JUDGE: Please have a seat.

JUDGE: Please state your full name.

WATBAN: Watban Ibrahim al-Hasan.

JUDGE: Year of birth?

WATBAN: 1952.

JUDGE: Mr. Watban, when did you become the Minister of Interior?

Watban Ibrahim Hasan al-Tikriti listens to charges against him. (Photo by Combat Camera)

WATBAN: At the end of 1991 in November.

JUDGE: How long were you in this position?

WATBAN: Until May of 1995.

JUDGE: Place of residence?

WATBAN: Baghdad. I have two families; I was living with my second family in al-Jadriyah.

JUDGE: Mother's name?

WATBAN: Subha Tulfah.

JUDGE (TO THE COURT REPORTER): After I introduce myself as the judge in charge of the investigation . . .

JUDGE (TO WATBAN): Mr. Watban, you are in front of the Iraqi judicial system to investigate with you the crimes of which you are accused. First, the court is going to explain the accusations. Second, the articles that pertain to these accusations and then your rights and guarantees. Then we will listen to any comments you have. First, the crimes you are accused of are you were part of the torture that was performed on Iraqi citizens during your tenure as Minister of Interior; you gave the orders for the killing of Iraqi businessmen while in your post as interior minister. The first crime goes under article number 333 of the punishment codes. The second crime goes under article 406/1/Y of the punishment codes. Your rights and guarantees will be explained to you as an accused in front of the Iraqi judicial system. You have the right to appoint an attorney. If you cannot afford an attorney, one will be appointed for you and the court will pay the fee. You have the right to be silent and it will not be held against you, and you have the right to question the witnesses and evidence. These are the crimes you are accused of, the articles they are under, and your rights and guarantees. Do you have an attorney to represent you?

WATBAN: Yes, I do. His name is Khudo al-Ouaadi and he is known as Khudo al-Ouaadi. I don't know his mother's name or father's name.

JUDGE: Yes. We will call the attorney union that he belongs to and get his information. I am sure they know him there.

WATBAN: This is my first choice in an attorney. In case we cannot reach him, my second choice is Talal Fundar al-Faisal.

JUDGE (TO THE COURT REPORTER): The court has addressed the defendant and reviewed the crimes he is accused of and the articles the crimes lay under and explained to him his rights and guarantees. Legally he has asked to appoint attorney Khudo al-Ouaadi or Talal Fundar al-Faisal.

JUDGE (TO WATBAN): If we try to contact them both and are unable to reach them, do you want us to appoint you an attorney?

WATBAN: No. Inform me if you cannot reach them and I will contact someone.

JUDGE (TO THE COURT REPORTER): Continuing with what I said last; if we cannot get hold of his attorneys, we will inform the defendant and he will make another selection. To guarantee the defendant's rights to an attorney, we will postpone this session until his attorney is present for further investigative sessions.

JUDGE (TO WATBAN): I am stamping the document stating all we have discussed. We need you to sign under your name.

(Watban signs.)

JUDGE: Thank you

WATBAN: Thank you.

(Watban exits courtroom.)

21
NINAWA–A KILLING FIELD

ON SEPTEMBER 15, 2004, A FEW MONTHS FOLLOWING THE arraignment of Saddam Hussein and the HVDs, I was in my office at the Presidential Palace in the Green Zone and had finished a long overdue report. It was time for dinner, and I left my office and headed to the dining facility located on the first floor.

The dining area served hundreds of uniformed and non-uniformed personnel three meals daily, seven days a week. State Department officials would get their meals here, too. The facility was managed and staffed by KBR (Kellogg, Brown, and Root), who secured the contract. They did a fantastic job. Although the menu seemed repetitive week after week, the quality of the food was always very good. Whenever trying to serve this large a number of personnel, there were always lines while waiting to select an entrée, but everything moved quickly, and the staff was always friendly. Most of the time I was joined at dinner by other members of my team: aide 2nd Lt. Brian Melanephy, executive assistant Maj. Mark Martin, and/or personal security detail (PSD) Sgt. Jason "Scotty" Scott. This evening it was the entire team.

Normally I would lead the conversation and would start by asking about their families—for instance, did they receive any mail from them today? From this point, table talk would fill the evening meal. Upon finishing dinner, we headed back to my office for my evening ritual of logging on to three computers:

the NIPR (NIPRNet: Non-secure Internet Protocol Router Network), SIPR (SIPRNet: Secret Internet Protocol Router network); and CENTRIX (CENTCOM Regional Intelligence exchange network (multi-national/coalition accessible)). The NIPR was a basic computer while the other two handled secured message traffic. CENTRIX was the only way to communicate with our coalition partners. At the time, there were thirty-five nations supporting the military operation.

On the way to the office I ran into Greg Kehoe, whom I first met at Saddam's court arraignment a couple of months earlier. He had been in attendance as an observer of the event. Kehoe headed up the US Army Corps of Engineers and the Defense Department's Joint POW/MIA Accounting Command (JPAC) exhumation, morgue, and forensics, under contract from the Regime Crimes Liaison Office.

"I just left your office," he said, "and thought you might be having dinner. How are you?"

"Fine, just another day in paradise," I replied.

"I'd like to invite you to join me on Saturday [September 17] on a trip up in Northern Iraq. I'm taking the Discovery Channel to a mass gravesite about 40 miles southwest of Mosul. Would you like to go?" Kehoe asked.

"It sounds like an all-day trip, correct?"

"Yes. We'll travel via helicopter, and it will probably be about a two-and-a-half-hour trip one way."

"Let me see what's on my schedule and if I can move a few things around. I'll get back with you in the morning."

"Great, let me know tomorrow," Kehoe replied.[1]

When I returned to my office, I checked my schedule for that day. It was another busy day but had some flexibility in it. I told Major Martin to shift things around so I could be out of Baghdad most of the day to go up north with Greg. This was a trip I really wanted to make if at all possible. I had read a lot about the many mass gravesites and wanted to see one for myself.

According to the group Archaeologists for Human Rights, more than 260 mass graves have been identified across Iraq.[2] The same group estimated the number of missing people in Iraq at 1.3 million.[3] Iraqi Foreign Minister Hoshyar Zebari told the United Nations that under Saddam Hussein, Iraq was a "murderous tyranny that lasted over 35 years." He went on to say, "Today we are unearthing thousands of victims in the horrifying testament."[4]

"Iraq's Legacy of Terror – Mass Graves," published by the US Agency for International Development (USAID), chronicles many of the unearthed grave sites. "The graves that Saddam Hussein's henchmen dug and filled with human beings are a bitter sign that mankind still has a long way to go before every person has the basic human rights promised by all our religions and cultures—the rights of life and liberty," stated Andrew Natsios, Administrator, USAID.[5]

The next morning, Friday, after the daily 06:30 General Officer/Flag Officer (GO/FO) briefing, I headed to Greg's office to inform him I could make the trip. I also asked if it might be possible to bring along Sgt. Scott. He said, "Sure, no problem."

We would always fly with two Army UH-60 Black Hawk helicopters, because I never knew when we might encounter mechanical issues necessitating a landing in the desert. Each helicopter had a .50-caliber mount near the door. Seating was always limited, but since we would be going to Northern Iraq and would be in an isolated area, I thought Sgt. Scott would be the person I would ask to accompany me as part of my security detail. Scotty came onboard as my security detail about a month after Lt. Cmdr. Kough's departure in July. Security was of extreme importance, and every flag officer had their own PSD. Some had one individual, while others had two or three providing protection depending on their rank. Of course, Kehoe had three security personnel as well.

The following morning, after breakfast and the daily GO/FO briefing, my aide took me and Sgt. Scott to Landing Zone (LZ) Washington, which was just a few blocks from the palace in the Green Zone. There we met Kehoe and others making the trip. We chatted while awaiting the arrival of two Army helicopters. Within a few minutes, both arrived. We boarded, lifted off a little after 8 a.m., and headed north. The route was usually the same, with noticeable landmarks always visible.

Most visible was Saddam's Republican Presidential Palace (the largest palace commissioned by Saddam), near the LZ and resting along the Tigris River. The palace measured some 1.7 square miles according to the United Nations. The river provided a natural boundary between the Green Zone and the Red Area (high-threat area). As we circled around, I could see the distinguishable landmark of the Crossed Swords monument, officially referred to as the Victory Arch. The arch consisted of a pair of hands holding crossed swords. The arch marks the entrance to the parade ground, which Saddam built to commemorate the Iran–Iraq War. He was often seen standing at the reviewing, waving or firing a weapon into the air. Also visible were the Monument to the Unknown Soldier, 14th of July Bridge, Convention Center, Adnan Palace, Council of Ministers Building, Al Rashid Hotel, and in the distance the Palestine and Sheraton Hotels.

As the helicopter turned and headed north over Baghdad, I could see the rooftops of several neighborhoods outside the Green Zone. There were TV satellite dishes for almost every home. Eighty percent of all Iraqis got their news from television. A majority of the homes were a desert tan color and either one or two stories tall. Palm trees were scattered around the neighborhoods. As we left the city, I could see the green sections of farming lands.

I always enjoyed my many trips outside of Baghdad via helicopter. Each one provided an opportunity to see the country of Iraq and the terrain. Sheepherders, camels, small green oases, and numerous date plantations dotted the landscape. These trips reminded me of my tour in the First Gulf War when I was deployed to the city of Dhahran in eastern Saudi Arabia. The desert terrain was very similar. My trips in Iraq covered most of the country, from Basra and Babylon in the south to Mosul in the northwest, to Ramadi in the west and to Tikrit in the northeast. The terrain always seemed the same: desert tan, whether flat or mountainous. But there were a handful of large lakes in Iraq, which certainly stood out. What was always very impressive to me was traveling over the Tigris or Euphrates Rivers, knowing that these two rivers are in the Bible as the center of early civilization some 2,500 years ago and often referred to as the "fertile crescent."

Our route took us first to the city of Taji, 30 miles northwest of Baghdad, a normal refueling stop for most of the trips I made around Iraq. We landed, refueled, and headed northwest for our two-hour flight. Our next stop would be Forward Operating Base (FOB) Jaguar. Upon making our approach to FOB Jaguar, the helicopters made a pass over the facility and headed to the landing zone. FOB Jaguar consisted of more than thirty prefabricated buildings that housed and fed Kehoe's staff who had worked on the mass grave excavation and identification project. Surrounding the compound were more than 100 CONEX boxes approximately eight feet by six feet and placed end to end that doubled as shipping containers and as the first line of defense for those inside.

Once we landed, we were greeted by staff members who escorted us to a large, air-conditioned tent where the first phase of the tour would begin. We were introduced and welcomed to FOB Jaguar by Michael "Sonny" Trimble, an award-winning archaeologist who led excavations and forensics teams across the globe. Jaguar was the primary receiving and processing facility of remains from the mass gravesite located about five miles away.

For the next hour and a half, Kehoe and Trimble would brief the group on the methods involved with exhumations and gathering evidence for the judicial process against Saddam and the HVDs. The exhumations at the Ninawa gravesite began September 1.

Because of security concerns, Kehoe said, "The team chose a mass gravesite that was remote and easy to protect." He explained that it takes four to six weeks to complete all work at a site. This site was critical to building the legal case against Saddam and Ali Hassan (Chemical Ali) since they were the individuals who gave the order to execute the people buried here as part of the 1985–1988 Anfal campaign.

Kehoe has a national and international law practice focusing on representation of individuals, corporations, and financial institutions. He was working as a lawyer in a private firm when he was asked by the US government to go to Iraq. Leading the team of lawyers and investigators, Kehoe was an advisor to the Iraqi Special Tribunal (IST) during the prosecution of Saddam Hussein. Kehoe was no stranger to this type of work. In 1995, he was the prosecutor at The Hague in the Netherlands for the war crimes committed in Bosnia. He helped convict a Bosnian general for massacring women and children.

Kehoe's team of experts in Iraq included: Dr. P. Willey, Professor of Anthropology, California State University–Chico State and in charge of operations at the morgue; Kirk Durgadin of the Joint Pacific Command Department of Defense Joint POW/MIA Accounting Command Central Identification Laboratory; Jessica Mondero, an artifact analyst; Eric J. Emery, forensic anthropologist; and Sonny Trimble, an archaeologist by training who ran the excavation site.

Kehoe said that because of limited budget and resources, his team could only excavate one mass grave at a time. This site was chosen due to the reliability of the information his team received about the location and an awareness of how critical the evidence would be to the legal process. His team planned to excavate at least ten more locations. The Ninawa site had nine trenches, each believed to contain hundreds of bodies. The team had exhumed only two bodies so far; these were women. "Only a representative sample is necessary for the judges," Kehoe explained to us. "That's why the team only removed 125 bodies [women and children] from a trench containing as many as 300." Kehoe continued, "That will be enough for the judges to conclude a fact pattern."

Kehoe, with a close-cut beard (slightly graying) and a shaved head, was wearing a black long-sleeve shirt and sunglasses hanging from a lanyard around his neck (and would don a New York Yankees baseball cap when outside). He gave a very informative PowerPoint presentation on how the remains were classified, identified, and stored. He explained, "We are confident there are many more bodies there that we haven't dug yet because we don't have the time at this point."

He explained how the bodies were exhumed from the mass grave (each placed in individual clear bags) and taken to the morgue at Jaguar. The clothes on the bodies were intact, and many still had flesh. First, the clothes were separated from body matter and sorted. The skeletons were cleaned and sorted, to determine sex and age. It is not possible to determine the gender from a skeleton of a pre-pubescent. Often, bone fragments and bullets are mixed in with clothes. On several occasions, fetal bones were found mixed in with clothes—the remains of pregnant woman mercilessly killed.

The clothes and personal belongings of everyone were photographed. The IST would then produce a book of photographs to show the area where the victims were and identify bodies by using their personal belongings, like a telltale piece of jewelry or scarf. Kehoe had used such books in Bosnia to help identify bodies exhumed there. Kehoe described the site we would shortly see as a "wadi," a bowl, not easily visible even from nearby. "It's a perfect place for executions," he said.

Trimble then discussed the mapping of the graves: "Cartographers map the position of the bodies at each layer of the depth of the grave." The result was a series of maps that lay out the exact position and location of each body before it was removed, in order to analyze how they landed there, (e.g., were they killed and then thrown in the grave or placed at the bottom of the grave and then shot, etc.). He described the process further: "The result is a series of bizarre-looking maps on posterboard-size paper that show bodies carefully drawn but without faces, contorted and wrapped around each other."

Trimble then pointed to different trenches each identified with a number. Kehoe explained details of each trench: "This is one has all women and children. We have taken more than 120 bodies out of there. This is something, in the time I've been working mass graves, I've never seen before. We have charted how the bodies were thrown into this grave at various levels. We are confident there was a bulldozer that just shoveled the bodies into the ground. You can see the teeth marks in the ground. Unlike bodies that you've seen in many mass graves, where they just look like cordwood, all lined up, that didn't happen here. These bodies were just pushed in." He reiterated, "It's been all women and children. No men. All these people were executed with small arms fire. Including pregnant women." Everyone was speechless, and the true emotional response to these comments would not really resonate with everyone until we visited the grave sites.

Kehoe estimated the killings occurred in late 1987 or early 1988, part of the first Anfal campaign. The victims were Kurdish, distinguishable by their dress and jewelry. "It's pretty clear the deceased were from the Dokan Lake area, near Suleimaniya, approximately 200 miles from the Ninawa site. ID cards on the bodies identify the victims as coming from that area. In the grave, over 100 bodies were removed—enough for a representative forensic sample—and about eighty more remains were exposed on the surface of the grave," Kehoe explained.

Kenneth Pollack, in his book *The Threatening Storm*, notes that during the 1987–1988 Anfal campaign, Iraqi Air Force helicopters sprayed scores of Kurdish villages with a combination of chemical weapons, including mustard gas, sarin, and VX. Scores of thousands of Kurds, most of them women and children, died horrible deaths. Of those who survived, many were left blind or sterile or crippled with agonizing lung damage. But most of the Kurd slaughtered in that season of mass murder were not gassed but rounded up and gunned down into mass graves. Those victims were mostly men and boys, and their bodies have been uncovered until now.[6]

Kehoe then shared, "It is my professional opinion this is a killing field. Someone used it on many occasions over time to take people up there to execute them." He went on to say, "People wonder why this takes so long. It's a very meticulous examination, and what you try to do is go through piece by piece, obviously keeping all the bodies together, trying to keep them intact as much as possible, while also preserving all this for evidentiary matters. It's a very tedious process; it's not just a matter of pulling bodies out of the ground. The women and children appear to have been taken from their villages with all their possessions. It's clear these people had all their belongings with them. You'll see pots and pans."

He showed slides, with close-up pictures of skulls, of both women and children. The clean entry wound in the skull, from point-blank range, left a neat round circle. The more ragged exit wound was a slightly larger hole with rough edges. Another slide showed a boy's skeleton and a red-and-white-striped plastic ball.

Kehoe commented. "This is a young boy, still holding onto his ball when we uncovered him. You see his little arm right here, this little ball, this little arm, this little boy . . ." Kehoe's voice trailed off. He resumed with the next slide, of a mother and baby who were found together, the mother's arm still around the infant. "The child was shot in the back of the head and the mother in the face."

Kehoe showed a slide of a woman's clothes, her headscarf, five pairs of gold earrings, and a pair of shoes. Alongside was a coin, a tube of tetracycline antibiotic cream, a matchbox, a small tin, and some decomposed paper money. "Jewelry is an important thing for us to analyze. That can be an identifying source," was all Kehoe said.

Dr. Willey, another valuable member of Kehoe's team, in charge of operations at the morgue, commented on one slide, stating "The mother's skeleton is shown laid out in anatomical order. The left hand is missing." Dr. Willey did not show emotion to the slide but maintained a calm, informative manner as he spoke. Kehoe had seen the results of brutality in Bosnia but did share with me that his experience in Bosnia did not fully prepare him for what he would experience in Iraq.

Once Kehoe finished his slide presentation, he presented a sign-in book for everyone. All visitors to the morgue or the exhumation site must sign in the logbook, to give the court a fully documented chain of custody for any evidence submitted.

I asked Kehoe why this mass grave, of all the ones in Iraq, was selected for exhumation.

Kehoe responded, "There are many places we could have chosen. The reason we selected this site was first and foremost because we felt we could move here safely. Security was a paramount concern. We can secure this location. That was a driving force. We had pretty good indications it would be a fruitful dig, which it has turned out to be. We're going to do them all over the country. But we must take these one at a time because of security. That's the way it is."

The morgue, which was one of the prefab metal buildings, had enough air conditioning to mitigate the punishing heat but not enough ventilation to eliminate the smell of decomposition. Although the bodies were sixteen or more years old, they still reeked of putrid flesh. The forensic team attributed the smell to the moisture in the ground at the wadi, which preserved much of the flesh on the bodies over the years, an effect they compared to that of a bog. I reflected back to the courtroom scene a few months earlier where Saddam, Chemical Ali, and Barzan Hasan had charges read against them for the killing of many of these individuals whose remains we were seeing.

Dr. Willey explained the procedure when remains arrived at the facility: "The remains come in a body bag with evidence tape over them. There's a sign over the evidence tape to make sure they haven't been tampered with. We take the body bags in here." He pointed toward the morgue tent that consisted of two long rows of rooms separated by a corridor. The morgue included a DNA room, a mapping room, a room where the bones were sorted and photographed, and a room where clothes were sorted and photographed. We followed him into the first room on the left.

Kirk Durgadin hunched over a pile of broken bones from which he was delicately removing dirt with a paintbrush. Clods of dirt and fragments of cloth clung to them. He had removed the clothing and placed it on a screen behind him. He then moved the remains onto another wire screen. As Durgadin worked, Willey explained, "They're photographed to make sure they're intact. The bag is opened and photographed again. Kirk then separates the remains from the clothing and cleans them up."

Dr. Willey pointed out the photographs pinned to the wall of the remains that were unearthed. I had never seen anything like this before. I looked around at the faces of those examining the images captured in these photographs; most everyone was horrified and speechless. These photographs would be submitted to the IST judges. "The youngest fetus we have was 18 to 20 fetal weeks," Willey said.

Jessica Mondero was sorting out several layers, working with a toothbrush to remove dirt from a Kurdish woman's blue dress. She stated, "In the clothing, we also found bullets and bone fragments. We find lots of items contained in the clothing." She continued, "Lots of children's clothing, medications, beads, money, change purses; all layered within the clothing. Whether they were robbed or not I can't say, but they are coming in with a lot of personal belongings still on their bodies."

In the bone room (officially called "Analysis") across the hall, Eric Emery, the forensic anthropologist, sorted a skeleton that appeared to be that of a woman. There was a black scarf still tied about the top of the bullet-pierced skull, worn tightly, the knot at the top of the neck. He laid out remains in anatomical order, looking for bones of others that were mixed in together. "We're looking for anything that doesn't fit this individual, based on size and on development," Emery said.

The other trench exhumed contained only men. About sixty bodies had been removed. "The men were tied together, blindfolded, and shot; their clothes are all torn up. They are all multiple gunshot wounds," Kehoe said. "They picked a very isolated spot. Literally, there's no place for them to run."

Once all the briefings concluded, we left the tent and walked to the landing area and loaded into the two helicopters for the five-minute flight to the gravesite (killing field). Upon landing, we offloaded the helicopters and Kehoe directed us about 1,000 yards to the excavation area, which was located in a remote desert area silted with fine sand. The wadi was dry. I was told when the river runs during the rainy season there is a ribbon of green with low shrubbery. The graves lay along the ridge, where it began sloping down to the wadi.

The site itself was flat and marked off with concertina wire, a type of barbed or razor wire that is formed in large coils and can be expanded across any area as a form of protection against individuals trying to gain access. In the distance was a Humvee with a .50 caliber gun mounted on top. Iraqi guards were positioned around the perimeter. As I looked around 360 degrees, I was glad I had brought Scotty along. If we were attacked, having an extra automatic rifle would be a plus.

The site with women and children was narrow, approximately four feet by twelve feet, and it ran on a downward slope. The bodies at the lowest point, where moisture collected, had the most flesh and hair still intact. The forty-odd uncollected bodies were visible on the surface fully clothed and piled on top of each other, in a pattern that suggested they were bulldozed into their position. As I looked closer, I could see a small skull with a single hole on its side. I was struck by the clothing wrapped around the bodies—how bright and vivid the colors—and that the clothing seemed damp. "Water comes out of that wadi and saturates most of this area," Trimble explained.

The males' site was further up the hill and dug much deeper; only thirty bodies were still visible, and they filled about half the exposed surface of the grave. Sonny Trimble oversaw the excavation site. "We want to finish this one before the rainy season," Trimble said.

On the day of our visit, clouds gathered overhead, and the atmosphere was humid in the brutal heat. Dr. Willey mentioned that sporadic rain had already begun. I knew that since my arrival in Iraq in mid-June, clouds were a rare sight, and I had not yet experienced the rainy season in Iraq.

"There's a ridge right along here and there is a really deep bowl, which means you can't see this site until you're right on top of the ridge. If you came driving in this direction due south, you wouldn't even know this place was here until you were right up on the ridge. It's the perfect killing field, as Mr. Kehoe stated earlier," Trimble said.

The men in Grave 009 were all adults, probably up to their forties in age. Shell casings were found in the grave from a machine gun, probably an AK-47. "All the men are bunched along one wall of the 13-foot by 30-foot grave," Trimble said. "They appear to have run and fallen atop each other." Their clothes—traditional Kurdish outfits—were ripped from machine gun fire. "Ninety percent of the men were blindfolded," Trimble continued. "Almost all of them were tied."

Trimble paused and then went on, "There are two groups of men in the grave. One group of men had their hands tied behind their backs; the other groups were tied together in front. This group of men was killed in the bottom of a much deeper grave dug by a backhoe, as evidenced by the teeth marks in this hard desert soil."

The approximate size of Grave 002 was fifteen feet by thirty feet according to Trimble. He went on to explain, "There were two or three more layers of bodies underneath the top, exposed layer."

"It takes about six weeks to exhume the grave, and several months to do the forensic analysis of all the bodies removed," Kehoe explained. "In the end, they hope to be able to identify bodies and return them to their families. We're try-ing to meet international standards that have been accepted by courts through-out the world. That's our benchmark. One of the reasons why we're going to stop digging now is because we have a lot of work to do back at the morgue. That takes time. We're putting a package together on each body removed that consists of pictures of bones, clothes, and the forensic report."

Kehoe paused as he gathered himself, then he continued, "We're going to present evidence that these people were systematically executed. These are not battle wounds, make no mistake about it. This was an execution. We've gone into two trenches, and there are more to dig—at least seven. How many bodies are in those seven? It's hard to say until you start digging. Iraqi officials, proba-bly Kurds, will take control of the site when the US leaves it."

In the adult male trench, there had been sixty-four bodies removed; there were thirty-two on the surface and sixty beneath, for a total of 156. "If you start to do the math on seven more trenches, the numbers get pretty staggering," Trimble said.

"If someone told us there are thousands of bodies buried up here, we wouldn't be shocked," Kehoe said. "Those were the rumors we heard when we came up here . . . that there were thousands of people buried here."

At the women's grave, Kehoe and Trimble pointed out that there were blindfolds, distinctive clothing, and personal belongings such as drinking glasses and cookware, mixed in with the bodies. "You can see very clearly the blindfold on her eyes," Trimble said, pointing at a still flesh-covered head along the edge of the grave. "I've been doing grave sites for a long time, but I've never seen anything like this, women and children executed for no apparent reason," Kehoe said.

At the male grave, the bodies wore dark-colored Kurdish-style pantaloons. "This was never touched until we got here," Trimble said. "It appears the men were shot from the top corner of the grave." He pointed out the entry and exit wounds and clothing shredded by machine gun fire. "All these guys still have blindfolds on," Trimble said, pointing at the crusty black cloths tied around the skulls and the frayed remnants of the rope that bound the men's hands.

As I stood there and viewed the site, I was amazed and aghast. Many of the skulls still had hair, even though the flesh had rotted away. The male grave was bigger and held fewer bodies, so the effect was not a pile of jumbled bodies but rather of scattered corpses captured in mid-movement.

"We found bullets that missed their mark," Trimble said, showing the line along the ground where cartridges were also found. "Once the shooting begins, people start to react and move—trying to get away—and that's when you get the odd person here or there with wounds that have a stranger trajectory . . . because they're hiding," Kehoe said.

A reporter asked whether the men were killed in the grave. Trimble, standing at the bottom of the grave, answered, "There are only two ways. Put them down here alive and shoot them, or shoot them up on the edge and throw them in. From what I see, I believe a lot of the people were already down here."

I asked Kehoe about the status for future mass gravesites throughout Iraq and he responded, "I have ten on the board right now that I'm going to move on. At each site, we'll do 125 bodies approximately. With that, we can come to a significant conclusion. Like with these women; we can conclude that this was a ritual killing."

Kehoe's objective was also to trace command responsibility to determine who ordered the killings: "I try to trace it back, to see where these people came from, to go back to the villages, and to make some determination as to when this killing took place, and then put it all together." Kehoe continued, "The orders were given, and soldiers went to take these villages and the people in them. You find the bodies and just try to connect the dots. If you have a series of orders that lay this out . . . the evidence on the ground that it took place, you just link it up together. Stuff on the ground like this doesn't take place systematically without somebody giving the command up top. That's why I'm confident this was a killing field. Someone on high had to give the order." As I listened and watched Kehoe give his presentation, his voice broke and visibly displayed his emotion on what happened at this site.

"Relatives have wanted to come to the site. It's a sensitive issue," Kehoe added somberly. "Lots of people, but it's a crime scene right now. We're going to leave all those issues to the Kurds who are preparing to exhume it. We and the British are giving them training."

Kehoe was then asked by a reporter if these sites were evidence of genocide. He responded firmly by saying, "Unlike in Bosnia, where the mass graves largely contained fighting-age men, this site contains the systematic execution of people being shot in the back of the head. You just didn't see that in Bosnia . . . two-year-old babies shot in the back of the head. I've never seen this before."

He shook his head. "Genocide is the attempt to eliminate, limit, or exterminate a religious, ethnic, national, or racial group. The Kurds are clearly a different nationality. So, could it be considered genocide? Killing, ethnic cleansing, property relocations, all of those were used to try to limit the Kurdish population. It is, fundamentally, downright murder." He continued, "Everybody said never again after the Holocaust. The world wasn't listening. That's how it happens again and again and again." Kehoe had witnessed mass killing scenes in

Bosnia, and now again in Iraq. He was truly the right person to lead this effort to ensure that those who committed these atrocities would be held accountable.

Another member of the press asked if this was more taxing than the five years he had spent excavating mass graves in Bosnia. "Sure," Kehoe said. His voice dropped to a whisper. "Sometimes you go in there, you see soldiers, and it's not to justify it, but my God, little babies, women with their little children, shot in the back of the head. Why? Because of who they were—they were Kurds? It's much different; it's more emotional because you just can't find any place to put it."

After about an hour and a half at the site, our visit came to end. We said our good-byes to Trimble and the other members of Kehoe's team. Kehoe escorted us back to the helicopters and we prepared to make our way back to Baghdad. He asked if we wanted to fly a few miles west over the ancient city of Hatra.[7] I said yes, but he informed us that we could not land due to security concerns and time restraints. The site was currently being excavated and I was excited to see it, even though it would be an aerial view. I had heard and studied a little about Hatra, and we were disappointed we couldn't land and see it up close.

Hatra, a 2,000-year-old city 68 miles southwest of Mosul, was a large, fortified city during the Parthian Empire and capital of the first Arab kingdom. Hatra is said to have withstood invasions by the Romans in AD 116 and 198 thanks to its high, thick walls reinforced by towers. The ancient trading center spanned four miles in circumference and was supported by more than 160 towers. At its heart was a series of temples with a grand temple at the center, a structure supported by columns that once rose to 100 feet.[8]

We approached and then flew over Hatra, which was visually stunning. Out in the desert was this city that had partly been excavated. Kehoe asked the pilots to make two large turns around the site. According to my research, only 10 percent of Hatra had been excavated. A scene at the beginning of the film *The Exorcist*, where the old man encounters a demon at an archaeological site, was filmed at Hatra.

In the spring of 2015, ISIS destroyed Hatra. "The destruction of Hatra marks a turning point in the appalling strategy of cultural cleansing underway in Iraq," said Irina Bokova, the director-general of UNESCO, and Abdulaziz Othman Altwaijri, director general of the Islamic Educational, Scientific and Cultural Organization (ICESCO) in a joint statement. "With this latest act of barbarism against Hatra, [the IS group] shows the contempt in which it holds the history and heritage of Arab people."[9]

As we lifted off and headed back to Baghdad, I opened the side door of the helicopter and sat back to view the landscape. With the door open it was like sitting in front of a fan blowing hot air. Within a few minutes, I was sweating through my uniform.

I reflected on my courtroom experience a few months earlier where I sat watching, observing, and hearing testimony from Saddam and Chemical Ali. The evidence obtained at this site would be processed, categorized, labeled, and used in the next phase of the legal proceedings against them. Knowing that the key charges read against both were related to the mass grave site I had just visited—being at a "killing field" and in the presence of men, women, and children who had been executed by them for no apparent reason—was a very moving experience. Conservative estimates put the number of killed during Saddam's twenty-four-year rule at 300,000. US officials had confirmed forty grave sites out of a possible 260. British Prime Minister Tony Blair told Parliament that the mass graves in Iraq were proof that Saddam's regime had to be removed. "I will not apologize for removing Saddam Hussein. I will not apologize for the conflict. I believe it was the right then, is right now, and is essential for the wider security of that region and the world," he said.[10]

I had read about mass killing fields but never thought I would see one. As I reflected on the events of the day, I wondered how this could happen without an intervention by the United Nations. I thought, how could a leader of 25 million Iraqis decide to kill so much of his population? It is one thing for him to kill men who are fighting against his reign, but to kill women and children randomly is hard to comprehend. This type of genocide has gone on for ages, not only in Iraq but also in other countries around the world. Would it continue in other areas of the world?

As the team boarded the helicopter and we departed, I knew this visit would remain with me. Every time I hear the word "Iraq," I reflect back on this memorable experience, and the visuals from this daytrip define my 2004 Iraq deployment.

POSTSCRIPT

AFTER THE ARRAIGNMENT, THE FOUNDATION WAS LAID FOR the Iraqi Special Tribunal. Saddam and his eleven cabinet members appeared before the tribunal, which consisted of a panel of judges. Charges would be read, witnesses would give testimony under oath, and the fate of the detainees would be determined by the rule of law. What follows is the final sentence each received and their status as of this writing.

SADDAM HUSSEIN

Before dawn on the morning of Saturday, December 30, 2006, Saddam was taken to the former headquarters of the Iraqi military intelligence service. As an official read aloud the death sentence, he interrupted: "Long live the people, long live jihad, and long live the nation." He added, "Down with the Persians and the Americans." The hangman arrived, and Saddam met with the Muslim cleric.[1]

Saddam's bizarre ending was illicitly captured by someone in the room using a cell phone camera. The condemned man, wearing a white shirt, black pants, and newly shined shoes, stepped to the gallows platform, his hands cuffed behind his back and his legs tied together. He appeared stone-faced, trying in his last act on earth to salvage whatever dignity he could from the day. A yellow noose was placed around his neck. Someone yelled "Moqtada! Moqtada! Moqtada!", a shout of triumph invoking Moqtada al-Sadr, the radical Shi'ite cleric who rose to great power in the wake of the American invasion.[2]

Saddam, who had never been free to witness the rise of Shi'ite power in post-Saddam Iraq, responded sarcastically, "Moqtada?"

"Go to hell!" someone shouted.[3]

"Long live Muhammad Baqir Sadr!" someone else shouted, referring to Moqtada al-Sadr's uncle, a founder of the Dawa Party.[4]

"The man is facing execution," pleaded Saddam's prosecutor, Munqith al-Faroun, who was also present. "Please don't."

Saddam dropped through the scaffold's trapdoor as more than one thousand pounds of torque snapped his neck. A few minutes later he was pronounced dead. In both its lethality and unruliness, the event was, somehow, a fitting end to 2006 in Iraq. (Two weeks later, when Saddam's half-brother was hanged, his head came off, provoking more disapproval.)[5]

ABID HAMID MAHMUD AL-TIKRITI

On October 26, 2010, Mahmud was sentenced to death by the Iraqi High Tribunal after being found guilty of organizing a crackdown against banned political parties in Iraq in the 1980s and 1990s, including assassinations and unlawful detentions.[6] He was executed by hanging on June 7, 2012, for crimes of genocide relating to the suppression of Iraqi Shi'a Muslims during the 1980s.[7]

ALI HASSAN AL-MAJID AL-TIKRITI

Ali Hassan was convicted in June 2007 and was sentenced to death for crimes of genocide against the Kurds committed in the Anfal campaign of the 1980s.[8] His appeal of his death sentence was rejected on September 4, 2007, and he was sentenced to death for the fourth time on January 17, 2010. He was hanged eight days later, on January 25, 2010.[9]

AZIZ SALEH AL-NUMAN

On March 2, 2009, al-Numan was sentenced to death. In 2011, he was transferred to Iraqi custody along with five others.[10] The sentence has yet to be carried out as of this writing.

MUHAMMAD HAMZA AL-ZUBAYDI

Al-Zubaydi, a Shi'ite Muslim, former Iraqi prime minister, and one of the top Saddam Hussein-era leaders, died Friday December 5, 2005, after being transferred to US 344th Corps Support Hospital in Baghdad. According to Lt. Col. Guy Rudisill, he began "complaining of chest pains" and it appeared he died of cardiac arrest, but an autopsy was expected before his body was transferred to his family. He was 67 years old.[11]

BARZAN IBRAHIM HASAN AL-TIKRITI

Barzan was former director of the notorious intelligence service Mukhabarat, which was believed to have tortured and murdered thousands of opponents of the regime. He was also a former ambassador to the UN in Geneva. Despite falling out of favor with Saddam Hussein, he was thought to have been a presidential advisor at the time of his capture.

During his trial, Barzan was known for his angry outbursts in court and was ejected on several occasions. Correspondents said, however, that he had learned the ways of the court well and was effectively poking holes in the prosecution. He was executed in Baghdad on January 15, 2007.[12]

SABIR ABDUL AZIZ AL-DOURI

The main surprise in the June 24, 2007, verdicts was that two defendants, both officials of Saddam Hussein's military intelligence directorate, were given life imprisonment instead of death. They were Sabir Abdul Aziz al-Douri and Farhan Mutlak al-Jubouri. Both were found guilty of involvement in the use of chemical weapons, including mustard and sarin gas. At the trial, prosecutors produced documents that showed that Mr. Douri conducted an inquiry for Mr. Hussein on the likely effectiveness of the chemical attacks and recommended targets and timings. He was given life imprisonment instead of a death sentence.[13]

SULTAN HASHIM AHMAD AL-TAI

Sultan Hashim Ahmad al-Tai, the general who commanded Iraq's First Army Corps during the attacks on the Kurds in 1988 and later served as Defense Minister during the American-led invasion of 2003, received three death sentences. Although Iraqi military officers have traditionally claimed the right to face a firing squad when sentenced to death, the court ordered him to be hanged.[14]

On June 24, 2007, Ahmad was sentenced to death by hanging for war crimes and crimes against humanity. However, his execution was not carried out because of public disapproval from Iraq's president Jalal Talabani. In May 2018, Iraq's Parliament speaker, Salim al-Jabouri, requested a pardon for Sultan al-Tai alleging medical reasons. He then was transferred from the prison in Nasiriyah to a prison in Baghdad. He died of a heart attack on July 19, 2020, at the Nasiriyah Central Prison.[15]

KAMAL MUSTAFA SULTAN AL-TIKRITI

On June 6, 2011, Kamal was sentenced to death for his role in the violent repression of a Shi'ite uprising in 1991.[16] His sentence is currently pending.

TAHA YASSIN RAMADAN

Born to a peasant family near Mosul, Ramadan took part in the 1968 coup that put the Ba'ath Party into power. The former Iraq vice president was hanged on the fourth anniversary of the US-led invasion that overthrew Saddam Hussein. The execution happened at a prison in northern Baghdad. According to his lawyer, he maintained his innocence, had no fear of death, and would "die bravely."

The execution was described as "a political assassination" by his son, Ahmad Ramadan, speaking to Al Jazeera TV from the Yemeni capital, Sanaa. He said his father would be buried in or near the Iraqi city of Tikrit, near Saddam's burial place.

Ramadan, who was thought to be in his late 60s, was the third senior former official to be hanged since Saddam Hussein was executed on December 30. He was found guilty of crimes against humanity. Ramadan lost his final appeal and under Iraqi law had to go to the gallows within thirty days. His execution was "smooth" to avoid a repeat of Barzan Ibrahim's bungled execution that led to his decapitation during the hanging.[17] He was executed on March 20, 2007.

TARIQ AZIZ

Tariq Aziz, the debonair Iraqi diplomat who made his name by staunchly defending Saddam Hussein to the world for three wars and was later sentenced to death as part of the regime that killed hundreds of thousands of its own people, died of a heart attack June 5, 2015, in a hospital in southern Iraq. He was 79.

Aziz died on Friday afternoon after he was taken to the al-Hussein hospital in the city of Nasiriyah, about 200 miles (320 kilometers) southeast of Baghdad, according to provincial governor Yahya al-Nassiri. Aziz had been in custody in a prison in the south, awaiting execution.[18] Aziz was the highest-ranking Christian in Saddam's regime and the international face of Saddam's regime for years. He was sentenced in October 2010 to hang for persecuting members of the Shi'ite Muslim religious parties that now dominate Iraq.[19]

WATBAN IBRAHIM HASAN AL-TIKRITI

Watban Ibrahim was the half-brother of Saddam Hussein and the brother of Barzan al-Tikriti. He was taken into coalition custody April 13, 2003, while attempting to flee to Syria.

On March 11, 2009, Ibrahim was sentenced to death by hanging for his role in the execution of forty-two merchants accused of manipulating food prices. On the morning of July 14, 2011, the US handed Ibrahim over to Iraqi authorities, expecting that he would be executed within a month. Instead, he remained imprisoned until his death from natural causes on August 13, 2015.[20]

NOTES

CHAPTER I

1. Michael A. Newton and Michael P. Scharf, *Enemy of the State: The Trial and Execution of Saddam Hussein* (New York: St. Martin's Press, 2008), 68–71.
2. Lt. Gen. David E. Quantock telephone interview, May 11, 2015.
3. Brig. Gen. David Phillips telephone interview, May 28, 2015.
4. Ibid.
5. John Burns interview, July 22, 2013.
6. Ibid.
7. John F. Burns, "Shrunk to Size, Hussein Faces His Reckoning," *New York Times*, July 4, 2004.
8. Col. (Ret.) Barry Johnson, telephone interview, March 2014.
9. Ibid.
10. Ibid.
11. Ibid.
12. Ibid.
13. John Burns interview, July 22, 2013.
14. Ibid.
15. Greg Kehoe telephone interview, July 13, 2013.
16. Karen Ballard telephone interview, June 3, 2014.
17. John Burns interview, July 22, 2013.
18. *New York Times*, July 1, 2004.
19. Ibid.
20. John Burns interview, July 22, 2013.
21. Ibid.

22. Ibid.
23. Ibid.
24. Ibid.
25. Ibid.
26. Newton and Scharf, *Enemy of the State*, 80.
27. Bobby Morgan interview, Oklahoma City, July 6, 2014.
28. Ibid.
29. Ibid.
30. Ibid.
31. Ibid.
32. John Burns interview, July 22, 2013.
33. Ibid.
34. Ibid.
35. Ibid.
36. Ibid.
37. Ibid.
38. *Stars & Stripes*, July 2, 2004.
39. Ibid.
40. Ibid.
41. Ibid.
42. *Variety*, June 20, 2004.
43. *New York Times*, July 4, 2004.
44. Kehoe interview, July 13, 2013.
45. John F. Burns, "Tables Turned, a Victim Sees Persecutor in Court," *New York Times*, July 5, 2004.
46. Ibid.
47. Ibid.
48. Ibid.
49. Newton and Scharf, *Enemy of the State*, 68–71.
50. John Burns interview, July 22, 2013.
51. Newton and Scharf, *Enemy of the State*, 68–71.
52. Ibid.
53. Ibid.

CHAPTER 2
1. Michael R. Gordon and Bernard E. Trainor, *Cobra II: The Inside Story of the Invasion and Occupation of Iraq* (New York: Pantheon Books, 2006), 176–77.
2. Ibid., 177.

3. Ibid.
4. L. Paul Bremer III, *My Year in Iraq: The Struggle to Build a Future of Hope* (New York: Threshold Editions, 2006), 107.
5. Con Coughlin, *Saddam: His Rise and Fall* (New York: Harper Perennial, 2002), 354.
6. Ibid., 355.
7. Ibid.
8. Eric Maddox interview, Las Vegas, June 7, 2013, and telephone interview July 3, 2014.
9. Ibid.
10. Ibid.
11. Ibid.
12. Lt. Col. Alan Troy interview, Oklahoma City, August 15, 2014.
13. Ibid.
14. Ibid.
15. Ibid.
16. Ibid.
17. Ibid.
18. Eric Maddox, *Mission: Black List #1: The Inside Story of the Search for Saddam Hussein—As Told by the Soldier Who Masterminded His Capture* (New York: HarperCollins, 2008), 234–45.
19. Ibid.
20. Ibid.
21. Ibid.
22. Ibid.
23. Ibid.
24. Troy interview, August 15, 2014.
25. Maddox interview, Las Vegas, June 7, 2013, and telephone interview July 3, 2014.
26. Troy interview, August 15, 2014.
27. Ibid.
28. Ibid.
29. Ibid.
30. Ibid.
31. Ibid.
32. Ibid.
33. Ibid.
34. Col. Barry Johnson, telephone interview, July 17, 2013.
35. Troy interview, August 15, 2014.

36. Ricardo S. Sanchez, *Wiser in Battle: A Soldier's Story* (New York: HarperCollins, 2008), 299–301.

37. Ibid.

38. Ibid.

39. Ibid.

40. Troy interview, August 15, 2014.

41. Maddox, *Mission: Black List #1*, 250–51.

42. Ibid.

43. Ibid.

44. Ibid.

45. Ibid.

46. Ibid.

47. George W. Bush, *Decision Points* (New York: Crown Publishing Group, 2010), 266–67.

48. Bremer, *My Year in Iraq*, 252–54.

49. Ibid.

50. Ibid.

51. CNN International.com, "UAE Official: Saddam Was Open to Exile," November 3, 2005, http://edition.cnn.com/2005/WORLD/meast/11/02/saddam.exile/.

52. Michael R. Gordon, "Official Takes Case to U.S., but Skeptics Don't Budge," *New York Times*, May 8, 2007, http://www.nytimes.com/2007/05/09/washington/09rubaie.html?ref=politics.

53. "From the Editor—The Brief," *Time* vol. 101, no. 11, November 11, 2018.

54. Bremer, *My Year in Iraq*, 256–61.

55. Ibid.

56. Ibid.

57. Ibid.

58. Ibid.

59. Ibid.

60. Ibid.

61. Ibid.

62. Ibid.

63. Ibid.

64. Ibid.

65. Bush, *Decision Points*, 267.

66. Ibid.

67. Ibid.

68. Troy interview, August 15, 2014.

69. Ibid.
70. Ibid.
71. Bush, *Decision Points*, 267.
72. Troy interview, August 15, 2014.
73. Ed Pilkington, "Saddam Hussein's Gun to Go on Display at Bush Library," *The Guardian*, July 6, 2010.
74. Bush, *Decision Points*, 267.
75. Ibid.
76. Maddox, *Mission: Black List #1*, 259–62.
77. Troy interview, August 15, 2014, and Maddox interviews, June 7, 2013, and July 3, 2014 .

CHAPTER 3

This chapter was drawn in its entirety from my notes, personal conversations, interviews, and personal perceptions. Because much of the activity covered an extended period, note-taking was the primary means of gathering information from meetings with many of the senior leaders.

CHAPTER 4

This chapter was drawn in its entirety from my notes, personal conversations, interviews, and personal perceptions. Because much of the activity covered an extended period, note-taking was the primary means of gathering information from meetings with many of the senior leaders.

CHAPTER 5

Much of this chapter was drawn from my notes, personal conversations, interviews, and personal perceptions. Because the activity covered a daylong event, note-taking was the primary means of gathering information from encounters with many of the senior leaders.

1. Radio Free Europe/Radio Liberty, Baghdad, November 20, 2003.
2. Valentinas Mite, Radio Free Europe/Global Security.
3. "Operational Update—Ask the White House," Defenselink, May 24, 2003.
4. Ibid.
5. *New York Times*, July 5, 2004.
6. Bremer, *My Year in Iraq*, 392–96.
7. Ibid.
8. Ibid.
9. Ibid.

10. Ibid.

CHAPTER 6

Much of this chapter was drawn from my notes, personal conversations, interviews, and personal perceptions. Because the activity covered a daylong event, note-taking was the primary means of gathering information from encounters with many of the senior leaders.

1. Steve Valley, *Inside the Fortress: A Soldier's Life in the Green Zone* (Salt Lake City: Millennial Mind Publishing, 2009), 199–201.
2. Sanchez, *Wiser in Battle*, 383–84.
3. Thomas E. Ricks, *Fiasco* (London: The Penguin Press, 2009), 324.
4. Ibid.
5. Ibid., 378–81.

CHAPTER 7

Much of this chapter was drawn from my notes, personal conversations, interviews, and personal perceptions. Because the activity covered a daylong event, note-taking was the primary means of gathering information from encounters with many of the senior leaders.

1. Newton and Scharf, *Enemy of the State*, 68–69.
2. Valley, *Inside the Fortress*, 199–202.

CHAPTER 8

Much of this chapter was drawn from my notes, personal conversations, interviews, and personal perceptions. Because the activity covered a daylong event, note-taking was the primary means of gathering information from these encounters with many of the senior leaders.

1. Col. (Ret.) Barry Johnson telephone interview, March 2014.
2. Ibid.
3. Ibid.
4. Brig. Gen. (Ret.) David Phillips telephone interview, May 28, 2015.
5. Ibid.
6. Barry Johnson interview, March 2014.
7. Ibid.
8. Ibid.
9. David Phillips interview, May 28, 2015.
10. Ibid.
11. Ibid.
12. General Tommy Franks, *American Soldier* (New York: Regan Books,

733352453328356482326265796568732754

2004), 411.

13. Franks, *American Soldier*, 413.
14. Jim Wilkinson telephone interview, September 27, 2014.
15. Franks, *American Soldier*, 413.
16. Jim Wilkinson interview, September 27, 2014.
17. David Phillips interview, May 28, 2015.
18. Ibid.
19. Ibid.
20. Ibid.

CHAPTER 9

1. William G. Pagonis, *Moving Mountains* (Boston: Harvard Business School Press, 1992), 3.
2. Elizabeth Bumiller, "Was a Tyrant Prefigured by Baby Saddam?" *New York Times*, May 15, 2004, http://www.nytimes.com/2004/05/15/books/was-a-tyrant-prefigured-by-baby-saddam.html.
3. Ibid.
4. Eric Davis, *Memories of State: Politics, History, and Collective Identity in Modern Iraq* (Oakland: University of California Press, 2005), 115.
5. Hanna Batatu, *The Old Social Classes and the Revolutionary Movements of Iraq: A Study of Iraq's Old Landed and Commercial Classes and of Its Communists, Ba'thists, and Free Officers* (Princeton, NJ: Princeton University Press, 1979), 120.
6. Coughlin, *Saddam: His Rise and Fall*, 24–27.
7. Ibid., 30.
8. US Congress, Senate, Select Committee on Intelligence, Alleged Assassination Plots Involving Foreign Leaders: An Interim Report, 94th Congress, 1st sess., 1975, S. Rep. 94-465, 181, http://www.intelligence.senate.gov/pdfs94th/94465.pdf.
9. Coughlin, *Saddam: His Rise and Fall*, 33–34.
10. Ibid., 35–39.
11. Robert W. Komer's Memo for the Record, February 8, 1963, President's Office Files, 117, John F. Kennedy Library, Boston.
12. "Abdel-Rahman Aref, 91, Former Iraqi President, Is Dead," *New York Times*, August 25, 2007, http://www.nytimes.com/2007/08/25/world/middleeast/25aref.html?_r=0
13. Coughlin, *Saddam: His Rise and Fall*, 52–55.
14. Olivier Guitta, "The Chirac Doctrine," *The Middle East Quarterly* (Fall 2005), http://www.meforum.org/772/the-chirac-doctrine.

15. Jack Healy, "Top Aide to Saddam Hussein Is Sentenced to Death," *New York Times*, October 26, 2010, http://www.nytimes.com/2010/10/27/world/middleeast/27iraq.html.

16. "A Documentary on Saddam Hussein 5," YouTube video, 9:54, posted by "Mohammed ABD EL HAI," January 12, 2007, http://www.youtube.com/watch?v=VHBF8EKt-zc.

17. Deborah Amos, *Lines in the Sand: Desert Storm and the Remaking of the Arab World* (New York: Simon & Schuster, 1992), 52.

18. John L. Esposito, ed., *Political Islam: Revolution, Radicalism, or Reform?* (Boulder, CO: Lynne Rienner Publishers, 1997), 56–58.

19. Coughlin, *Saddam: His Rise and Fall*, 248–50.

20. Ibid.

21. Amos, *Lines in the Sand*, 53–55.

22. Ibid., 56–57.

23. "Saddam's Chemical Weapons Campaign: Halabja, 16 March 1988," United States Department of State Bureau of Public Affairs, March 14, 2003, http://2001-2009.state.gov/r/pa/ei/rls/18714.htm.

24. Stephen C. Pelletiere, "A War Crime or an Act of War?" *New York Times*, January 31, 2003, http://www.nytimes.com/2003/01/31/opinion/a-war-crime-or-an-act-of-war.html; "Genocide in Iraq: The Anfal Campaign Against the Kurds," Human Rights Watch, July 1993, http://www.hrw.org/reports/1993/iraqanfal; "Ethnic Cleansing and the Kurds," The Jewish Agency for Israel, https://archive.jewishagency.org/peace-and-conflict/content/36921/, accessed May 15, 2005.

25. White House Office of Global Security, *The Global Messenger*, Special Edition, March 16, 2003.

26. Ibid.

27. Norman Friedman, *Desert Victory* (Annapolis, MD: Naval Institute Press, 1991), 372.

28. The National Security Archive of George Washington University. The Mount Holyoke International Relations Program; Peter W. Galbraith, "The True Iraq Appeasers," *Boston Globe*, August 31, 2006, http://www.boston.com/news/globe/editorial_opinion/oped/articles/2006/08/31/the_true_iraq_appeasers.

29. Alan Cowell, "Iraq Chief, Boasting of Poison Gas, Warns of Disaster if Israelis Strike," *New York Times*, April 3, 1990, http://www.nytimes.com/1990/04/03/world/iraq-chief-boasting-of-poison-gas-warns-of-disaster-if-israelis-strike.html; Alan Cowell, "Iraqi Takes Harsh Line at Meeting," *New York Times*, May 29, 1990, http://www.nytimes.

com/1990/05/29/world/iraqi-takes-harsh-line-at-meeting.html; Youssef M. Ibrahim, "Iraq Threatens Emirates and Kuwait on Oil Glut," *New York Times*, July 18, 1990, http://www.nytimes.com/1990/07/18/business/iraq-threatens-emirates-and-kuwait-on-oil-glut.html?module=Search&mabReward=relbias%3Ar; Michael R. Gordon, "U.S. Deploys Air and Sea Forces After Iraq Threatens 2 Neighbors," *New York Times*, July 25, 1990, http://www.nytimes.com/1990/07/25/world/us-deploys-air-and-sea-forces-after-iraq-threatens-2-neighbors.html?module=Search&mabReward=relbias%3Ar.

30. James F. Dunnigan and Austin Bay, *From Shield to Storm* (New York: William Morrow and Company 1992), 27–28.

31. Molly Moore, *A Woman at War* (New York: Charles Scribner's Sons, 1993), 49.

32. General H. Norman Schwarzkopf, *It Doesn't Take a Hero* (New York: Linda Grey-Bantam Books, 1992), 345.

33. Moore, *A Woman at War*, 49.

34. "In Memoriam—David Hackworth," Military.com, May 6, 2003; David H. Hackworth, *Hazardous Duty* (New York: William Morrow and Company, 1996), 85.

35. Ibid., 86.

36. Ibid.

37. Ibid., 87.

38. Rick Atkinson, *Crusade: The Untold Story of the Persian Gulf War* (Boston: Houghton Mifflin Company, 1993), 27.

39. Amos, *Lines in the Sand*, 160–62.

40. Schwarzkopf, *It Doesn't Take a Hero*, 393.

41. "Iraqi Leader's Koran 'Written in Blood,'" BBC News, September 25, 2000, http://news.bbc.co.uk/2/hi/world/monitoring/media_reports/941490.stm.

42. Bush, *Decision Points*, 269–70.

43. George W. Bush, State of the Union Address, January 29, 2002, http://georgewbush-whitehouse.archives.gov/stateoftheunion/2002/index.html; George W. Bush, "Full text: State of the Union address," BBC News, January 30, 2002, http://news.bbc.co.uk/2/hi/americas/1790537.stm.

44. Richard Engel, *A Fist in the Hornet's Nest* (New York: Hyperion Books, 2004), 37.

45. "CNN Transcript of Blix's remarks," CNN.com, January 27, 2003, http://www.cnn.com/2003/US/01/27/sprj.irq.transcript.blix/index.

html?_s=PM.

46. Sue Chan, "Behind the Scenes with Saddam," CBS News, February 24, 2003, http://www.cbsnews.com/news/behind-the-scenes-with-saddam; Joanne Allen, "FBI Says Saddam's Weapons Bluff Aimed at Iran," Reuters, http://www.reuters.com/article/2009/07/02/us-iran-sadd-am-idUSTRE56113O20090702. July 2, 2009.

47. "Smashing Statues through the Ages," *Socialist Worker*, August 13, 2005, http://socialistworker.co.uk/art/6930/Smashing+statues+through+the+ages

CHAPTER 10

1. Rajiv Chandrasekaran, "U.S. Captures Key Hussein Aide; No. 4 on List Found Near Tikrit; GI and Two Protesters Killed in Capital," *Washington Post*, June 19, 2003.

2. Mike Dorning and Paul Salopek, Special Report to the *Baltimore Sun*, June 19, 2003.

3. "Profile: Abid Hamid Mahmud al-Tikriti," BBC, June 6, 2003.

4. Toby Harnden, "Net Closing on Saddam As Top Aide Is Captured," *The Telegraph* (London), June 18, 2003.

CHAPTER 11

1. Patrick Cockburn, "Chemical Ali: The End of an Overlord," *The Independent* (London), June 25, 2007.

2. "Rise and Fall of Chemical Ali," Aswat al-Iraq (Voices of Iraq), June 25, 2007.

3. Gordon and Trainor, *Cobra II*, 60.

4. Charles Moore, "General Ali Hassan al-Majid," *Daily Telegraph* (London), April 7, 2003, retrieved April 23, 2010.

5. Alex Efty, "Rebels Welcome Safe Haven Promise," Associated Press, April 17, 1991.

6. "The Anfal Campaign Against the Kurds. A Middle East Watch Report," Human Rights Watch, 1993.

7. Ibid.

8. Ibid.

9. Ibid.

10. Said K. Aburish, *Saddam Hussein: The Politics of Revenge* (London: Bloomsbury Publishing, 2000), 289.

11. Coughlin, *Saddam: His Rise and Fall*, 257–80.

12. Gordon and Trainor, *Cobra II*, 122.

13. Coughlin, *Saddam: His Rise and Fall*, 280–81.
14. Ibid.
15. Ibid.
16. Gordon and Trainor, *Cobra II*, 456.
17. Gordon and Trainor, *Cobra II*, 455.
18. John Burns interview, July 22, 2013.
19. Ibid.

CHAPTER 12
1. Robert Burns, "Senior Baath Members Arrested," Associated Press, May 23, 2003.
2. "U.S. Hands over Saddam-era Officials to Iraqis," CNN, July 15, 2011.

CHAPTER 13
1. Trial, www.trial-ch.org/en/resources/trial-watch/trial-watch.
2. "Postwar Phase Begins," *Lubbock Avalanche-Journal*, lubbockonline.com, April 22, 2003.
3. Muhammad Hamza al-Zubaydi, GlobalSecurity.org, September 7, 2001, http://www.globalsecurity.org/military/world/iraq/zubaydi.htm.
4. GlobalSecurity.org, February 22, 1999, https://www.globalsecurity.org/wmd/library/news/iraq/1999/990222-in2.htm.
5. Muhammad Hamza al-Zubaydi," GlobalSecurity.org.
6. Trial, February 29, 2012.

CHAPTER 14
1. Coughlin, *Saddam: His Rise and Fall*, 101.
2. "Saddam Hussein's Half-brother, Intelligence Chief and Intimate Ally from the First Days of Baath Rule," *Independent*, January 16, 2007.
3. Coughlin, *Saddam: His Rise and Fall*, 160–61.
4. "Saddam Hussein's Half-brother."
5. Coughlin, *Saddam: His Rise and Fall*, 186.
6. Newton and Scharf, *Enemy of the State*, 30–31.
7. Newton and Scharf, *Enemy of the State*, 31–32.
8. Coughlin, *Saddam: His Rise and Fall*, 199–200.
9. Aburish, *Saddam Hussein: The Politics of Revenge*, 326.
10. Coughlin, *Saddam: His Rise and Fall*, 204.
11. Ibid., 205.
12. Ibid.
13. Aburish, *Saddam Hussein: The Politics of Revenge*, 319–20.

14. "Saddam Hussein's Half-brother."
15. Ibid.

CHAPTER 16

1. Aburish, *Saddam Hussein: The Politics of Revenge*, 306–7.
2. Atkinson, *Crusade*, 8–9.
3. Atkinson, *Crusade*, 8.
4. Atkinson, *Crusade*, 9.
5. Ibid.
6. Gordon and Trainor, *Cobra II*, 60–61.
7. Ibid.
8. Joel Roberts, CBS news, CBS/AP, September 20, 2003.
9. Gordon and Trainor, *Cobra II*, 118.
10. Robert Windrem, "Lt. Col. Rick Francona," NBC News, December 14, 2007.
11. Ibid.
12. Ibid.
13. John Burns interview, July 22, 2013.
14. Ibid.
15. Personal observation.

CHAPTER 17

1. "No. 10 on Iraq Most-Wanted List Captured," *Lubbock Avalanche-Journal*, May 18, 2003, lubbockonline.com.

CHAPTER 18

1. Joffe, "Taha Yassin Ramadan," *The Guardian* (London), March 20, 2007.
2. Ibid.
3. Ibid.
4. Coughlin, *Saddam: His Rise and Fall*, 156–59.
5. Joffe, "Taha Yassin Ramadan."
6. Ibid.
7. Coughlin, *Saddam: His Rise and Fall*, 206–7.
8. Ibid., 208.
9. Joffe, "Taha Yassin Ramadan."
10. "Iraqi Court Upholds Saddam's Death Sentence," Associated Press/MSNBC, December 28, 2006.
11. "Top Saddam Aide Sentenced to Hang," BBC News, February 12, 2007.

12. Joffe, "Taha Yassin Ramadan."
13. Engel, *A Fist in the Hornet's Nest*, 110.
14. "Saddam's VP Is Captured," CBS/Associated Press, August 19, 2003.

CHAPTER 19

1. Coughlin, *Saddam: His Rise and Fall*, 121.
2. Ibid.
3. Phebe Marr, *The Modern History of Iraq* (Boulder, CO: Westview Press, 2004), 175.
4. Marr, *The Modern History of Iraq*, 195.
5. Coughlin, *Saddam: His Rise and Fall*, 214–15.
6. Ibid.
7. Ibid., 245.
8. Edward J. Marolda and Robert J. Schneller Jr., *Shield and Sword* (Washington: Naval Historical Center, Department of the Navy, 1998), 48–49.
9. Ibid.
10. Amos, *Lines in the Sand*, 84.
11. Ibid.
12. Coughlin, *Saddam: His Rise and Fall*, 262–63.
13. Atkinson, *Crusade*, 55–56.
14. Ibid., 87.
15. Coughlin, *Saddam: His Rise and Fall*, 262–63.
16. Moore, *A Woman at War*, 164.
17. Aburish, *Saddam Hussein: The Politics of Revenge*, 302–4.
18. Ibid.
19. Atkinson, *Crusade*, 348–49.
20. Aburish, *Saddam Hussein: The Politics of Revenge*, 303–4.
21. Ibid., 304.
22. Coughlin, *Saddam: His Rise and Fall*, 283.
23. Marr, *The Modern History of Iraq*, 23.
24. Ibid.
25. Coughlin, *Saddam: His Rise and Fall*, 283.
26. Ibid.
27. "Tariq Aziz to Meet with Pope," *Irish Examiner*, February 5, 2003, https://www.irishexaminer.com/world/arid-30087158.html.
28. "CNN Live Event/Special: Tariq Aziz Speaks Out," CNN.com, March 24, 2003, https://transcripts.cnn.com/show/se/date/2003-03-24/segment/13.

29. "Tariq Aziz Surrenders to US Forces," Meed.com, April 25, 2003, https:// www.meed.com/tariq-aziz-surrenders-to-us-forces/.

30. Jane Perlez and John Kifner, "Tariq Aziz Surrenders; Interim Government Near," *New York Times*, April 24, 2003, https://www. nytimes.com/2003/04/24/international/worldspecial/tariq-aziz-surren- ders-interim-government-near.html.

31. "Son of Tariq Aziz Negotiated Surrender," ABC News, April 25, 2003, https://abcnews.go.com/International/story?id=79511&page=1.

32. Coughlin, *Saddam: His Rise and Fall*, 355–56.

33. Gordon and Trainor, *Cobra II*, 59–121

34. Son of Tariq Aziz Negotiated Surrender.

35. John Burns interview, July 22, 2013.

36. Ibid.

37. Ibid.

38. Ibid.

39. Ibid.

CHAPTER 20

1. Coughlin, *Saddam: His Rise and Fall*, 9.

2. Ibid., 63.

3. Ibid., 42.

4. Aburish, *Saddam Hussein: The Politics of Revenge*, 161.

5. Trail Watch, April 26, 2001.

6. Ibid.

7. Coughlin, *Saddam: His Rise and Fall*, 306.

8. Trail Watch, April 26, 2001.

CHAPTER 21

Much of this chapter was drawn in large part from my notes, personal con- versations, interviews, and personal perceptions. Because much of the activity covered fifteen-hour periods, notetaking was the primary means of gathering information from these meetings with many of the participants.

1. Kehoe interview, July 13, 2013.

2. "Iraq's Legacy of Terror – Mass Graves," US Agency for International Development (USAID), January 2004, 1.

3. Ibid.

4. Jeff Jacoby, "Saddam's Shop of Horrors," *Boston Globe*, October 31, 2002.

5. "Iraq's Legacy of Terror – Mass Graves," January 2004, 1.

6. Ibid.

7. Kehoe interview, July 13, 2013.

8. Sameer N. Yacoub and Vivian Salama, "IS Destroying Another Ancient Archaeological Site in Iraq," Associated Press, March 7, 2015, https://apnews.com/article/aaec29198d1246e1951a38a39d13302d.

9. Ibid.

10. AP, pool report.

POSTSCRIPT

1. Thomas E. Ricks, *The Gamble* (New York: The Penguin Press, 2009), 105.

2. Ibid.

3. Ibid.

4. Ibid.

5. Ibid.

6. "Senior Saddam Aide Executed in Iraq," *Financial Times*, June 8, 2012.

7. "Iraq Executes Saddam Hussein's Aide Abid Hamid Mahmud," BBC News June 7, 2012.

8. "Genocide in Iraq - The Anfal Campaign Against the Kurds."

9. "Saddam Hussein's Henchman 'Chemical Ali' Executed," *The Telegraph*, January 25, 2010, www.telegraph.co.uk/news/worldnews/middleeast/iraq/7072155/Saddam-Husseins-henchman-Chemical-Ali-executed.html.

10. "Aziz Saleh Al-Numan," Wikipedia.com, https://en.wikipedia.org/wiki/Aziz_Saleh_Al-Numan.

11. "Former Iraqi PM al-Zubaydi Dies at 67," Chinadaily.com, December 6, 2005, http://www.chinadaily.com.cn/english/doc/2005-12/06/content_500850.htm.

12. "Watban [*sic*] Ibrahim al-Hassan, Half Brother of Saddam Hussein, Has Died," Iraqi News, August 13, 2015, retrieved March 2, 2019.

13. "Obituary: Barzan Ibrahim Hasan al-Tikriti," BBC News, January 15, 2007, http://news.bbc.co.uk/2/hi/middle_east/6230177.stm.

14. John F. Burns, "Hussein Cousin Gets Death Sentence for Mass Killings," *New York Times*, June 24, 2007, https://www.nytimes.com/2007/06/24/world/middleeast/24cnd-verdict.html.

15. "Saddam's Former Minister Pleads for Clemency As Health Deteriorates," *The National*, May 28, 2018, retrieved March 17, 2020.

16. "Kamal Mustafa Abdullah," Wikipedia.com, https://en.wikipedia.org/wiki/Kamal_Mustafa_Abdullah.

17. "Former Iraq Vice-President Hanged," BBC News, March 20, 2007, http://news.bbc.co.uk/2/hi/middle_east/6468495.stm.

18. Qassim Abdul-Zahra and Sameer N. Yacoub, "Tariq Aziz dead: Saddam
    Hussein's deputy dies of heart attack while awaiting death sentence,"
    Independent, June 5, 2015, https://www.independent.co.uk/news/world/
    middle-east/tariq-aziz-dead-saddam-hussein-s-deputy-dies-heart-attack-
    while-awaiting-death-sentence-10300769.html.
19. "Saddam's Deputy PM Tariq Aziz Gets 15-year Prison Sentence," CBC
    News, https://www.cbc.ca/news/world/saddam-s-deputy-pm-tariq-aziz-
    gets-15-year-prison-sentence-1.789502, March 11, 2009, retrieved March
    2, 2019.
20. "Half Brothers of Saddam Hussein To Be Executed in Iraq Within a
    Month," *New York Post*, https://nypost.com/2011/07/15/half-brothers-
    of-saddam-hussein-to-be-executed-in-iraq-within-a-month/, July 15, 2011,
    retrieved March 2, 2019.

BIBLIOGRAPHY

BOOKS

Aburish, Said K. *Saddam Hussein: The Politics of Revenge*. London: Bloomsbury Publishing, 2000.

Amos, Deborah. *Lines in the Sand: Desert Storm and the Remaking of the Arab World*. New York: Simon & Schuster, 1992.

Atkinson, Rick. *Crusade: The Untold Story of the Persian Gulf War*. Boston: Houghton Mifflin, 1993.

Batatu, Hanna. *The Old Social Classes and the Revolutionary Movements of Iraq: A Study of Iraq's Old Landed and Commercial Classes and of Its Communists, Ba'thists, and Free Officers*. Princeton University Press, 1979.

Bremer, L. Paul, III. *My Year in Iraq: The Struggle to Build a Future of Hope*. New York: Threshold Editions, 2006.

Bush, George W. *Decision Points*. New York: Crown Publishing Group, 2010.

Coughlin, Con. *Saddam: His Rise and Fall*. New York: Harper Perennial, 2002.

Davis, Eric. *Memories of State: Politics, History, and Collective Identity in Modern Iraq*. Oakland: University of California Press, 2005.

Dunnigan, James F., and Austin Bay. *From Shield to Storm*. New York: William Morrow, 1992.

Engel, Richard. *A Fist in the Hornet's Nest*. New York: Hyperion Books, 2004.

Esposito, John L, ed. *Political Islam: Revolution, Radicalism, or Reform?* Boulder, CO: Lynne Rienner Publishers, 1997.

Franks, Tommy (General). *American Soldier*. New York: Regan Books, 2004.

Friedman, Norman. *Desert Victory*. Annapolis, MD: Naval Institute Press, 1991.

Gordon, Michael R., and Bernard E. Trainor. *Cobra II: The Inside Story of the Invasion and Occupation of Iraq*. New York: Pantheon Books, 2006.

Hackworth, David H. *Hazardous Duty*. New York: William Morrow and Company, 1996.

Maddox, Eric. *Mission: Black List #1: The Inside Story of the Search for Saddam Hussein—As Told by the Soldier Who Masterminded His Capture*. New York: HarperCollins, 2008.

Marolda, Edward J., and Robert J. Schneller Jr. *Shield and Sword*. Washington, DC: Naval Historical Center, Department of the Navy, 1998.

Marr, Phebe. *The Modern History of Iraq*. Boulder, CO: Westview Press, 2004.

Moore, Molly. *A Woman at War*. New York: Charles Scribner's Sons, 1993.

Newton, Michael A., and Michael P. Scharf. *Enemy of the State: The Trial and Execution of Saddam Hussein*. New York: St. Martin's Press, 2008.

Pagonis, William G. *Moving Mountains*. Boston: Harvard Business School Press, 1992.

Pollack, Kenneth M. *The Threatening Storm: The Case for Invading Iraq*. New York: Random House, 2002.

Ricks, Thomas E. *Fiasco*. London: The Penguin Press, 2009.

———. *The Gamble*. New York: The Penguin Press, 2009.

Sanchez, Ricardo S. *Wiser in Battle: A Soldier's Story*. New York: HarperCollins, 2008.

Schwarzkopf, Norman H. (General). *It Doesn't Take a Hero*. New York: Linda Grey-Bantam Books, 1992.

Valley, Steve. *Inside the Fortress: A Soldier's Life in the Green Zone*. Salt Lake City: Millennium Mind Publishing, 2009.

INTERVIEWS

Ballard, Karen, telephone interview, June 3, 2014.

Burns, John Fisher, telephone interview, July 22, 2013.

Johnson, Barry, Col. (Ret.), telephone interviews, July 17, 2013, March 2014.

Kehoe, Greg, telephone interview, July 13, 2013.

Maddox, Eric, Las Vegas, June 7, 2013; telephone interview, July 3, 2014.

Morgan, Bobby, Oklahoma City, July 6, 2014.

Phillips, David, Brig. Gen. (Ret.), telephone interview, May 28, 2015.

Quantock, David, Lt. Gen., telephone interview, May 11, 2015.

Troy, Alan, Lt. Col. (Ret.), Oklahoma City, August 15, 2014.

Wilkinson, Jim, telephone interview, September 27, 2014.

ARTICLES AND DOCUMENTS

Abd El Hai, Mohammed. "A Documentary on Saddam Hussein 5." YouTube, January 12, 2007.

"Abdel-Rahman Aref, 91, Former Iraqi President, Is Dead." *New York Times*, August 25, 2007.

Allen, Joanne. "FBI Says Saddam's Weapons Bluff Aimed at Iran." Reuters, July 2, 2009.

"The Anfal Campaign Against the Kurds: A Middle East Watch Report." Human Rights Watch, 1993.

"Aziz on Trial over Iraqi Killings Role." *Financial Times*, April 30, 2008.

Bumiller, Elizabeth. "Was a Tyrant Prefigured by Baby Saddam?" *New York Times*, May 15, 2004.

Burns, Robert. "Senior Baath Members Arrested." Associated Press, May 23, 2003.

Bush, George W. "Full Text: State of the Union Address." BBC News, January 30, 2002.

Bush, George W. State of the Union Address, January 29, 2002.

"Bush Challenged to 'Duel' with Saddam." BBC News, October 3, 2002.

Central Intelligence Agency. "Addendums to the Comprehensive Report of the Special Advisor to the DCI on Iraq's WMD," March 2005.

Chan, Sue. "Behind the Scenes with Saddam." CBS News, February 24, 2003. http://www.cbsnews.com/news/behind-the-scenes-with-saddam.

Chandrasekaran, Rajiv. "U.S. Captures Key Hussein Aide; No. 4 on List Found Near Tikrit; GI and Two Protesters Killed in Capital." *Washington Post*, June 19, 2003.

CNN International.com. "UAE Official: Saddam Was Open to Exile." http://edition.cnn.com/2005/WORLD/meast/11/02/saddam.exile/, November 3, 2005.

"CNN Transcript of Blix's Remarks." CNN.com, January 27, 2003.

Cockburn, Patrick. "Chemical Ali: The End of an Overlord." *The Independent* (London), June 25, 2007.

Cowell, Alan. "Iraq Chief, Boasting of Poison Gas, Warns of Disaster if Israelis Strike." *New York Times*, April 3, 1990.

———. "Iraqi Takes Harsh Line at Meeting." *New York Times*, May 29, 1990.

Dorning, Mike, and Paul Salopek. Special Report to the *Baltimore Sun*, June 19, 2003.

Efty, Alex. "Rebels Welcome Safe Haven Promise." Associated Press, April 17, 1991.

"Ethnic Cleansing and the Kurds." The Jewish Agency for Israel. https://
    archive.jewishagency.org/peace-and-conflict/content/36921/. Accessed
    May 15, 2005.

"From the Editor—The Brief." *Time* vol. 101, no. 11, November 11, 2018.

Galbraith, Peter W. "The True Iraq Appeasers." *Boston Globe*,
    August 31, 2006.

"Genocide in Iraq: The Anfal Campaign Against the Kurds." Human Rights
    Watch, http://www.hrw.org/reports/1993/iraqanfal, July 1993.

GlobalSecurity.org. http://www.globalsecurity.org/military/world/iraq/
    zubaydi.html, September 7, 2001.

GlobalSecurity.org. *RFE/RL Iraq Report* 4, no. 19, June 1, 2001.

Gordon, Michael R. "Official Takes Case to U.S., but Skeptics Don't Budge."
    New York Times, May 8, 2007.

———. "U.S. Deploys Air and Sea Forces After Iraq Threatens 2 Neighbors."
    New York Times, July 25, 1990.

Guitta, Olivier. "The Chirac Doctrine." *The Middle East Quarterly*
    (Fall 2005).

Harnden, Toby. "Net Closing on Saddam As Top Aide Is Captured." *The
    Telegraph* (London), June 18, 2003.

Healy, Jack. "Top Aide to Saddam Hussein Is Sentenced to Death." *New York
    Times*, October 26, 2010.

Ibrahim, Youssef M. "Iraq Threatens Emirates and Kuwait on Oil Glut." *New
    York Times*, July 18, 1990.

"In Memoriam – David Hackworth." Military.com, May 6, 2003.

"Iraq Executes Saddam Hussein's Aide Abid Hamid Mahmud." BBC News,
    June 7, 2012.

"Iraqi Court Upholds Saddam's Death Sentence." Associated Press/MSNBC,
    December 28, 2006.

"Iraqi Leader's Koran 'Written in Blood.'" BBC News, September 25, 2000.

"Iraq's Legacy of Terror – Mass Graves." US Agency for International
    Development (USAID), January 2004.

Jacoby, Jeff. "Saddam's Shop of Horrors." *Boston Globe*, October 31, 2002.

Joffe, Lawrence. "Taha Yassin Ramadan." *The Guardian* (London),
    March 20, 2007.

Mite, Valentinas. Radio Free Europe/Global Security.

Moore, Charles. "General Ali Hassan al-Majid." *Daily Telegraph* (London),
    April 7, 2003.

"No. 10 on Iraq Most-Wanted List Captured." *Lubbock Avalanche-Journal*,
    lubbockonline.com, May 18, 2003.

"Operational Update—Ask the White House." Defenselink, May 24, 2003.

Pelletiere, Stephen C. "A War Crime or an Act of War?" *New York Times*, January 31, 2003.

Pilkington, Ed. '"Saddam Hussein's Gun to Go on Display at Bush Library." *The Guardian* (London), July 6, 2010.

"Postwar Phase Begins." *Lubbock Avalanche-Journal*, lubbockonline.com, April 22, 2003.

"Profile: Abid Hamid Mahmud al-Tikriti." BBC, June 6, 2003.

Radio Free Europe/Radio Liberty, Baghdad, November 20, 2003.

"Rise and Fall of Chemical Ali." Aswat al-Iraq (Voices of Iraq), June 25, 2007.

Robert W. Komer's Memo for the Record, February 8, 1963. President's Office Files, 117, John F. Kennedy Library, Boston.

Roberts, Joel. CBS News. CBS/AP, September 20, 2003.

"Saddam Appears in Iraqi Court." *Stars & Stripes* (Mideast Edition), Friday, July 2, 2004.

"Saddam Hussein's Half-Brother, Intelligence Chief and Intimate Ally from the First Days of Baath Rule." *Independent*, January 16, 2007.

"Saddam's Deputy PM Tariq Aziz Gets 15-Year Prison Sentence." CBC News. https://www.cbc.ca/news/world/saddam-s-deputy-pm-tariq-aziz-gets-15-year-prison-sentence-1.789502, March 11, 2009.

"Saddam's VP Is Captured." CBS News. CBS News/Associated Press, August 19, 2003.

"Senior Saddam Aide Executed in Iraq." *Financial Times*, June 8, 2012.

"Smashing Statues through the Ages." *Socialist Worker*, August 13, 2005.

"Son of Tariq Aziz Negotiated Surrender." ABC News, April 25, 2003.

"Taha Yassin Ramadan, Saddam's Deputy, Is Hanged Before Dawn." Associated Press, retrieved April 24, 2008.

"Top Saddam Aide Sentenced to Hang." BBC News, February 12, 2007.

Trial, www.trial-ch.org/en/ressources/trial-watch/trial-watch.

United States Department of State Bureau of Public Affairs. "Saddam's Chemical Weapons Campaign: Halabja, 16 March 1988," March 14, 2003.

US Congress, Senate, Select Committee on Intelligence. "Alleged Assassination Plots Involving Foreign Leaders: An Interim Report." 94th Congress, 1st sess., S. Rep. 94-465, 1975.

"U.S. Hands over Saddam-era Officials to Iraqis." CNN, July 15, 2011.

Wallace, Kelly. "W.H. Rejects Bush-Saddam Duel Offer." CNN.com, October 3, 2002.

White House Office of Global Security. *The Global Messenger*, Special Edition, March 16, 2003.

Windrem, Robert. "Lt. Col. Rick Francona." NBC News, December 17, 2007.

Yacoub, Sameer N., and Vivian Salama. "IS Destroying Another Ancient Archaeological Site in Iraq." Associated Press, March 7, 2015. https://apnews.com/article/aaec29198d1246e1951a38a39d13302d.

INDEX

Note: Page numbers in italics refer to images.

1st Battalion, 22nd Infantry Regiment of the 1st Brigade, 4th Infantry Division, 135
1st Cavalry Division, 511st Naval Construction Division, 84
1st Marine Expeditionary Force Engineer Group, 84
4th Infantry Division (4th ID), 35, 45
24th Infantry (Division) Mechanized, 84
82nd Airborne Division, 31
89th Military Police (MP), 99
101st Airborne Division (Air Assault), 183
197th Infantry Brigade (Mechanized), 84

A Fist in the Hornet's Nest (Engel), 199
ABC News, 76, 79
Abdel-Hussein, Muhyi, 114
Abid Hamid Mahmud al-Tikriti, *13*, 30, 38, *98*, 133–39, *134*, 236
    Ace of Diamonds (#4 on Iraq's Most Wanted), 133
    executed by hanging, 236
    knowledge of Saddam's WMD program, 133
    mother's name, 136
    oversaw presidential secretariat, 133
Abizaid, John, 38–39, 54, 57, 84
Abu Ghraib prison, 86, 98
    propaganda for terrorists, 86
    soldiers not properly trained, 85
Abu Shalal (Father of Waterfall), 173
Ace of Clubs, 30
Ace of Diamonds, 30, 133
Ace of Hearts, 30
Ace of Spades, 29–30, 36
Ad-Dawr, Iraq, 175
Ad-Dawr farm, 34–35
Adnan Palace, 223
Afghanistan, 54, 102, 115
Aflaq, Michel, 113
Agence France-Presse (AFP), 134
AK-47, 36, 69
Al Faw Palace, 64, *65*, *66*, 83, 93, 116
Al Faw (Iraq city), 116
al Hassan, Malik Dohan, 136, 138
Al Iraqiya, 8, 79, 102
Al Jabouri, Fatma Ahmad, 201
Al Jazeera, 8, 23, 80, 102, 238
Al Mansur, 164
Al Rashid Hotel, 223

Al Yarmuk (neighborhood), 201
Al-Adel, Aziz (pseudonym), 32, 43
Al-Arabiya, 40
al-Assad, Hafez, 114
al-Awja, Iraq, 111, 141
al-Bakr, Ahmed Hassan, 113–14, 161
al-Barzani tribe, 169
al-Bazzaz, Abd al-Rahman, 113
al-Bu Nasir tribe, 141
Albu Haidar tribe, 175
al-Dour, 162
al-Douri, Sabir Abdul Aziz. *See* Sabir
   Abdul Aziz al-Douri
Alexander, John, 45
Alexandria, Virginia, 49
Alfaisal, Tallal Fahad, 138
al-Faisal, Talal Fundar, 219
Al-Faw Peninsula, 65
al-Hamad, Nasma Jasser, 187
al-Hasan, Ibrahim, 111
al-Hilla, 79
al-Hussein, Faisal, 110–11
al-Hussein, Faisal II, 111
al-Hussein Hospital, 238
Ali, Abdul Karim, 170
Ali Hassan al-Majid al-Tikriti
   ("Chemical Ali"), *13*, 38, *98*,
   141–50, *143, 145, 146,* 216, 225,
   228, 234, 236
   accused of crimes in Halabja
     attack, 146
   "Butcher of Kurdistan," 142
   executed by hanging, 236
   genocidal campaign, 142
   Governor of 19th Province of Iraq
     (Kuwait), 142
   King of Spades (#5 on Iraq's
     Most-Wanted List), 141
   manslaughter of Iraqis, 148
   Minister of Defense, 144
   mother's name, 148
   Saddam's closest military

     advisor, 142
   Sunni Muslim, 141
al-Jabouri, Salim, 237
al-Jadida (New Baghdad), 170
al-Jadriyah, 136, 218
Al-Jassim, Tala, 170
al-Jubouri, Farhan Mutlak, 237
al-Khasawna, Hani, 149
al-Khasawneh, Ziad, 24
Allah, Sajeda Kheit, 161
Allah, Thuria Abid, 137
Allahu Akbar ("God is great"), 121
Allawi, Iyad, 73–74, 76, 78–81
al-Mahmoudi, Midhat, 74, 76, 78, 81
al-Majids, 164
Al-Mansur neighborhood, 30
al-Muslit, Mohammed
   Ibrahim, 33–36, 44
al-Mussallat, Subha Tulfa (Saddam
   Hussein's mother), 111,
   124, 169, 219
al-Nahda (the Awakening), 216
Al-Nahyan, Zayed bin Sultan, 40
al-Najaf Province, 159
al-Nassiri, Yahya, 238
al-Nayef, Abdul Razzaq, 161–62
al-Nihayah, Qasr, 215
al-Numan, Aziz Saleh. *See* Aziz
   Saleh al-Numan
al-Ouaadi, Khudo, 219
al-Qaeda, 121
Al-Rashid Street, 112
Al-Rawi, Hamid Salih, 148–49
al-Rikabi, Fuad, 113
al-Rubaie, Mowaffak, *7,* 7–8,
   25–26, 40–43
   Iraqi Governing Council, 40
   National Security Advisor, 40–41
   rope to hang Saddam Hussein, 41
Al-Sabah, Sheikh Saad, Prime Minister
   (Kuwait), 205
al-Sadr, Ayatollah Grand, 156

al-Sadr, Mohammed Bak, 162, 236
al-Sadr, Moqtada, 27, 92, 235
al-Saedi, Ra'id Juhi Hamadi. *See* Ra'id
　　Juhi Hamadi al-Saedi
Al-Tabakchali Nazar, 171
al-Tai, Sultan. *See* Sultan Hashim
　　Ahmad al-Tai
al-Tai, Sultan Hashim Ahmad. *See*
　　Sultan Hashim Ahmad al-Tai
Al-Thawra (Ba'ath newspaper), 203
al-Tikriti, Abid Hamid Mahmud. *See*
　　Abid Hamid Mahmud al-Tikriti
al-Tikriti, Ali Hassan al-Majid
　　("Chemical Ali"). *See* Ali Hassan
　　al-Majid al-Tikriti
al-Tikriti, Barzan Ibrahim Hasan. *See*
　　Barzan Ibrahim Hasan al-Tikriti
al-Tikriti, Kamal Mustafa Sultan. *See*
　　Kamal Mustafa Sultan al-Tikriti
Al-Tikriti, Sabawi Ibrahim, 111, 166
al-Tikriti, Saddam Hussein al-Majid. *See*
　　Saddam Hussein
al-Tikriti, Watban Ibrahim al-Hasan.
　　See Watban Ibrahim al-Hasan
　　al-Tikriti
Altwaijri, Abdulaziz Othman, 233
Alvarez, Everett, Jr., 47
al-Yawer, Ghazi, 74–75, 78–81
al-Zubaydi, Muhammad Hamza. *See*
　　Muhammad Hamza al-Zubaydi
Amanpour, Christiane, 8–9, 23–24, 76,
　　80–81, 89, 92–94, *93*
　　allowed in courtroom, 94
　　did not follow ground rules, 94–95
Amara, Iraq, 156
"Ambush Alley," 68
American Airlines, 59
American Soldier (Franks), 104
Amin, Bakhtiar, 99
Amman, Jordan, 24, 118
Amos, Deborah, 116
an Najaf, 113, 162

Anbar Province, 188
Anfal campaign, 18, 41–42, 117, 142,
　　155, 186, 216, 225, 227
　　chemical weapons used
　　　　against Kurds, 42
　　Surah al-Anfal (the spoils
　　　　of war), 117
Anfal attacks, 128
Annan, Kofi, 198–99
anthrax, 122
Apache helicopters, 9
Arab League, 40
Arab Socialist Ba'ath Party, 30, 203
Arabian (Persian) Gulf, 115
Arabic, 123
Arab-Israeli conflict, 204
"Arabization," 142
Aref, Abdul Rahman, 161
Argov, Shlomo, 204
Arif, Abdul Salam, 113
Army Intelligence, 45
As Sayliyah, Qatar, 29
Assistant Director of Mukhabarat, 168
Assistant to the Joint Chief of Staff, 193
Assistant to National Security
　　Advisor, 104
Assyrian Christian, 203
Assyrians, 117
Attempts to Assassinate Saddam Hussein
　　(Barzan), 163
Austria, 21
axis of evil, 122
Aziz Saleh al-Numan, *13*, *98*, 151–
　　54, *152*, 236
　　"dirty dozen," 151
　　Governor of Karbala, 151
　　Governor of Najaf, 151
　　King of Diamonds (#8 on Iraq's
　　　　Most-Wanted list), 151
　　Minister of Agriculture, 153
　　mother's name, 153
　　regional Commander of the Ba'ath

Party, 151

Aziz, Tariq. *See* Tariq Aziz

Azzaman (Time), 8, 102

Ba'ath militia, 144

Ba'ath Party, 75, 112, 141, 143, 151,
    197–98, 210, 238

Ba'ath Party Regional Commander
    (West Baghdad), 151

Ba'athist, 20, 42, 112–15, 162

Ba'athist Iraqi Defense Minister, 142

Babel (newspaper), 216

Babel, Iraq, 201

Babylon, Iraq, 155

Bachelor Officers Quarters (BOQ), 56

Baghdad, Iraq, 11, 17, 25, 27, 30–32, 37,
    61, 69, 75, 92, 110–11, 123, 142, 153,
    159, 163, 169, 185, 204–5, 207, 209,
    223–33, 238

Baghdad Bureau Chief, 101

Baghdad Convention Center, 69, 102

Baghdad International Airport (BIAP),
    6, 32–33, 37–38, 41, 62–63,
    81, 86, 99

Baghdad/Karada (Iraq), 159

Baghdad Law School, 92

Baghdad Pact, 111

Baghdad Press Corps, 100

Baghdad University, 203

Baghistani, Dawood, 183

Bahrain, 118

Baier, Bret, 76

Baker, Brent, 48

Baker, James, 205–6

Ballard, Karen, 8, 12, 16, 75,
    77–78, 101, 187

Barzan Ibrahim Hasan al-Tikriti, *13,
    98*, 111, 161–73, *165*, 228, 237
    Chief of Intelligence, 164
    complex personality, 164
    crimes attributed, 169
    executed by hanging, 237

Five of Clubs (#38 on Iraq's
    Most-Wanted List), 161
    half-brothers, 163
    head of Mukhabarat (Secret
    Police), 163
    hire hit teams, 162
    medals for bravery, 166
    mother's name, 169

Barzani family, 18

Basra, Iraq, 84, 143, 156

Battle Update Assessment (BUA), 83

BBC, 23

Beirut, Lebanon, 118

Beirut marine barracks bombing
    (1983), 118

Bejat clan, 141

Bentson, Clark, 62

Beretta (9mm), 56

Big 12 football, 66

bin Laden, Osama, 199

Black Hawk Down (film), 63

Blair, Tony, 44, 234

Blix, Hans, 122

"Blood Qur'an," 121

Bokova, Irina, 233

bombing of US Marine Corps com-
    pound (Beirut), 118, 204

Bosnia, 23, 225, 228, 232–33

Bosnian Serb wars, 21

Boucher, Richard, 49

Bowling Green State University, 99

Brashear, Carl, 47

Bremer, Paul, 31, 40–41, 72–74, 77, 79,
    81–82, 85–86, 92

Brezhnev, Leonid, 115

Brooks, Vincent, 30, 50

Bubiyan (Kuwaiti Island), 115

Bucher, Lloyd ("Pete"), 47

Burns, John Fisher, 5, *7*, 8–9, 13–14,
    16–18, 21–22, 25–26, *26*, 101, 144,
    186, 209–10

Bush, George W., 25, 29, 39, 43–44,

72–73, 120–22, 128, 198, 205–6
"Butcher of Kurdistan," 142

C-130 Hercules, 82
Camp As Sayliyah, 62
Camp Ashraf, 100
Camp Cropper, 37, 99–100
    square footprint facility, 37
Camp Victory, 66, 68, 72, 84, 86,
    89, 97, 100
Casey, George, Jr., 50–52, 61,
    82–84, 105
    44th Chief of Staff of the Army, 51
    Georgetown graduate, 51
Casey, George, Sr., 51
    West Point graduate, 51
    Korean and Vietnam Wars, 51
CBS, 122
Central Criminal Court of Iraq
    (CCCI), 92
Central Intelligence Agency (CIA), 32,
    75, 121, 134, 164, 183–86, 204–5
CENTRIX (CENTCOM Regional
    Intelligence exchange network–mul-
    tinational/coalition accessible), 222
CH-47 Chinook, 81
Chalabi, Ahmad, 40–42, 94, 135
Chalabi, Salem "Sam," 7, 7–8, 48, 92
Chaldean Catholic Church, 203
change of command cere-
    mony, 83–87, 87
"Chemical Ali" (Ali Kimyawi), 142
"Chemical Ali." See Ali Hassan al-Majid
    al-Tikriti
chemical attack on Halabja, 117
Chief of Information (CHINFO), 48
Chief of Intelligence, 164
Chief of Staff, Multi-National
    Force–Iraq, 66
Chief of Staff USCENTCOM, 57
China, 101, 115
Chirac, Jacques (French Prime

Minister), 114
Churchill, Winston, 110
    British House of Commons, 110
    invited Prince Faisal al-Hussein, 110
Clarke, Victoria (Torie), 104
CNN, 11–12, 13, 24, 54, 76, 91,
    93, 95, 102
    live report from outside
        courtroom, 11
    porta-john incident, 11
    violation of ground rules, 24
Coalition Provisional Authority (CPA),
    40, 67, 72, 76–77, 85, 102
Combat Camera, 8, 13, 15, 18–19, 22,
    103, 134, 143, 145–46, 152, 157,
    165–66, 176–77, 176–77, 184–85,
    192, 200, 218
Combat Correspondent Pool
    (CCP), 119
Combined Press Information Center
    (CPIC), 8, 23, 68–69, 86, 95, 101
Commander, Navy Reserve Force, 61
Commander 10th Armored
    Brigade, 175
Commander 14th Tank Battalion, 175
Commander 17th Armored
    Division, 175
Commander Iraqi Army First
    Corps, 181, 237
Commander Joint Task Force 7
    (CJTF-7), 38, 49, 57, 83–84
Commander of the Central Euphrates
    Region, 156
Commanders Emergency Response
    Program (CERP), 103–4
Committee for Strategic
    Development, 164
CONEX boxes, 224
Congressional Delegations
    (CODEL), 82, 119
Convention Center (Green Zone), 223
CONUS Replacement

Center (CRC), 55
Cotton, John, 61
Coughlin, Con, 112
Council of Ministers Building, 223
coup d'état, 113
Court of Cassation, 76
Crossed Swords monument, 116, 223
Crystal City, 49
Crummell, Brenda, 55–56
Culler, Dave, 62
Custer, John, 35, 39
Cutler, Dawn, 50
Czechoslovakia, 21

Damascus, Syria, 112
Dawa Party, 40, 204, 236
DBACHILLES, 183
deck of cards, 30
Decision Points (Bush), 44
Defense Intelligence Agency (DIA), 45
Delta Force, 32, 35–36, 44
Department of Defense POW/MIA
    Accounting Command (JPAC), 225
Deputy Chief of Public Affairs,
    US Army, 51
Deputy Commander-in-Chief
    (DCINC), 57
Deputy Commander of Detainee
    Operations, 97
Deputy Director for Operations/Chief
    Military Spokesman, 100
Deputy Director of the Institute for the
    Study of War, 104
Deputy Prime Minister, 156, 198, 204
Deputy Prime Minister of Najaf, 162
Dhahran, Saudi Arabia, 61, 63, 89,
    116, 119, 224
Dhi Qar province, 148
DiRita, Larry, 50
Discovery Channel, 222
Director of military strategy (Iraqi
    Ministry of Defense), 175

Director of Public Affairs Secretary of
    the Air Force, 50
Director of Public Affairs/Strategic
    Communications, 49
Director of Public Affairs, US
    Marine Corps, 50
"dirty dozen" (Saddam's group of
    thugs), 151
DNA, 36–37, 228
Doenitz, Karl, 21
Doha, Qatar, 27, 34, 57, 60, 102
Dokan Lake, 226
Dujail (town), 142, 163, 169, 172
Dujail trial, 92
Dujailis, 163
Durand, Carolyn, 62
Durgadin, Kirk, 222, 228

Egypt, 198, 202
Egyptian president, 112
Eight of Hearts, 181
Eight of Spades, 203
El Silaa, Taleb, 178–79
Emerson, Steve, 135
Emery, Eric J., 225, 229
Engel, Richard, 122, 199
Escobar, Pablo, 63
ethnic cleansing, 216
Euphrates River, 224
Exorcist, The, 233
Expendables, The, 103

Fallujah, Iraq, 33
Farlow, David, 62
Fedayeen, 144
Federal Bureau of
    Investigation (FBI), 43
fertile crescent, 224
Fiasco (Ricks), 85
First Deputy Prime Minister, 201
First Gulf War, 89, 119, 198, 224
First Gulf War ceasefire, 182

Five of Clubs, 161

Five of Spades, 215

Fleischer, Ari, 198

Forward Operating Base (FOB)
Jaguar, 224

Fox News, 11, 76, 79

frag (fragmentation) grenades, 68

Francona, Rick, 183, 185

Franks, Tommy, 29, 102, 104–5

French Quarter, 47

Fort Benning, Georgia, 54–55

Fort Carson, Colorado, 35

Gaddafi, Muammar, 204

General Commander of the Armed
Forces (Iraq), 130, 175

General Director of the Iraqi Special
Tribunal, 92

Geneva, Switzerland, 164, 166,
172, 205, 237

Geneva Conventions, 36, 127

genocide, 155, 232, 236

George Washington University, 110

Gibson, Mel, 55

Giuliani, Rudy, 105

Glock (9mm), 36

Goering, Hermann, 21

Gorbachev, Mikhail, 115, 206

Goss, Porter, 43

Governing Council (GC), 40, 72

Governor of Baghdad Province, 175

Governor of Karbala Province, 175

Governor of Kirkuk, 158

Governor of Kuwait, 153

Governor of Tikrit, 215

Green Room, 72, 81

Green Zone, 6, 13, 23, 27, 63, 65–69,
72, 84–85, 87, 92, 221, 223

Greenstock, Jeremy, 75

ground rules (for media coverage of the
arraignment), 8, 11–12, 24, 100
legal repatriations at arraignment, 24

violation of, 24

Gulf War, 43, 114, 116, 120–21, 146,
155, 164, 210, 216

Hackworth, David ("Hack"), 119

Hafia, 153

Hague, The (Netherlands), 225

Hain, Peter, 207

Haiphong Harbor, 49

Haj, Iraq, 188

Hakimiya, Iraq, 163

Halabja (Kurdish town in Iraq), 18, 42,
79, 117, 128, 142, 146, 148, 186
poisoned with mustard gas and
nerve agents, 117

Hamdani, 162

Hamza, Athia, 159

Hamza, Muthana Muhammad, 160

"Hands of Victory," 116

Haretheya (Baghdad), 193

Harrell, Gary, 63
assisted with rescue of
Kurt Muse, 63
Special Operations Command, 63

Hartsfield International Airport, 54

Hasan, Hadlah, 194

Hashin al-Jabburi, 98

Hatra, Iraq, 233

Head of CPA Strategic
Communications, 72

Head of National Security, 215

Head of State Internal Security, 216

Heathrow (London) Airport,
39, 43, 59–61

Heatley, Charles, 40

Hess, Rudolf, 21

Hickey, Jim, 35–36, 44

High Value Detainees (HVDs), xi,
5, 8, 13–14, 23, 36–37, 71, 97,
98, 99–100, 104–5, 156, 187,
211, 221, 224

High Value Target (HVT), 30, 37, 45

Highway of Death, 120
"Highway to Hell," 68
Hillah, Iraq, 156
Hitler, Adolf, 21, 120
Holocaust, 232
House of Commons, 110
Hudner, Tom, 47
Hughes, Tim, 24
human bombs, 198–99
Human Rights Watch, 117
HUMIT (Human Intelligence), 34
Humvee, 229
Hunter, Duncan, 82
Hurriya Bayya' district (Baghdad), 216
Hussein, Hala, 191
Hussein, Qusay, 30, 85, 135, 182
Hussein, Sabawi, 216
Hussein, Saja, 164
Hussein, Sajidah, 24
Hussein, Uday, 30, 85, 135, 164, 216

Ibrahim, Sabawi al-Tikriti, 111, 162
Ibrahims (family), 216
Imam Ali, 127
improvised explosive device (IED), 68
India, 198
"Inshallah," 173, 195, 212
International Atomic Energy Agency
    (IAEA), 122, 207
International Military
    Tribunal (IMT), 20
invasion of Kuwait, 18–19, 128, 130
Iran, 122, 198
Iran–Iraq War, 65, 116, 223
Iraq, 54
    admitted to League of Nations, 111
    annexation of Kuwait, 198
Iraq Ambassador to the United
    Nations, 237
Iraq Council of Representative (Iraq's
    Parliament), 40–41
Iraq Governing Council (IGC), 40, 72

Iraq National Police Academy, 100
Iraq Parliament speaker, 237
Iraq Special Security Organization, 135
Iraq Special Tribunal (IST), 5, 8, 48,
    225, 229, 235
Iraqi Army Chief of Staff, 187
Iraqi Barzanian, 128
Iraqi Christians, 204
Iraqi Defense Minister, 183, 237
Iraqi Embassy (Damascus, Jordan), 31
Iraqi Foreign Minister, 222
Iraqi Governor of al-Najaf, 151
Iraqi Governor of Karbala, 151
Iraqi Governor of Kuwait, 151
Iraqi High Tribunal (IHT), 20
Iraqi Intelligence Service, 142
Iraqi Interim Government (IIG),
    5, 99, 156
Iraqi Kurdish editor, 183
Iraqi Kurds, 186
Iraqi Media Network, 102
Iraqi Military Academy, 175
Iraqi Military Academy Staff
    College, 175
Iraqi Scud missile launchers, 63
Iraq–Kuwait border, 205
"Iraq's Legacy of Terror – Mass
    Graves," 222
Iraq's Most Wanted, 27
Islamic Educational, Scientific
    and Cultural Organization
    (ICESCO), 233
Islamic Revolution, 115
ISIS (Islamic State of Iraq), 233
Israel-Kurd (magazine), 183
Italy, 21

Jack Reacher (film), 103
Jacoby, Lowell, 45
Jasim, Qies Niemic, 34–35
Jennings, Peter, 9, 23, 79, 89, 92–94, *93*
Jews, 197

Jizani (Iraq), 169, 172

Johnson, Barry, 6, 11–12, 97, 99–101, 105

Johnson, Jim (pseudonym), 32, 43

Joint Information Bureau (JIB), 104, 119

Joint Special Operations Command (JSOC), 32

Joint Task Force-Guantanamo Bay (JTF-GTMO)

Jordan, 31, 198

Judgment at Nuremberg, 20

July 14th Bridge, 223

Kamal Mustafa Sultan al-Tikriti, *13, 98*, 191–95, *192*, 237
  mother's name, 194
  Queen of Clubs (#10 on Iraq's Most-Wanted list)
  Secretary General of the Republican Guard, 191
  sentenced to death (currently pending), 237

Kansas State University, 51

Karbala (province), 153

Kazzar, Nadhim, 215

KBR (Kellogg, Brown, Root), 221

Keating, Timothy J., 50

Kehoe, Greg, *7,* 7–8, 14, 25, 222–28, 231–33
  HVDs needing suits, 14

Kevlar vest, 60

Khalabja, Iraq, 188

Khomeini, Ayatollah Ruhollah, 113–15

Khoury, Dina, 110

"killing field," 229, 234

Kimmitt, Mark, 48, 57, 67, 72–77, *73,* 81, 89, 100–101, 105
  Deputy Director for Operations/ Chief Military Spokesman, 100
  press conference after Transfer of Sovereignty, 81

King Hussein, 197

Kirkuk, Iraq, 111

Kitchens, Mark, 105

Komarow, Steven, 100

Korean War, 51

Kough, Lindsay, 56–57, 62–64, 67–68, 223

Krussa-Dossin, Mary Ann, 50

Kubic, Chuck, 84

Kufa, Iraq, 156

Kurdish genocide, 18

Kurdish peshmerga, 117

Kurdistan Region, 110

Kurds, 216, 232–33, 237

Kut, Iraq, 156, 162

Kuwait, 43, 112, 115–16, 148, 154

Kuwait Armed Forces, 118

Kuwait City, 120–21

Kuwaiti oil fields, 207

Landing Zone (LZ) Washington, 23, 81, 223

League of Nations, 111

Legion of Merit Medal, 43

Liebermann, Joe, 85

Lippold, Kirk, 47

Liya (compound), 163

Los Angeles Rams, 45

MacDill Air Force Base, 29, 54

Maddox, Eric, 31–32, 34–35, 38–39, 43
  4th ID taking credit, 45
  and Barry Sanders, 39
  Operation Red Dawn, 38
  presented with awards, 43

Mahdi, Adel, 40–42

Mahmoudiya district, 216

Makhlif, Amina, 178

Manchuria, 120

Mandeans, 117

Marr, Phebe, 109

Marshall, George Catlett, 120

Marshall Plan, 205
Martin, Mark, 221–22
Massachusetts Institute of
    Technology (MIT), 40
Maude, Frederick Stanley, 110
MC-130, 35
McClellan, Scott, 24–25
McCreary, Terry, 50, 52
McRaven, Bill, 32, 34, 37
media pool, 14, 89, 91–92, 95
Melanephy, Brian, 64, 67–68, 72–73,
    89, 92, 221
Memorandum of
    Understanding (MOU), 99
Metz, Tom, 57, 84
MH-6 Little Birds, 35
Middle Euphrates Office, 159
Military Police (MP), 11–12
Miller, Geoff, 6, 97, 101, 106
Milosevic, Slobodan, 21
Minister of Agriculture, 153–54
Minister of Communications, 155, 158
Minister of Defense, 144, 182
Minister of Education, 211
Minister of Housing, 201
Minister of Industry, 197, 201
Minister of Information, 203
Minister of Interior, 148, 216, 218–19
Minister of Justice, 99
Minister of Transportation, 158
Mission-oriented protective posture
    (MOPP), 55
Modern History of Iraq, The (Marr), 109
Mogadishu (Somalia), 63
Mondalek, Mr. and Mrs. Joe, xi
Mondero, Jessica, 225, 229
Monument to the Unknown
    Soldier, 223
Moore, Hal, 55
    We Were Soldiers (film), 55
Moore, Molly, 118–19
Morgan, Bobby, 21

mosque courthouse, 90
Mosul, Iraq, 110, 116, 181, 183, 188,
    197, 222, 233, 238
MSNBC, 135
Muhammad (Prophet), 111
Muhammad Hamza al-Zubaydi, 13, 98,
    144, 155–60, 157, 236
    59th Prime Minister of Iraq, 155
    Commander of Central Euphrates
        Region, 156
    died of cardiac arrest, 236
    Governor of Kirkuk, 158
    grandfathers' names, 158
    mother's name, 159
    Queen of Spades (#9 on Iraq's
        Most-Wanted list), 155
    Saddam's dirty dozen, 155
    Saddam's Shi'a thug, 155
Mujahedin e-Khalq (MEK), 100
Mukhabarat (Secret Police), 161,
    163, 168, 237
Multi-National Corps–Iraq (MNC–I),
    57, 64, 84
Multi-National Force–Iraq (MNF–I),
    6, 49, 51, 57, 64, 65, 76, 79, 84, 86,
    91, 97, 99
    165,000 troops/140,00 US, 83
Murderers' Row, 12
Muse, Kurt, 63
mustard gas, 65, 227
Myers, Richard, 48, 50–51
    Chairman Joint Chiefs of
        Staff, 50–51
    Kansas State University, 51

Naaman (village), 153
Najaf, Iraq, 27, 92, 156, 201
Najma, 153
Nasiriyah, Iraq, 151, 153, 156, 237–38
Nasiriyah Central Prison, 237
Nasser, Gamal Abdel, 112
National Defense University, 134

National Football League (NFL), 45

National Intelligence Medal of
Achievement, 43

National Security Advisor (NSA), 40

National Security Institute, 181

Natsios, Andrew, 223

Nation of Iraq, 79

Navy Military Processing Station
(NMPS), 50

Navy Reserve public affairs officers
(PAO), 61, 104–5

Nazi leadership, 20, 186

Nazis, 162

NBC, 25, 122, 183, 199

Negroponte, John, 79, 82, 85

nerve gas, 122

Newsweek, 119

New York Times, 5, 8, 45, 101

Nickles, Don, *85*

Nidal, Abu, 204

Ninawa, Iraq, 220, 226
ancient city of Hatra, 233
Dokar Lake area, 226
Fertile Crescent, 224
Forward Operating Base (FOB)
Jaguar, 224
IS shows contempt,
KBR managed property, 221
killing field, 221, 234
mass graves, 222–32
war crimes, 225

NIPR (Non-secure Internet Protocol
Router Network), 222

Normandy, 35

Norris, Tom, 47

Notre Dame, 45

Northwestern University School
of Law, 94

Nuremberg, Germany, 20–21, 186

O'Hare International Airport, 59

Oklahoma State University, 39

Operation Desert Shield, 48, 120

Operation Desert Storm, 48, 84, 120

Operation Iraqi Freedom (OIF),
29, 79, 104–5

Operation Red Dawn, 35, 38

Organization of Special Security
(OSS), 217

Ottoman Empire, 109
oil discovered (Kirkuk) in 1927, 111

Ottoman Turks, 110

Pace, Peter, 45, 50, 52
Vice Chairman and Chairman Joint
Chiefs of Staff, 52

Pachachi, Adnan, 40–42

Palace of the End, 215

Palkot, Greg, 76, 79

Palestine Hotel, 23

Palestinians, 204

Paris, France, 114, 204

Patriotic Union of Kurdistan
(PUK), 76, 199

Payne, Bill, 56

PC-3, 206

Pentagon, 53, 91

"perp walk," *10*, 105

Persian Gulf, 118

Persian Gulf War, 142, 183

Personal Security Detail (PSD), 57, 221

Petraeus, David, 183

Phillips, Barry, 99–100, 103–4, 106

Phillips, David, 6

Pittman, Hal, 54, 57

Pittsburgh Steelers, 45

Plan of Attack (Woodward), 121

Pollack, Kenneth, 111, 227

pool rules (media coverage), 103

Poole, Linda, xii

Pope John Paul II, 207

Powell, Colin, 48, 120

President of Iraq, 17, 19, 123

President of Syria, 114

Presidential Palace, 205, 221, 223
Presidential Palace (Green Zone),
   65, 68, 74
Presidential Secretary, 133
Press Secretary, 211
Prime Minister of Great Britain, 44
Prime Minister of Iraq, 155
Principal Deputy Assistant Secretary of
   Defense for Media Operations, 50
Province of Hofaz, 153
Puerto Rico National Guard, 100
Pulitzer Prize, 101
Putin, Vladimir, 121

Qasim, Karim Abdul, 112
Qatar Airlines, 61–62
Quantum of Solace, 103
Queen of Clubs, 191
Queen of Spades, 155
Qur'an, 125
Qur'an (Red), 78

Ra'id Juhi Hamadi al-Saedi, xi, 8, 10,
   18–19, 22, 26–27, 90, 92–94, 94,
   123–32, 145–50, 152–54, 157–60,
   167–73, 177–79, 187–89, 193–95,
   199–202, 208, 210–14, 217–20
   admonished Saddam, 19
   seven general charges, 18
Ramadan, Ahmad, 238
Ramadan, Taha Yassin. See Taha
   Yassin Ramadan
Ramadi, Iraq, 166, 224
Rand, Ron, 50
Rather, Dan 122
Reagan, Ronald, 54, 199, 205
   death of, 54
   funeral at Reagan Library, 54
Reagan administration, 118
Regime Crimes Liaison Office, 222
Revolutionary Command Council
   (RCC), 23, 30, 158, 197–98,

204, 206, 210
Rhino bus, 6, 9, 11, 14, 22, 100
Rhino Runner, 6
   fully protected, 6
   Saddam departing, 9
Rice, Condoleezza, 25, 39, 104
Richmond, David, 74, 78
Ricks, Thomas, 85
Ritz Carlton (Doha), 62
Riyadh, Saudi Arabia, 119
Robinson, John, 57
Rocket-Propelled Grenade
   (RPG) Alley, 68
Rodney, "Stretch," 62
Romans, 233
Rosenberg, Alfred, 21
Route Irish, 6, 67–68, 72
Royal Cultural Center, 118
Royal Navy, 110
Rudisill, Guy, 236
Rumaila oil field, 205
Rumsfeld, Donald, 39, 43–44, 99, 104
Russia, 198

Saad 16 (missile program), 116
Sabir Abdul Aziz al-Douri, 13, 98,
   175–80, 176, 177, 237
   Governor of Karbala Province, 178
   graduate from Iraq Military
      Academy, 175
   held numerous military
      positions, 175
   life imprisonment instead of death
      sentence, 237
   mother's name, 178
Saddam Hussein: The Politics of Revenge
   (Aburish), 164
Saddam Hussein, 5–6, 8, 8–11, 13–20,
   15, 16, 19, 20, 22, 22–27, 29–33,
   36–45, 48, 71, 75–78, 84–86, 89,
   92, 97, 98, 100, 105–6, 109, 111–12,
   114–18, 120–35, 141, 144, 163–65,

183–84, 186, 191, 198, 203–7,
210–11, 215–16, 222, 225, 228,
234–35, 237–38
Ace of Spades (#1 on Iraq's
Most-Wanted List), 29
Anfal campaign, 117
bounty on ($25 million),
30–31, *31*, 44
capture, 36
death by hanging, 235
denied legal representation at
arraignment, 24
denies possessing WMD, 122
fixed mobile Scud launchers, 121
General of Iraq Armed Forces, 114
genocide of Kurds, 117
hiding, 31
invasion of Kuwait, 130
killing Iraqi Barzanian, 128
lost control of Iraq, 122
miscalculated international reaction
to invade Kuwait, 118
mother's name, 124
participation in Ahmed Hassan
al-Bakr coup, 113
"perp walk," *10*
President of Iraq, 17
rarely left Iraq, 114
refused to review or sign
document, 20
Revolutionary pan-Ba'ath Party, 111
seized power, 14
uncovers traitors and conspirators, 114
Safwan (Iraqi village), 181
Safwan Agreement, 182
Salaheddine (Muslim warrior
Saladin), 216
Saleh, Barham, 74, 76, 78, 81–82
Samawa, Iraq, 156
Sanchez, Ricardo, 14, 38, 40–42, 51, 77,
81, 83–84, 86, 103

Sanders, Barry, 39
Sapulpa, Oklahoma, 31
sarin gas, 227
Sattler, John, 62
Saudi Arabia, 116, 119
Saudi Defense Ministry, 118
Schmierer, Richard ("Rich"), 72–74,
74, 76, 81
Schwarzkopf, H. Norman, 50, 104, 119,
121, 181–82
Scott, Jason ("Scotty"), 221, 223, 229
Scud missiles, 120–21
Secretary General of the Northern
Bureau of the Ba'ath Party, 142, 155
Secretary General of the Republican
Guard, 191
Secretary of Defense, 99
Secretary of State, 48, 49, 211
Secretary of State spokesman, 49
Senor, Dan, 67, 81, 89
Shabaks, 117
Shatt al-Arab River, 65
Sheppard, Cullen (JAG), 103
Sheraton Hotel, 223
Shi'a, 155
Shi'a Muslims, 197, 236, 238
Shields, Guy, 51
Shi'ites, 76, 113–14, 162, 235
Shi'ite Muslim Dawa Party, 162
Shu'la district (Baghdad), 216
Shultz, George, 204
Shultz-Aziz meeting, 204
SIPR (Secret Internet Protocol Router
network), 222
Slavonic, Greg, *26*, *73*, *74*, *85*, *94*
Slavonic, Molly (author's wife), xi,
49, 53, 57
Slavonic collection (images), 26, 31,
73–74, 85, 93–94
Smith, Greg, 51
Solarz, Stephen, 204
Soviet Union, 114–15

Special Assistant to Chairman Joint
   Chiefs of Staff for Public Affairs, 48
Special Operations Force (SOF),
   32, 35, 156
Special Republican Guards, 156, 216
Speer, Albert, 21
"Spoils of War" (Surah
   al-Anfal), 117, 142
Stalin, Joseph, 162
Starr, Barbara, 54
Streicher, Julius, 21
Suleimaniya, Iraq, 76, 226
Sullivan, Mareisa, 104
Sultan, Amouna, 148
Sultan Hashim Ahmad al-Tai, 181–89,
   184, *185*, 237
   commanded several military
      units, 182
   convicted of war crimes, 183
   died of a heart attack, 237
   Eight of Hearts (#27 on Iraq's
      Most-Wanted List), 181
   highest ranking general, 181
   met with Gen. Schwarzkopf to sign
      cease of Gulf War, 181
   Minister of Defense, 182
   most admired officer in Iraqi officer
      corps, 182
   mother's name, 187
Summer Olympic Games, 69
Sunni Muslim, 141, 203
Sunnis, 76, 141
Surah al-Anfal ("the Spoils of
   War"), 117
Swaika, Iraq, 162
Switzerland, 17
Swords of Qadisiyah, 116
Syria, 31, 198, 238

Taguba, Antonio (Tony), 86
"Taguba Report," 86
Taha Yassin Ramadan, *13*, *98*,
   197–202, *200*, 238
   Deputy Prime Minister, 198
   executed by hanging, 238
   Minister of Industry, 197
   mother's name, 201
   Ten of Diamonds (#20 on Iraq's
      Most-Wanted List), 197
   Vice President, 201
Taheri, Amir, 198
Taji, Iraq, 224
Talabani, Jalal, 185, 237
Talfah, Khairallah, 111
Taliban, 102, 121
Tappan, Rob, 72–74, *74*, 76, 81
Tariq Aziz, *13*, 38, *98*, 162, 186,
   203–14, *208*, *209*, 238
   audience with Pope John
      Paul II, 207
   Christo, Manuel (baptized
      name), 203
   code name PC-3, 206
   Deputy Prime Minister, 204
   died of a heart attack, 238
   editor of Ba'ath newspaper, 203
   Eight of Spades (#43 on Iraq's
      Most-Wanted list), 203
   member of Chaldean Catholic
      Church, 203
   mother's name, 211
Task Force 121 (TF 121), 32
Task Force 134 (TF 134), 6, 98, 100
Tehran, Iran, 204
Tel Keppe (Northern Iraq town), 203
temporary screening facility (TSF), 37
Ten of Diamonds, 197
Texas A&I University, 84
Texas A&M University, 66
Thawra Council, 211
Thawra district (Baghdad), 216
Thomas, Clendon, 45
   47-game winning streak, 45
Thorp, Frank, 48–49, 51, 76

Threatening Storm, The
  (Pollack), 111, 227
Three Blue Dots, 36
Tigris River, 69, 159, 223–24
Tikrit, Iraq, 31–34, 45, 162, 191, 238
Time, 8, 77
Today Show, 25
Tojo, 120
Transfer of Sovereignty (TOS), 71, 73,
  75, 77, 78, 80
Tribe of Khafaja, 153
Trimble, Michael ("Sonny"),
  224, 230–32
Troutman, George, III, 62
Troy, Alan (pseudonym), 32–37, 44–45
  Camp Cropper, 37
  4th Infantry Division (4th
    ID), 35–36
  Saddam's pistol to
    President Bush, 44
  Temporary screening facil-
    ity (TSF), 37
Tulfa, Subha, 124, 169, 219
Tulsa, Oklahoma, 31
Turkoman, 117

UH-60 Black Hawks, 35, 37, 223
United Arab Emirates (UAE), 40, 205
United States Navy admiral, 16
United Arab Emirates (UAE), 205
United Arab Republic, 112
United Kingdom, 40, 113
United Nations (UN), 222, 234
United Nations Educational, Scientific
  and Cultural Organization
  (UNESCO), 233
United Nations Secretary General, 198
United Nations Security Council
  (UNSC), 127, 206–7
United Nations Security Council
  Resolution 660, 206
United Nations Security Council

Resolution 1441, 122
University of Chicago, 40
University of Oklahoma, 31, 38, 45
  47-game winning streak, 45
US 344th Corps Support Hospital
  (Baghdad), 236
US Agency for International
  Development (USAID), 222–23
US Air Force, 183
US Army Corps of Engineers, 222
US Army War College (Carlisle, PA), 72
US Central Command (CENTCOM),
  29–30, 39, 55, 84, 181, 191
US Central Command (CENTCOM)
  Forward (Doha, Qatar), 105
US Central Command Forward J-2
  (Intelligence), 35
US Embassy (Beijing), 31
US Special Operations Command
  (USSOCOM), 34
US State Department, 221
US-led occupation, 17
USS *Cole* (DDG 67), 47
USS *Constellation* (CVA 64), 49
USS *Pueblo* (AGER 2), 47

V Corps 1st Armored Division, 84
Vatican City (Rome), 207
Valley, Steve, 86–87, 95
Vice Chairman Joint Chiefs of Staff, 45
Vice Prime Minister, 211
Victory Base, 6
Victory Corps (V Corps), 6
Vietnam, 35
Vietnam War, 51
von Papen, Franz, 21
VX, 227

wadi (bowl), 226
Wagner, John, 64, 66–68, 87
Wallmark, Gwen, 54
Warbah (Kuwaiti Islands), 115

Warren, Mark, 103

Washington, DC, 39, 45, 47, 49

Washington Navy Yard, 50, 54

Washington Post, 80

Watban Ibrahim al-Hasan al-Tikriti, *13*, *98*, 111, 215–20, *218*, 238
  died of natural causes, 239
  Five of Spades (#37 on Iraq's Most-Wanted List)
  Governor of Tikrit, 215
  Head of State of Internal Security, 216
  mother's name, 219
  Saddam's half-brother, 215

Water Palace. *See* Al Faw Palace

We Were Soldiers (film), 55

weapons of mass destruction (WMD), 122

Weber, Joe, 66–67

West Point, 51, 84

Whitcomb, Steve, 57

White House, 25, 44, 101–2, 117, 164

Whitman, Bryan, 50

Whitmire, Lyndon, xi

Wilkinson, Jim, 24, 104–6
  discussion of "perp walk," 105

Willey, P., 225, 227–30

Woodward, Bob, 121

World War I, 110

World War II, 21, 35, 84

World War II Memorial, 49

Yacoub, Zakia, 211

Yale University, 92

Yaphe, Judith, 134

Yazidis, 117

Yousiffiya (Iraqi village), 216

Youssef, Mohammed, 30

Yugoslavia, 21

Yugoslavia tribunal, 21

Zebari, Hoshyar, 222

Printed in the USA
CPSIA information can be obtained
at www.ICGtesting.com
CBHW022229220424
7386CB00002B/127